Movement and Experimentation in Young Children's Learning

In contemporary educational contexts young children and learning are tamed, predicted, supervised, controlled and evaluated according to predetermined standards. Contesting such intense governing of the learning child, this book argues that the challenge to practice and research is to find ways of regaining movement and experimentation in subjectivity and learning.

Vivid examples from Swedish preschools – involving children, teachers, teacher students, educators and researchers – are woven together with the theories of French philosophers Gilles Deleuze and Félix Guattari, bringing important new concepts and practices to the early childhood field. This ground-breaking book investigates three key areas:

- the need to focus on 'process' rather than 'position', as positioning of any kind, such as learning goals or developmental stages, hampers movement;
- working with methods that recognize science's inventiveness and productivity, demonstrating how the events in which children take part can remain open-ended and in movement;
- re-considering the dichotomy between the individual and society as a 'cause and effect' relationship, which immobilizes subjectivity and learning and hinders experimentation.

Challenging dominant ways of thinking, *Movement and Experimentation in Young Children's Learning* offers new possibilities for change and provokes a re-evaluation of the educational system's current emphasis on predetermined outcomes and fixed positions.

This book provides researchers and students with a sound theoretical framework for re-conceptualizing significant aspects of movement and experimentation in early childhood. Its many practical illustrations make this a compelling and provocative read for any student taking a course in Early Childhood Studies.

Liselott Mariett Olsson is in the Department of Didactic Science and Early Childhood Education at the University of Stockholm, Sweden.

Contesting Early Childhood

This groundbreaking new series questions the current dominant discourses surrounding early childhood, and offers instead alternative narratives of an area that is now made up of a multitude of perspectives and debates.

The series examines the possibilities and risks arising from the accelerated development of early childhood services and policies, and illustrates how it has become increasingly steeped in regulation and control. Insightfully, this collection of books shows how early childhood services can in fact contribute to ethical and democratic practices. The authors explore new ideas taken from alternative working practices in both the Western and developing world, and from other academic disciplines such as developmental psychology. Current theories and best practice are placed in relation to the major processes of political, social, economic, cultural and technological change occurring in the world today.

Other titles in the series:

Art and Creativity in Reggio Emilia
Exploring the role and potential of ateliers in early childhood education (Forthcoming)
Vea Vecchi

Contesting Early Childhood ... and Opening for Change (Forthcoming)
Gunilla Dahlberg and Peter Moss

Going Beyond the Theory/Practice Divide in Early Childhood Education
Using studies of reconceptualisation to help bridge the gap (Forthcoming)
Hillevi Lenz-Taguchi

Doing Foucault in Early Childhood Studies
Applying post-structural ideas
Glenda MacNaughton

Ethics and Politics in Early Childhood Education
Gunilla Dahlberg and Peter Moss

Forming Ethical Identities in Early Childhood Play
Brian Edmiston

In Dialogue with Reggio Emilia
Listening, researching and learning
Carlina Rinaldi

Unequal Childhoods
Young children's lives in poor countries
Helen Penn

Movement and Experimentation in Young Children's Learning

Deleuze and Guattari in early childhood education

Liselott Mariett Olsson

Routledge
Taylor & Francis Group

LONDON AND NEW YORK

First published 2009
by Routledge
2 Park Square, Milton Park, Abingdon, Oxon OX14 4RN

Simultaneously published in the USA and Canada
by Routledge
711 Third Avenue, New York, NY 10017

*Routledge is an imprint of the Taylor & Francis Group,
an informa business*

© 2009 Liselott Mariett Olsson

Typeset in Baskerville by
HWA Text and Data Management, London

British Library Cataloguing in Publication Data
A catalogue record for this book is available from the
British Library

Library of Congress Cataloging in Publication Data
Olsson, Liselott Mariett, 1970–
  Movement and experimentation in young children's
  learning : Deleuze and Guattari in early childhood
  education/ Liselott Mariett Olsson.
    p. cm. – (Contesting early childhood)
  Includes bibliographical references and index.
  1. Early childhood education. 2. Poststructuralism.
  3. Deleuze, Gilles, 1925–1995. 4. Guattari, Félix,
  1930–1992. I. Title.
  LB1139.23.O48 2009
  372.2101– dc22   2008038709

ISBN 13: 978-0-415-46866-4 (hbk)
ISBN 13: 978-0-415-46867-1 (pbk)
ISBN 13: 978-0-203-88123-1 (ebk)

This book is dedicated to Karim

Contents

Figures

Foreword

Gunilla Dahlberg and Peter Moss

> Society is an experiment and a labyrinthine construction that we must enter and exist in many ways since 'the way' does not exist.
>
> Rajchman

Why this book is in our series

This series, *Contesting Early Childhood*, opens up space for questioning the current dominant discourses in early childhood education and for offering alternative narratives that demonstrate the multiplicity of theories and perspectives that are not just being written about, but are also being put to work in everyday practice. This is a series, therefore, very much about new ideas, new knowledge and new ways of working. This book fits the bill very well. The author is a preschool teacher herself and has worked, from a Swedish university base, with teachers in different preschools, as well as with teacher students. In this book Liselott Mariett Olsson investigates the potential contribution of the thinking of Gilles Deleuze and Félix Guattari in the field of early childhood education. Their thought has until now received little attention in our field, and their thinking may seem far away from young children's everyday lives and from the work going on in early childhood services. However, as is shown in this book, their challenging philosophical and theoretical thought offers very important new perspectives to our field, and actually presents concepts and tools that are particularly suited for work with young children.

Drawing on Deleuze and Guattari, Liselott Olsson makes a strong indictment of our societies today: that they put a tremendous effort into taming, predicting, preparing, supervising and evaluating learning. This resonates with our earlier work and other books published or forthcoming in this series (cf. MacNaughton, 2005; Dahlberg and Moss, 2005; Rinaldi,

2006; Dahlberg, Moss and Pence, 2007; Lenz Taguchi, forthcoming). This body of work has commented critically on the extent to which procedures such as standards and tests prevail in contemporary educational reforms, the product of an instrumental rationality that seeks the best methods for delivering predetermined outcomes including a stable, defined and transmittable body of knowledge. Complex and contestable concepts, such as the child, knowledge, learning and evaluation, are reduced to a simplified technical discourse – often expressed in such terms as 'quality', 'excellence', 'best practice', 'benchmarks', as well as 'children at risk' and 'children with special needs' – that produces processes of normalization, exclusion and marginalization, while truth claims based on expertise, technology and management seek to impose consensus and to close down the contestability of subjects. By questioning and deconstructing the discourse and its truth claims, this body of work has opened up a new space in early childhood education, a space that transgresses the restricted horizon that the reforms offer to us.

The present book takes this critical perspective still further, through questioning other assumptions that often lie behind our ideas of what constitutes a pedagogical relationship. With support from Deleuze and Guattari, the author challenges our need and desire – we might say our will – to represent and recognize. This is what Nietzsche called a will to power: a will to judge and control that reduces difference to the same or the negative and runs the risk of moralizing piety and of what Deleuze talks about as the 'indignity of speaking for others' (Rajchman, 2001: 97).

Instead of representation and recognition, which Liselott Olsson argues subtracts and reduces thought and learning, she proposes to re-establish an affirming and experimenting attitude that can put movement, the unpredictable and the new into education. Through affirming the complexity that exists in an educational situation, she shows, both theoretically and in practice, how the conditions and the horizon of early childhood education can be extended instead of reduced and subtracted, and how learning can run wild rather than being tamed. She holds out the prospect of extending not only children's learning, but also their existential conditions and lives, opening up children's potentialities through engagement in processes of intensification and becoming.

Modern schooling

The work that is presented in this book has emerged in a scientific context that for half a century has conceptualized and reconceptualized the constitution of education in so-called pre-modern, modern and post-modern societies. Looking back historically, we can see that modern schooling, including early childhood education, has been caught up in a representational logic resulting in, as Deleuze would say, a taming of children's vitality. By its way of understanding knowledge and learning, this logic has infantilized children. We think that it is valuable to readers of this book to give a short description of how modern schooling has become constituted and how in this process the logic of representation has become predominant.

In the scientific context just mentioned, the Swedish researcher and curriculum theorist Ulf P. Lundgren has written extensively on this issue. He argues that the history of schooling can be seen as a continuous struggle between different views of what knowledge is, what is worth knowing and what different individuals and groups are able to learn (Lundgren, 1979, 1991; see also Dahlberg, 1982; Dahlberg and Lenz Taguchi, 1994). Lundgren relates modern schooling to the development of the modern state. He argues that the school system, as we know it today in the Western world, is formed when societies are organized and a visible state apparatus develops.

He often starts his reasoning by arguing that for the existence and development of society two basic processes are necessary: societal production and societal reproduction. Societal production implies not only the production of necessities of life, but also the creation of symbols and knowledge that can give meaning to these things and develop them, as well as the conditions within which production takes place. Societal reproduction refers to the processes which reproduce both the material base as well as the culture; the reproduction of knowledge, skills and values, and the reproduction of societal power in a broad sense. In a society characterized by a restricted social division of labour and a relatively homogeneous culture, children's upbringing and education in the primary group, in the village community and the family, is sufficient for cultural reproduction. In this context children learn both the value and meaning and the moral and ethics of work, and at the same time they learn different skills needed for work. In these societies production and reproduction are in close relation.

Although looking back historically the mandates of early childhood services and schools have been different, we can see that both types of institution have mainly been established from a similar societal need and have had a similar societal purpose: namely to bring up and educate those children who, due to historical and social developments, have ended up outside a 'natural' context of upbringing and education because production increasingly became divided from the reproduction of knowledge and skills (Dahlberg and Lenz Taguchi, 1994). This tearing away of reproduction from production takes place at different points of time for different strata of society. Initially the modern state is only interested to educate those who are supposed to work in the state apparatus, as those who are supposed to govern, legislate, administer and defend the law must be acquainted with earlier laws, be able to interpret their basic meaning and hence need to master written language. This requires an organized form of education and, in this situation, texts for education become important, not only for representing and reproducing things, but also to ensure that laws and the basic foundation of societies will last, e.g. be reproduced.

When the task of societal reproduction is taken away from the primary group to be placed in specific institutions, such as schools, established with the sole purpose of upbringing, texts for pedagogy are created. The objects and processes that children are supposed to learn are represented with words and pictures. This requires a specific selection and a specific organization and evaluation of what knowledge children are supposed to learn the teachers are supposed to teach. In this context what Lundgren (1979) has called *the problem of representation and transmission* is established.

For the broad mass of the people, it was not until the beginning of the nineteenth century that the state took this responsibility in most countries. It is Lundgren's contention that modern schooling emerges when a separate educational world is constructed. It was only then that it became possible for modern curricular questions to emerge.

What we can learn from this background is that the school system has a long history of representational logic, and that the tradition of the school has been to reproduce that which has been or might be lost. The idea behind this logic is that, when reproduction and production are divided, it is necessary to represent in the most accurate way the world – the world out there – and transmit this 'knowledge' to children, knowledge that has been lost through the process of societal change. Even a progressive thinker like John Dewey, at the beginning of the last century, stressed the reproductive function of education and saw it as a process of necessity. In his book *Democracy and Education*, Dewey says that society exists through a process of transmission quite as much as biological life. This transmission occurs, he says, by means of communication of habits of doing, thinking and feeling from older to younger, and without this communication to the young of ideals, hopes, expectations, standards, and opinions, social life would not exist. He also says that 'if the members who compose a society lived on continuously, they might educate the new-born members, but it would be a task directed by personal interest, rather than social need. Now it is a work of necessity' (Dewey, 1916: 3–4).

At the beginning of the last century, Lundgren argues, we experienced the strongest change there had been until then in the idea of schooling. The school came to be understood more and more as an institution that was supposed to reproduce what had been lost, and it should also have a forward-looking direction and give knowledge of utility not only for society but also for the individual. Focus was then displaced from given subject matters towards a content that was supposed to be evaluated for its utility. Learning, to a greater extent, was then supposed to emanate from the child and be based in scientific knowledge.

Lundgren considers that this was radical thought, but, he asks, did the last century become 'the century of the child', as the Swedish writer Ellen Key proposed in her eponymous book published in 1900 (Key, 1900)? Indeed, a strong idea behind the historical development described above was that the production of knowledge takes place within the scientific community and *not* among children in schools. Even the important ideas of *bildung* connected to the establishment of the Humboldt University in Germany saw institutions of science as knowledge-producing institutions and schools as institutions where this knowledge should be used and reproduced – hence, constructing a theory–practice binary.

This short historical overview shows us a model of how education should be pursued and what it should contain that is deeply embedded in modern schooling. It is a model that is very obvious today in early childhood education, especially as processes of 'schoolification' (the demands and expectations of compulsory schooling pressing down into early childhood education) are becoming more and more prevalent (Dahlberg, Lundgren and Åsén, 1991; OECD, 2001).

Although there has been some awareness that the processes of naming and speaking do not represent a 'true' reality, the logic of representation has remained very influential. For this logic characterizes most Western thought and inquiry, assuming as it does the possibility of a more or less accurate representation of a world that exists 'in itself', prior to and independent of the knower's experience of it. It is a way of thinking that keeps the world, both physically and socially, at a distance, as 'an independently existing *universe*, and which holds knowledge as reflecting, or even corresponding, to *the* world' (Steier, 1991).

Deleuze and Guattari, like poststructuralist thinkers, reacted strongly against this idea that to know means having a 'true' and objective representation of reality. And they are not alone. In cognitive science Varela, Thompson and Rosch (1993), for example, argue that cognition is not a representation of a pre-given world by a pre-given mind, but is rather the enactment of a world and a mind – we are bringing forth a world. Others who have demonstrated the situated character of knowledge have argued that in the 'process of naming', where things going on in one context are supposed to be used and understood in other contexts, then the meaning of the situation is likely to get lost as it will be de-contextualized. Likewise the child will be de-contextualized from its 'natural' context (Dahlberg, 1985; Lave and Wenger, 1991).

To construct a more meaningful education, several researchers in recent decades have also taken a constructionist stance, questioning the idea that knowledge, as well as our construction of the world represents an independent, 'objective' reality that exists apart from our own experiencing. Instead of language as a given and the words as directly corresponding to a reality 'out there', these researchers talk about 'meaning making', which implies that each individual creates and constructs meaning in relation to a specific society and context. Von Glasersfeld (1991), the main proponent of what has been called a radical constructivism, has said of his idea of learning as construction:

> the constructivist teacher will not be primarily interested in observable results, but rather in what students *think* they are doing and *why* they believe that their way of operating will lead to the solution of the problem at hand … If one wants to generate understanding, the reasons why the student operates in a certain way are far more indicative of the child's stage of conceptual development than whether or not these operations lead to a result that the teacher finds acceptable. … The most widespread effect, however, has been achieved by the very simple constructivist principle that consists in taking whatever the student produces as a manifestation of something that *makes sense* to the student. (p. 24)

Highly relevant to Deleuze and Guattari and the present book, another important development taking place in recent decades, within different disciplines (e.g. bio-physics (von Foerster, 1991); neurophysiology and biology (Bateson, 1972; Maturana and Varela, 1987), radical constructivism (Von Glasersfeld, 1996)), has been what is called 'second-order cybernetics'. Klaus Krippendorff (1991), in his discussion of cybernetic epistemology, locates knowledge neither in someone's head, as solipsists do; nor in an external and observer-independent universe (literally a singular version of reality), as objectivist or natural scientists insist on; nor in text, as many hermeneutics and discourse analysts argue.

Instead he argues that knowledge is located in an essentially circular social practice involving perceiving, thinking and acting (including languaging) beings.

Cybernetics recognizes the importance of self-reflexivity, the participation of the knower in the process of knowing, and seeks to understand knowing as a circular process constructing realities. Here we have come a long way from the representational logic and the reproductive role of the modern school.

A new image of thought

Big/small
relative

> Whereas a finger always calls for recognition and is never more than a finger, that which is hard is never hard without also being soft, since it is inseparable from a becoming or a relation which includes the opposite within it (the same is true of the large and small, the one and the many). The sign or point of departure for that which forces thought is thus the coexistence of contraries, the coexistence of more and less in an unlimited qualitative becoming. Recognition, by contrast, measures and limits the quality by relating it to something, thereby interrupting the mad-becoming.
>
> (Deleuze, 1994: 141)

The author of this book has taken inspiration from Deleuze's statement that the classical image of thought is a real betrayal of what it means to think, as it subordinates thought and action to representations. To characterize this kind of thinking Deleuze uses the image of a tree, with its roots as a point of origin from which everything develops in a linear way following a principle of dichotomy. The tree is deeply embedded in our way of thinking – the tree of life, the tree of knowledge, the family tree – while the disciplines are also organized in arboreal schemas similar to Linnaeus's hierarchical system of ordering living things.

According to Deleuze this image of thought has played a repressive role: it stops us thinking (Deleuze and Parnet, 1987: 13). Education, then, becomes more of an apparatus of taming instead of a place for learning. Deleuze wanted to claim thought as a different activity. With inspiration from Nietzsche, he saw thought as a matter of creation that takes place when the mind is provoked by an encounter with the unknown or the unfamiliar, forcing us to think.

Because we cannot have secure and stable foundations for knowledge, we are given the opportunity to invent, create and experiment. This points the way towards a non-representational and nomadic conception of thought, a rhizomatic thought that is not like a staircase, where you have to take the first step before you move onto and reach the next, which is similar to the tree metaphor that remains so prominent in education. Rhizomatic thought is more like a tangle of spaghetti, as Loris Malaguzzi (the philosopher and first head of the world-famous preschools in the Italian city of Reggio Emilia) spoke of their idea of knowledge in Reggio Emilia (Dahlberg and Moss, 2005).

> A rhizome has no beginning or end; it is always in the middle, in between things, interbeing, *intermezzo*. The tree is filiation, but the rhizome is alliance, uniquely alliance. The tree imposes the verb 'to be', but the fabric of the rhizome is the conjunction 'and ... and ... and'. This conjunction carries enough force to shake and uproot the verb 'to be'.
>
> (Deleuze and Guattari, 1999: 25)

This image of thought also suggests a more nomadic subject who enters into the domain of potentialities. To connect is to work with potentialities, with unpredictable becomings, as a way of breaking with that which we take to be natural and necessary: 'what counts is the present-becoming' (Deleuze and Parnet, 1987: 23). And the nomadic conception points the way to another idea of what thought and education is about. Instead of representation, recognition and identification it points towards how learning processes are produced and function and what social effects they have. It directs us towards the processes, the becomings – and these becomings are not to be judged by their results, but rather by how they proceed and continue.

Deleuze argues that we have to flee representations, the striated as he calls them, even if that is never wholly possible. Instead of searching for what a child is, as a person and individual, we have to search for the '*and*' through augmenting the numbers of connections, or encounters, that provoke something new to be thought; we need to explore the trajectories, the forces, the lines of flight and how they intersect.

Liselott Olsson, with support from the Swedish philosopher Fredrika Spindler (2006), makes us notice that this thinking is not the opposite of sedentary thinking. It is inevitable that we need to deal in one way or another with representations; so by acknowledging that representations are never stable constructions, but rather temporary and leaking constructions, we can pay attention to that which leaks, flees and adds to a situation in what she calls open-ended and unstable collective assemblages of desire. Similarly, Deleuze and Guattari argue that speaking and thinking do not belong to a subject that is the origin of thought. In their book *A Thousand Plateaus*, they state that 'Before the interiority of a subject, or the inner space of consciousness and the unconsciousness there is an utterance which creates an assemblage, an act of becoming, an unconscious and collective production' (Deleuze and Guattari, 1987: 38).

Following these lines of thought, the work presented in this book, both by the author herself as a researcher and by the Swedish preschool teachers, is characterized by a struggle on two fronts: first, to move away from the idea of knowledge as a representation and as a transmission; second, to move away from ideas of representing children in terms of what kind of subject they are – not trying to know what a child *is*, as a person and as an individual. Rather than assuming a subject as the origin of everything or deconstructing our 'readings' of the child to get hold of supplementary images of the child and learning, the author and the teachers have moved towards a pedagogy where the teacher is installed in the here-and-now, in the event, through listening and with the use of pedagogical documentation.

To do away with the subject! Doesn't that sound dangerous for our field of early childhood education? Just when we have managed to provide children with a stronger identity, for example through the idea of a competent and rich child, and through the United Nations Convention on the Rights of the Child. However, like Foucault, Deleuze and Guattari are not doing away with the subject, but with the way in which we construct the subject, as the essentialist and stable subject. It is this subject, they argue, that limits what we are able to do. Instead they want to move towards a way of speaking and acting that can open up a more vitalistic vision of the self – for a subject as a process of becomings that are all the time part of active processes of movement and transformation. This relates to their ideas of life and the world as a complex set of assemblages that continuously connect, bifurcate, combine and transform: life from the perspective of emergence and potentiality, which leads towards a more emergent pedagogy.

Children are already plunged into this

As the preschool practices described in this book show us, it is particularly productive to use the thinking of Deleuze and Guattari when it comes to very young children as they are not already too 'grounded'. For Deleuze, childhood was a state of 'overabundant extravagant force, supple, plastic, capable of metamorphosis, but doomed to dry up and settle down in the face of reactive demands of the social and familial world' (Zourabichvili,

1996: 211). In the essay 'What children say', Deleuze (1997: 61–64) points out that children are already plunged into an actual milieu, with its qualities, substances, power and events.

To extend the horizon of early childhood education Liselott Olsson and the teachers that she has been working with have tried to take care of this force and vitality, its mode of becoming, by directing attention to the processes. The primary focus has not been to judge their final result. The focus has rather been to follow how the learning processes proceed and their power to continue. In these processes children and teachers, as well as materials, such as drawings, documentations, play tools, furniture, overhead projectors, smells, light, and sounds and noises, such as children talking, singing, walking and their dramas, are pathways that merge not only with the subjectivity of the child, but also with the subjectivity of the milieu itself, insofar as it is reflected in those who travel through it. In this respect other children and pedagogues are a milieu that children travel through – they pass through its qualities and powers. In this milieu other children, pedagogues and objects play the roles of openers or closers of doors, guardians of thresholds, connectors or disconnectors of zones; they act as navigators.

Subjectivity and learning as a relational field

The author states that it is important for teachers to hook onto these trajectories through installing themselves in the here-and-now and not positioning themselves outside through representing, commenting, interpreting or reflecting. Rather than representing the children and interpreting the meaning of different events in the preschool in relation to a pre-planned programme (e.g. developmental stages or learning goals), they have to be attentive to the conditions under which something new is produced. This is a pedagogue who arranges environments that give conditions for experimentation and for making ever more unforeseen and complex connections.

Pedagogical work then not only becomes a narrative of children's intentions and children's meaning-making, but is also about intensity, movement and energy. Besides following the processes, the trajectories, teachers, according to the author, need to let themselves become affected so intensity and vitality can be opened up. In this context Olsson draws on Deleuze's way of working with Spinoza's concept of 'affectus'. What a body is, Spinoza says, is what it can do as it goes along, and affectus stands for a body's capacity for affecting and being affected. When you affect something, at the same time you are opening yourself up to being affected in turn, but in a slightly different way than you might have been the moment before (Massumi, 2006: 4). The capacity to multiply connections is a capacity to become affected that may be realized by a given 'body' to varying degrees in different situations. It may be thought of as a scale of intensity or fullness of existence.

Affect cannot be reduced to personal feelings or emotions in the everyday sense. Feelings and emotions are just one very partial expression of affect. Affect concerns the very moment of transition; when a body (human or non-human) reaches a threshold and manages to pass it. It is the virtual co-presence of potentials. It isn't actually there – only virtually. It is like a swarm of potential that follows us through life. And having more affect available intensifies our lives. Every transition is accompanied by a feeling of change in capacity and potential, but of all our complex experiences we are only able to feel parts of what we have experienced. An emotional state or a conscious thought cannot encompass all the depth and breadth of our experiences. When the logic of affect is activated it gives rise to collective experimenting, intensity and unpredictability. It functions like a sort of contagion that people get involved in, or rather 'hooked on' (Massumi, 2006).

This is not a progressive build-up of knowledge based on 'the foundations'. It is respect for the singular. It is not the application of a method, but rather an involuntary activity. Its primary characteristic is that it can only be sensed.

In writing about affect Liselott Olsson elaborates on the concept of 'collective assemblages of desire' put forward by Deleuze and Guattari. Desire, in their discussion, is not seen as a lack, but as a positive force – a force that creates new compositions. A collective assemblage of desire denotes a certain kind of 'non-personal individuation', always assembled, which cannot be reduced to personal feelings as events take place *in between* people. Olsson says that desire hits upon us, in singular ways, because desire and the movements it produces take place in between people in a continuously changing and polyphonic way. As it happens in between people this is not something that we can plan or control. It is never conscious. It is like machinery that is put into motion and it hits, and this hitting makes us *sense difference* which can trigger new self-organizing and self-producing processes, like in a network model. In this respect affect escapes language and functions more at the level of the real and of life. It is immanent.

Massumi (1996: 226) says that Deleuze's work, together with Spinoza's, could profitably be read together with recent theories of complexity and chaos. For they are all concerned with a question of emergence, which is the focus of the science-derived theories that converge around the notion of self-organization, e.g. the spontaneous production of a level of reality having its own rules of formation and order of connection. He continues by saying that affect and intensity are akin to what is called a critical point, or a bifurcation point, or singular point, in chaos theory and the theory of dissipative structures. Related to this, the author states that self-organizing processes push the system towards a limit where it is forced to start to produce new events and the system is self-organizing and self-producing in an open network model. More like complex systems within physics, these systems combine internal complexity and outer organizing factors, but where none functions as a higher organizing principle. As said before, it is seeing life and the world from the perspective of emergence, potentiality, and connections – as a complex set of assemblages that continuously connects, bifurcates, combines and transforms.

Project works as rhizomes

Following this way of reasoning, the projects described in this book which the children are working with differ from our understanding of how project work is usually carried out in early childhood education, i.e. as pre-planned and where pre-formed questions are worked out on the basis of the answers that are assumed to be probable according to dominant meanings. Even in what is called an emergent curriculum this approach to project work is very common.

This pattern of 'question and answer' has the effect of forcing the children into a position, as the questions are most often aimed at a future or a past. Many teachers, as well as parents, have seen that in such a situation children very often have nothing to say. However, while you turn in circles among these questions, there are becomings which are silently at work, which are almost imperceptible since 'movement always happens behind the thinker's back, or in the moment when he blinks' (Deleuze and Parnet, 1987: 1).

To get away from this pattern of question and answering, the teachers featured in this book have tried to construct an open space in the preschools, a space where the children and the teachers invent a problem before they search for solutions. This gives a space for experimentation, movement and the unexpected, and is in line with Deleuze's thinking when he says that encountering is to find and to steal instead of regulating, recognizing and judging. But there is no method, no rules, no recipes for finding and stealing other than a long preparation. It is the opposite of plagiarizing, copying, imitating, or doing such like. It is a space where children actually do not work together, as a theft does not happen between persons, it happens between ideas, each one being deterritorialized in the other. It does not create something mutual, but an asymmetrical block, an a-parallel evolution, always outside and between. It is difficult to tell what comes from one child, or another child, or the teachers, or the clay or the overhead projector when lines are encountering each other and responding to each other.

The assemblages that we can follow in this book look more like the subterranean shoots of a rhizome, as opposed to the unity of the tree and its binary logic. It looks like a production studio that is highly populated and when the children are bringing in their own loot a becoming is sketched out and a block starts moving, which no longer belongs to anyone, but is between everyone, 'like a little boat which children let slip and lose, and is stolen by others' (Deleuze and Parnet, 1987: 9).

Liselott Olsson states that to detect and to use desire, either as a teacher or as a researcher, is an ethical and a political choice that concerns a certain kind of experimentation and a certain kind of listening. This listening must go beyond the need to explain or define an Other, beyond the indignity of speaking for the Other, and it must admit polyphonic interpretations of what is taking place.

In this context she makes us aware that movements and transformations are already taking place through flows of belief and desire – even in the most rigid of governing systems. So, from her perspective teachers and researchers have to be prepared to work with the potentialities already inherent and immanent to a preschool. This sounds very much like how Rabinow (1994: xix), referring to Foucault, understands the work of a committed intellectual:

> Who one is, Foucault wrote, emerges acutely out of the problems with which one struggles. He talks about experience *with* instead of engagement *in* and through this he privileges experience over engagement and this makes it difficult to remain absolutely in accord with oneself. For identities are defined by trajectories, not by position taking. His attitude is rooted in an ethics not a morality, a practice, an active experience rather than a passive waiting.

Rabinow continues by saying that Foucault did not want to replace one certitude with another. He wanted instead to cultivate an 'attention to the conditions under which things become "evident", ceasing to be objects of non-attention and therefore seemingly fixed, and unchangeable'.

However, Liselott Olsson also makes us aware that this kind of micro-politics has inherent risks as thought opens up to new sensations and forces, which pushes us outside the dogmatic thought of clichés, rules and conventions. The lived experience, the impersonal and singular becomings that the children are expressing, confronts our orthodox thinking and often becomes difficult for us to bear. It becomes violent. You get 'goose bumps' as the author says in relation to her work and the teachers' work. But this is a risk we have to take if we want to work like this. Or as Foucault often said: everything is dangerous, but not always bad. And if we have already started it means that there is no way back – something that we have heard many teachers say who have started to experiment in this way.

However, do we really 'listen' to children (Dahlberg and Moss, 2005)? This is a question that occupied Deleuze. In a conversation, he praises Foucault's endeavour to teach us the fundamental fact that we so often are speaking for others (Deleuze, 1980); again, the indignity of speaking for others. Perhaps this is even more obvious when it comes to small children as the representations that we have of small children produce images of children being immature and lacking. Deleuze says that children in the school system are submitted to a form of infantilization, despite the fact that they can, more than we think, speak and act on their own behalf. Very often children have lost in advance, even though the teachers are acting in good will. He even argues that if the protests of children were heard in kindergarten, if their questions were attended to, it would be enough to explode the entire educational system.

In a challenging paper Liane Mozère (2008) draws on Spinoza's saying that we must not look at childhood from the adult down. Instead we need to put the child back on its feet and look at children from the child up. While saying that our thoughts go to Loris Malaguzzi. He once said in a speech that all children have a lot of potentialities and they are actually able to walk from birth, but they do not do so as that would intimidate their parents. From this thinking about the competent child the pedagogues in Reggio Emilia have tried to build their pedagogy on an ethics of listening, research and experimentation.

In relation to Deleuze's work, Francois Zourabichvili (1996: 211) has said that adults often say that a child is someone to whom everything must be given, but who gives nothing in return. Following the work presented in the present book we come to wonder if it is not the reverse. If this is 'true', if the child has so much to give, it has real consequences for institutions for early childhood education. It puts in question the tradition of representation and reproduction, and the practice of transmission. It implies a change in the role of teachers and in the role of the curriculum, as well as the educational system as a whole.

Is this what has started to happen in the preschools with which Liselott Mariett Olsson has been working?

References

Bateson, G. (1972) *Steps to an Ecology of Mind*. New York: Ballantine Books.

Dahlberg, G. (1982) *Kulturöverföringens rationalisering (The Rationalization of Cultural Reproduction)*. Stockholm: Institute of Education.

Dahlberg, G. (1985) *Context and the Child's Orientation to Meaning*. Stockholm: Almqvist and Wiksell.

Dahlberg, G. and Lenz Taguchi, H. (1994) *Förskola och skola – två skilda traditioner och visionen om ett möte (Preschool and School – Two Different Traditions and a Vision of an Encounter)*. Stockholm: HLS Förlag.

Dahlberg, G. and Moss, P. (2005). *Ethics and Politics in Early Childhood Education*. London: Routledge.

Dahlberg, G. and Moss, P. (2008) 'Beyond Quality in Early Childhood Education and Care: Languages of evaluation', *CESifo DICE Report 2/2008*, pp.3–8.

Dahlberg, G., Lundgren, U. P. and Åsén, G. (1991) *Att utvärdera barnomsorg (To Evaluate Early Childhood Education and Care)*. Stockholm: HLS Förlag.

Dahlberg, G., Moss, P. and Pence, A. (2007) *Beyond Quality in Early Childhood Education and Care: Languages of evaluation*. 2nd edition. London: Routledge.

Deleuze, G. (1980) 'Intellectuals and Power: A conversation between Michel Foucault and Gilles Deleuze', *L'Arc, 49*, pp. 3–10.

Deleuze, G. (1994a) *Difference and Repetition*. New York: Columbia University Press.

Deleuze, G. (1997) *Essays Critical and Clinical*. Minneapolis: University of Minnesota Press.

Deleuze, G. and Guattari, F. (1987) *A Thousand Plateaus: Capitalism and schizophrenia*. Minneapolis: University of Minnesota Press.

Deleuze, G. and Guattari, F. (1999) *A Thousand Plateaus: Capitalism and schizophrenia*. London: The Athlone Press.

Deleuze, G. and Parnet, C. (1987) *Dialogues*. London: Athlone Press.

Dewey, J. (1916) *Democracy and Education*. New York: Macmillan.

Durkheim, E. (1916) *The Division of Labour in Society*. New York: Macmillan.

Key, E. (1900) *Barnets århundrade (The Century of the Child)*. Stockholm: Bonnier.

Krippendorff, K. (1991) 'Reconstructing Communication Research Methods'. In F. Steier (ed.) *Research and Reflexivity*. London: Sage Publications. pp. 115–143.

Lave, J. and Wenger, E. (1991) *Situated Learning: Legitimate peripheral participation*. Cambridge: Cambridge University Press.

Lenz Taguchi, H. (forthcoming) *Going Beyond the Theory/Practice Divide in Early Childhood Education: Introducing an intra-active pedagogy*.

Lundgren, U. P. (1979) *Att organisera omvärlden (To Organize the Surrounding World)*. Borås: Publica.

Lundgren, U. P. (1991) *Between Education and Schooling: Outlines of a diachronic curriculum theory.* Geelong: Deakin University Press.

Massumi, B. (1996) 'The Autonomy of Affect'. In P. Patton (ed.) *Deleuze: A critical reader.* Oxford: Blackwell. pp. 217–240.

Massumi, B. (2006) *Navigating Movements: An interview with Brian Massumi.* By Mary Zournazi. Available online: http://www.21magazine.com/issue2/massumi.html (accessed 29 March 2006).

Maturana, H. R. and Varela, F. (1987) *Tree of Knowledge: Biological roots of human understanding.* London: New Science Library.

MacNaughton, G. (2005)*Doing Foucault in Early Childhood Studies: Applying Poststructural Ideas.* Routledge, London.

Mozère, L. (2008). Paper presented at the 15th International Reconceptualizing Early Childhood Education Conference. Hong Kong Institute of Education, 13–17 December 2007.

OECD (2001) *Starting Strong.* Paris: OECD.

Rabinow, P. (1994) (ed.) *Foucault – Ethics, Subjectivity and Truth: Essential works of Foucault, 1954–1984.* New York: New Press.

Rajchman, J. (2001) *The Deleuze Connections.* Cambridge: MA: MIT Press.

Rinaldi, C. (2006) *In Dialogue with Reggio Emilia: Listening, researching and learning.* London: Routledge.

Spindler, F. (2006) 'Att förlora fotfästet : om tänkandets territorier' ('To lose one's foothold: about the territories of thinking'). In S. Gromark and F. Nilsson (eds) *Utforskande arkitektur.* Stockholm: Axl Books.

Steier, F. (1991) (ed.) *Research and Reflexivity.* London: Sage Publications.

Varela, F. J., Thompson, E. and Rosch, E. (1993) *The Embodied Mind: Cognitive science and human experience.* Cambridge, MA: MIT Press.

Von Foerster, H. (1991) 'Through the eyes of the Other'. In F. Steier (ed.) *Research and Reflexivity.* London: Sage Publications.

Von Glasersfeld, E. (1991) 'Knowing without Metaphysics: Aspects of the radical constructivist position'. In F. Steier (ed.) *Research and Reflexivity.* London: Sage Publications, pp. 12–30.

Von Glasersfeld, E. (1996). *Radical Constructivism: A Way of Learning.* London: Routledge

Wiener, N. (1948) *Cybernetics.* Cambridge, MA: MIT Press.

Zourabichvili, F. (1996) 'Six Notes on the Percept'. In P. Patton (ed.) *Deleuze: A critical reader.* Oxford: Blackwell. pp. 188–217.

Acknowledgements

I would like to thank the children, teachers and head teachers in Trångsund, where assemblages of desire never stop invading the whole place, as well as children, teachers, teacher students, teacher educators and researchers in in-service training courses and in 'Pedagogical and Theoretical Spaces' for the joy of experimenting together; Sanna, Sussa and Lottie for generously sharing your material; my supervisor Gunilla Dahlberg for support, joyful work and for incarnating a logic of affirmation and creation; Liane Mozère for sharing her experiences and for insisting upon the weaving together of theory and practice; Peter Moss for valuable commentaries and for helping out with the English; everybody in the Research School in Pedagogical Work for a creative working environment with lots of humour and less prestige; the research group for 'The Ethics and Aesthetics of Learning': Ingela, Eva, Bodil, old and new members, for fun, hard-working and interesting seminars, as well as everybody who has contributed to the developing of the study in different seminars along the way; the Reggio Emilia Institute and the schools in Reggio Emilia for inspiration; Ann Åberg for intelligent work and humour; Thor Jonsson for letting Stella Nona invade your artwork; Monica Sand for your incapability to be simultaneous and thereby instead being totally focused. And finally I would like to thank my family and friends in Sweden and France simply because I cannot do without you.

Prologue
Entering a problem

Walking and surfing

I saw my little niece Stella Nona's attempts to start walking.[1] She was lying on her stomach, arms and hands level with her armpits, a sudden jump up to a squat position, the slight raising of the legs, the arms balancing horizontal to the body. And then, all of a sudden, I came to think about my surf class on the west coast two years earlier. Stella Nona's movements seemed to have something to do with the movements I had so much trouble mastering in surfing: lying on the board with the hands level with the armpits, the fast jump up into a squat position with the feet close to

Figure 0.1 Stella Nona and surfer. (Copyright Thor Jonsson 3 Oceans)

the hands, the slight raising of the legs, the arms balancing horizontally to the body (Figure 0.0).

When Stella Nona started to walk she had so many different ways of moving; she would drag herself across the floor with the help of her arms, she would sit on her bum and use her legs and arms and jump. She would crawl on all fours, she would use toys, cars, wagons on wheels, install her body on them and push with her arms and legs. She would use furniture or people around her. Each time I saw her she had changed something about her walking; she moved faster or slower, she would, even when she no longer needed it, drag herself with the help of furniture, she would drag furniture after her. She would walk sideways or backwards, she would take pauses standing up, sitting down. She would change her walking according to the ground, she would stumble and fall. She would use walking for different purposes; to enjoy different speeds, to enjoy the challenge of climbing the stairs. She would use walking to discover a room or a space outside in different ways; she would use walking in different ways to adapt her body, to make her body one with the different spaces.

Nobody has to tell a child how to start walking, they do it anyway. There seems to be a strong drive for children to learn how to walk. Who has not served as a 'walking tool' for a little child that tirelessly uses your body to be able to move its own body around? What is this drive? What is at stake that makes a child move around with such frenetic eagerness? Seeing a child using her or his body in relation to everything that surrounds that body, it seems that learning to walk is about the joy of increasing your body's capacity to move through joining your body with other bodies and forces.

Learning to surf might be something that somebody needs to tell you how to do. Perhaps this is because we have lost the eagerness and desire to extend our bodily capacities, maybe otherwise we would all be surfers. When learning to surf, everything is about joining your body with the movements of the sea. Even if somebody explains to you how to move your body on the board – and they indeed try to, a lot of the training actually takes place on the beach before taking the board into the water – once you're in the water you are left with experimenting and nothing else. Nobody can totally predict the movements of the waves and what you learnt on the board on the beach serves you little unless you are capable of joining the movements of the sea; you need to become one with the water. You will discover that this is never predictable or controllable; learning to surf literally hits you from behind, you never know how it happens, all of a sudden you are just doing it.

If you do succeed in walking or surfing, you feel a tremendous feeling of joy; you have increased your body's capacity, you have joined other forces and together with these your body is capable of doing more. Walking and surfing take place *in between* child and ground, surfer and sea. To the same extent that the sea is unpredictable, the ground is in continuous movement. The ground walks with the child and the sea surfs with the surfer.

That the ground walks with the child and the sea surfs with the surfer transforms the child's and the surfer's body, they become plastic and elastic. They stretch their physical bodies in resonance with the movements of the sea and the ground. This is what reminds the walking child and the surfer of each other; they both extend their bodies in relation with other forces and bodies. Otherwise there is no point in comparing them; the other comparative likenesses and differences pale in comparison to this relationship to ground and sea. The child and the surfer find themselves in continuous movement just as the sea and the ground and when they learn to walk and surf they do so through intense experimenting.

Joining the child and the surfer in this way, departing from the relationship between child and ground and surfer and sea when learning to walk and surf, has nothing to do with establishing a metaphor or an analogy.[2] It is simply a question of focusing the movement and experimentation in subjectivity and learning through the encounter of bits of walking that has something to do with parts of surfing. Neither is there any particular interest in wanting to make the child take the position of the surfer and the surfer that of the child. The child's development into an adult is of course already coded in, but what actually takes place along that path of growing from child to adult? We have quite clear conceptions of the differences between adult and child, but that is only from the point of view of their respective positions and all the attributes we give to them. What is more interesting is what actually takes place in between child and ground and surfer and sea in the very moment they are learning. We tend to focus a lot on the moment when the child does not walk and then when she or he walks, and all the intermediate stops on the way to walking that are so familiar to us; reflexes, crawling in specific patterns, raising up etc. But what takes place in between these predetermined stops? What is at stake when a child learns to walk or a surfer learns to surf?

At the least, there seems to be something else than what we normally associate with a learning subject: conscious thinking. There seems to be another logic at stake, a bodily logic. The effects for sure are more or less conscious; we have a feeling of joy when our body joins another force and increases its capacity to move, but the actual movement of forces joining each other is much more interesting: this is when learning takes place, unconsciously, bodily. This does not mean that the brain is left on the beach or figures only once the child actually walks. It just gives another role to the brain. It is no longer above or outside the body, with the role to explain. But instead it participates as an inseparable part of the body, the ground and the sea.

That the body of the surfer and the child become plastic and elastic should not be confounded with an imaginary image. It is not that they are fantasized artificial bodies. Their bodies are perfectly real. It is just that they are here seen through the point of view of a continuous relation with the sea and the ground. This relation is not that of a mix between entities, it is not hybridization, the relation itself is in a continuously changing and becoming state. Ground *and* child change, surfer *and* sea change, simultaneously. In this respect they are not really natural biological bodies either, since those have restricted limits of what they are capable of doing and are sharply distinguished from the culture surrounding them. The plastic elastic body of the child and the surfer is simultaneously nature and culture.

Plastic and elastic can also be thought of in relation to the surf board. The board is a technical attribute that permits the body of the surfer to increase its capacities. Does this mean that every technical attribute that leads to increased capacities also leads to joy? Not necessarily, there are many ways to increase your body's capacity: computers, technical innovations, surgery, drugs, … . But the point is that it is not these innovations in themselves that are interesting. We cannot rely on them if we are interested in increasing bodily potential and joy. The increase of one body's capacity might imply the decrease of another one and what seems to be new sometimes turns out to be more of the same. Technique in itself has no particular potential, it might just as well lead to disaster for some bodies. And anyway, isn't the increasing of your ordinary everyday body's capacity a large enough challenge? It might not be a very flashy or philosophically stringent point of view to speak of children's and surfers' bodies, joining ground and sea through plastic and elastic principles, but it does come with some interesting pragmatic and ethical consequences; to take seriously the potential of everyday life and bodies. To be even more cautious about saying 'bring on the drugs, the surgery, the artificial lives, the technical innovations, …', in favour of saying more modestly: 'How can we raise the potential of our everyday bodies?' It is true that not all children learn how to walk. For some reason they might not. But the question of bodily potential becomes even more urgent in relation to these children. What, for example, can a body without legs do? What is potentiality for each singular and unique body? It is only as long as we keep the nature/culture divide intact that these bodies will be reduced in their capacities to act. From the point of view of bodies joining other bodies the important thing becomes to seek to open for potentiality in every situation, in relation to *every body*, not in relation to *everybody*.

Maybe walking is one of the functions supporting the illusion that we are heading somewhere in life, but do we really walk ahead? Does everything develop for the better? What if we walk and walk and never get anywhere? When children walk, very often they do not walk with the purpose of getting ahead. So many things can happen on the way; something interesting is found on the sidewalk – a snail or a branch, or there is the discovery of walking being done backwards or in circles, or jumping on one leg. It seems as if children's walking is more a question of exploring rhythm than of getting ahead.[3] The surfer surfs, not to get somewhere, but for the moment. Surfing is about living the moment to the fullest capacity of one's body, and to stretch beyond that.

When they learn to walk and surf, children and surfers explore the potential of their bodies, and the encounter of bodies and forces. But this goes for more than learning to walk and surf. Very often when children learn they do so by bodily logic, potential and the joining of forces. Everything becomes ground and sea when children learn; everything becomes movement and experimentation. Letters, light, numbers, colours, everything is thrown up in the air, nothing is wrong and everything is potentiality. Sense and nonsense walk together hand in hand. Answers and solutions are never really interesting, goals serve nothing if they are not anchored in the exact present moment. The important thing is to *construct* a problem, this is what children do when they are walking backwards, sideways, in circles; they are constructing the problem of walking. This is a *creative* response to one of the problems the world presents us with: the problem of walking. The creative response is not an act of imitation, or a desperate search for a given solution. The creative response lies in the way children vibrate and resonate together with the world in staying in the process of constructing problems.

Children, just as surfers, all have their specific style when learning how to walk and surf. Actually they all have their specific style when learning anything whatsoever. But we rarely pay attention to these different styles. Walking, once you know how to do it, is domesticated by other imperatives, it is tamed to achieve a specific goal of some sort or other. The movement and process of walking in itself becomes a mediator, and it becomes without importance. It is automatic and forgotten movement.

The actual movement of walking just serves as a preparation for other things to come. We focus on the goal to be attained: to be a walker.

In this way, a lot of effort is put into taming subjectivities as well as learning processes; predicting, controlling, supervising and evaluating according to predetermined standards. This is very much what haunts all subjectivity and learning today; movement in subjectivity and learning becomes automatic and forgotten and experimentation becomes tamed, lifeless and predictable. Movement and experimentation in subjectivity and learning seem to find themselves somewhat in a theoretical and practical no-man's-land. There are few theoretical and practical tools available for thinking movement and experimentation as a principle that is more important than the intermediate stops on the way to the goal. The goal or the position is all that counts; movement and experimentation are reduced to mediating devices. If we try to bring forward critique to be able to make room for change, we again lose movement; critique can only take place from position. Positioning always starts by distracting movement. Even if we try to make room for change by insisting on the crossing of borders and hybridization of identities and learning processes, we will end up having lost movement. Moving from one position to another is just shadow movement; it is a change of position and not continuous movement. Movement and experimentation in subjectivity and learning are subordinated to the outcome and to position.

To return to styles, of children or surfers, is of the highest importance and interest. They can tell us something about how subjectivities and learning find themselves in movement. The styles can tell something about continuous and continuously varying processes open for vital, intense and unpredictable experimentation. In the middle of this particular time and space, they can bring back some hope to us, a hope that is directed nowhere else but into the present moment. Going back and picking up the different styles can give us access to a hope that really is nothing more than a trust in the moment. This trust consists of a conviction and belief in things *already* finding themselves in movement. This does not mean that we no longer have anything to do. If it is true that everything is already moving, then that is some of the best news for a long time because that means that there is always and will always be so much to do.

Purpose of the study: the construction of a problem

The story just told concerns movement and experimentation as features of subjectivity and learning. It was possible to tell the story because of experiences in some preschools in Sweden.[4] Preschools are early childhood centres for children from one to five years of age, and most Swedish children of this age attend. The preschools referred to here in this book have been engaged, since the beginning of the 1990s, in collective experimentation concerning subjectivity and learning, bringing together children, preschool teachers, teacher students, teacher educators and researchers.

In 1993 a government-funded project was started up in some preschools in Skarpnäck, a commune (local authority) in Stockholm, where ideas about children, teachers, and preschool environments, content and form were questioned and experimented with (Barsotti, Dahlberg, Göthson and Åsén, 1993). The research group 'The Ethics and Aesthetics of Learning', at the Stockholm Institute of Education, led by Professor Gunilla Dahlberg, was inspired by the French philosopher Michel Foucault (1926–84) and worked with the preschools using post-structural discourse analysis. This made it possible to challenge the dominant discourse of developmental psychology,[5] in which the child already has its position and predetermined development, and where learning is seen as a question of transmission and reproductive imitation. Taken-for-granted images of the child were deconstructed. The image of the child as a rich child capable of constructing knowledge, presented in the preschools in the Italian city of Reggio Emilia, was offered to the Swedish preschools as an alternative image of the child (for more about Reggio Emilia, see Rinaldi, 2005).

All this was done as a way of inspiring and giving tools to the preschools to be able to begin a process of changing their practices (Dahlberg and Moss, 2005). Many other Swedish communes followed up the efforts being made in Skarpnäck, for instance Trångsund, south of Stockholm, and Bromma, west of Stockholm. The research group served as a meeting place for practice and research. In the mid-1990s, a network was created called 'Pedagogical and Theoretical Spaces'. In this context teachers, teacher students, teacher educators and researchers met together to work with questioning preschool practices and making room for them to change. The Swedish preschools involved in these efforts now have many years of experience of how to question and deconstruct one's own practice, and they have produced alternative ways of thinking of the child, the teacher and the preschool's environment, content and form.

However, during later years, questions were raised in the context of cooperative work between teachers and researchers about the changes that have been achieved possibly becoming new and somewhat rigid 'mappings' of young children and learning. These changes sometimes seemed to function as new predetermined schemes, new 'maps' of children and teachers replacing the old ones, in which subjectivity and learning were again becoming immobilized and stereotyped. So what started off as vital, intense and unpredictable experimentation sometimes seemed to have turned into a somewhat lifeless experimentation with the controlling of all parameters as well as the expected outcomes. Recent efforts, therefore, have been made to challenge, both practically and theoretically, the notion of change in relation to subjectivity and learning. What has been looked for both in practice and theory are ways of working with change as something continuously ongoing and as something more than effecting a move from one predefined position to another. Questions have been asked about how to work, practically and theoretically, with the driving forces at stake before everything has settled again into new patterns. In short, what has become the latest challenge to practice and research is finding ways of regaining movement and experimentation in subjectivity and learning.

The study described in this book sets out to contribute to these recent efforts by having as its purpose to construct the problem of how to work with movement and experimentation in subjectivity and learning in the field of early childhood education practice and research.

The problem is contextualized in the first part of the book. Chapter 1 and Chapter 2 give a closer description of the practical and theoretical resources used in this study; why they have been chosen and how they are of importance for the purpose of the study. By the end of the description of the theoretical resources, three decisive points are identified that will function as research questions guiding the construction of the problem. In Chapter 3 a political perspective is drawn up, situating the study in relation to the features of ethics and politics in contemporary society.

The second part of the book deals with methodological questions. In Chapter 4, an attempt is made to account for the close relationship, marked by collective and intense experimentation, between theory and practice taking place in the study presented in this book. In Chapter 5 a pedagogical and scientific methodological perspective is presented and discussed that can possibly account for movement when approaching documented events in preschool.

The third part of the book contains analysis and conclusions. Chapter 6 presents and analyses a documented project in a preschool class with children around the age of two years, working with an overhead projector machine over a period of two years. In Chapter 7 the study is summed up and some conclusions are offered.

Part I

Contextualizing the problem

Chapter 1

Practical resources

Preschools in Stockholm and its suburbs where subjectivity and learning take on the features of a relational field

Introduction

In many of the preschools in the city of Stockholm and its suburbs and at the Stockholm Institute of Education,[1] 'everyday magical moments' take place. Children, preschool teachers, teacher students, teacher educators and researchers come together and are literally caught up in the desire to experiment with subjectivity and learning. In these practices experimentations and intense, unpredictable events are taking place concerning the idea of what a child is, what a teacher should do, the purpose of a preschool and its organization, contents and forms.

As earlier described, the network 'Pedagogical and Theoretical Spaces' serves as a meeting place for practice and research. Also important is the research group's connection and exchange with the preschools in the Italian city of Reggio Emilia. The preschools in Reggio Emilia have been a source of inspiration for many Swedish preschools, by challenging their image of the child, the teacher and the preschool. In these Italian preschools the child is looked upon as rich, capable and knowledge constructing. With this image, the teacher has the role of listening carefully to children as well as arranging situations where children can work with their questions and problems. The preschool is seen as a place where children, together with their peers and teachers, can be engaged in the collective construction of knowledge and values.

One important tool for working with this pedagogical approach consists of continuous project work on different contents of knowledge, where children and teachers collectively are constructing problems in intense learning processes and where the content of knowledge is constructed and negotiated rather than transmitted and reproductively imitated. The focus in the projects is on the multiplicity of perspectives that all participants can bring, and many different means to approach the content of knowledge are used; aesthetic, ethical, political and scientific approaches are all employed and put to work in the learning processes that are taking place. In relation to the content of knowledge, children's thinking, talking and doing are as valued as any other perspective and are often seen as important and additional perspectives on the content of knowledge as it is known and already defined by adults, culture and history.

Working in projects is accompanied by pedagogical documentation – observations, photos, video films, artefacts from different kinds of learning processes. This visualization of learning processes serves as a meeting place for all participants and plays a crucial role in these intense learning processes (Lenz-Taguchi, 2000; Giudici, Rinaldi and Krechevsky, 2001; Dahlberg, Moss and Pence, 2007). As stated earlier, in many preschools in Stockholm and some of its suburbs the inspiration from Reggio Emilia has been of great importance and a network structure has been built up, where preschool teachers, teacher students, teacher educators and researchers meet regularly to experiment with and widen the domains for political action in the preschools. This collaboration is realized through cooperative work with pedagogical documentation in the preschools.

This is a complex process, and the work takes place at many levels at the same time. Historical and cultural issues of how children are seen in relation to different theoretical paradigms about identity and knowledge are discussed, as well as questions of ethics and politics in early childhood education.[2] There is questioning and experimenting with the ways and means by which the teacher takes part in children's learning processes. There are also discussions and the trying out of alternative ways to understand and work with the task of a preschool. There is ongoing work to invent new pedagogical environments suitable for the different features of children, teachers and preschools that are now being experimented with. There is an organization of the content of knowledge in projects and there is an ongoing development of new techniques for observation and documentation.

Recently, Swedish preschools, teachers and researchers began to face new challenges as it seems that what started out as new and vital ideas about children, teachers and preschools sometimes became, quite quickly, new standardized maps. The child is now very often talked about as the 'competent child', in a somewhat taken for granted way that is not very different from the stereotypical thought of recognition and representation that was originally challenged. In the same way, the teacher is talked about as a 'co-researcher' and the teacher's role as well as the task of preschool seem to have become, quite unquestionably, about putting into practice the idea of learning as simply following the children's interest.

Pedagogical environments sometimes look very similar even though preschools are very different and, of course, have very different inhabitants. The work in projects seems to present the preschools with great difficulties; most of the time the projects work with the same kind of content of knowledge and they eventually seem to become quite standardized, in that learning quite often turns out to be treated through a somewhat simplified logic of transmission and imitative reproduction; or the trans-disciplinary work in the projects that was thought to be able to transgress the established borders between different contents of knowledge turns into a somewhat confused and shallow treatment of the different disciplines. Pedagogical documentation presents maybe even greater difficulties as it seems to get easily stuck within the logic of telling the obvious or telling new truths about children. Faced by this situation, many preschools have felt the need for alternative ways of working with their practices and efforts have been made to regain vitality in practice.

Recently, efforts have been made in some of the communities where teachers and researchers try to challenge all these complex areas within the field of early childhood education. In different projects – for instance, *Children's Dialogue with Nature – The Challenges of the Knowledge Society and the Possibilities for Learning* (Dahlberg and Theorell, forthcoming), *Transculturalism and Communication* (Barsotti *et al.*, forthcoming) and *The Magic of Language – Young Children's Relations to Language, Reading and Writing* (Dahlberg and Olsson, forthcoming) – attempts have been made to reactivate movement and experimentation in relation to the image of the child, the role of the teacher, the task of the preschool, the pedagogical environment as well as in relation to the work in projects with pedagogical documentation. These attempts are briefly described below.

Image of the child

In recent efforts, teachers and researchers have struggled to imagine the child in more open and complex ways, trying to avoid falling into the trap of thinking, talking and acting in a simplified way through the notion of the 'competent child'. The ambition has been to open up this image of the child to many other expressions; to find more and unknown ways of being a child than being defined through one's competencies. There has been recognition of the fact that the 'competent child' might be a predetermined map, as strongly regulating as the image of the child earlier defined through the workings of developmental psychology. The ongoing struggle involves an ambition to avoid defining the child beforehand, either through theories of developmental psychology, or through the more or less outspoken definitions of competency.

The focus in recent efforts is the idea of the child as perpetually becoming and not being defined once and for all. To work practically with this perspective, the focus has become less the individual child and more what takes place in between the children – what kinds of thoughts, speech, actions, interests, questions, and desires preoccupy the children at the present moment? Which part of the preschool environment is being used by the children and in what way? What kinds of products or processes from popular culture engage the children; which television programmes, which toys, which figures are they using and how? Are some of these processes and products picked up by groups of children, and through transmission creating a collective culture amongst the children? Where does this take place and how?

Role of the teacher

With respect to the role of the teachers, the ambition in current efforts has been to complicate the idea of the co-researcher, as this role has quite often come to imply that teachers simply followed the children's interest. This has presented difficulties, first of all because it has turned out to be very hard to detect with what kind of interests children actually are preoccupied. It seems difficult, as a teacher, not to use one's own predetermined ideas of what children are doing, and extremely difficult to really listen to children's thoughts, speech and actions in such a way that one gets a glimpse of what is at stake. This also leads to difficulties when trying to connect to and act with the children through arranging situations and proposing new materials to continue the process. Very often teachers and researchers feel that this is the hardest part of their work: how to understand what the children are working with and how to know when to engage with the children and in what way, so that a process of learning where children and teachers are collectively engaged can take place.

This has led to more careful preparatory work before encountering the children, for instance through studying from many different perspectives the actual content of knowledge at stake. For example, if the children seem particularly interested in the characteristics of the physical phenomenon of light and they often gather around the overhead projector, the teachers need to start off by studying these characteristics from many different perspectives: read theories on light from physics, discuss with architects about the function of light in building and design, discuss and read about how light influences our daily lives and environments etc. At the same time, the teachers need to start observing how the children, in their own specific ways, treat all these perspectives on light. These preparations then enable teachers to understand more about children's unique and singular ways of learning.

In recent efforts the ambition has been through such preparations to be capable of listening carefully to verbal, as well as other expressions of children, which very often do not resemble the way we use language as adults, so as to be able to understand in what way children use these to express how they think. Through cooperation with people in other fields such as physicists, designers, and architects, the receptiveness of teachers to children has been raised, and it has also permitted the collection of many ideas and much material that can serve as a source when trying to create situations where children can continue working on the content of knowledge at stake. The misconception of learning as simply a question of following the children's interest has also been challenged through the recognition of the fact that everything does not have to start with the children. Teachers can also propose to children a content of knowledge to be worked upon, the important thing being when and how this content of knowledge is approached.

Task of the preschool

Through all these efforts, the struggle has been to really make something out of the notion of the preschool as a place for the collective construction of knowledge and values. There has been an acknowledgement of the fact that co-construction only means something if teachers and researchers also engage and invest themselves in the content of knowledge at stake in the ways described above. Preschool as a place for the collective construction of knowledge and values also concerns preschool's role as an institution in society. Efforts have been made to treat preschool no longer as a smaller world protected and cut off from the rest of the world. Everything that happens in the world influences preschool, but it can also be the other way around; preschool can also in turn influence the world. Teachers and researchers have worked a lot with trying to connect the ongoing processes and projects in preschool with what goes on in society and to make children's thoughts, speech and actions visible in society. In this respect preschool has become much more of a political institution in the sense that the preschool is considered as a place where children and teachers are active political actors, rather than as a target for political intervention.

Connect to outside. Should be moelable /

Pedagogical environment /

Recent efforts have also touched on questions about the pedagogical environment. The pedagogical environment in its stereotyped form has been challenged through struggling with the need to make it transformable and connective, not only as possible for the children to influence and combine in different ways, but also in relation to the different contents of knowledge at stake and ongoing events in society. Recently it has become important to make preschool an environment that not only reflects the ongoing processes within preschool, but also takes into account what is going on outside preschool. So, for example, the construction corner in the preschool could include elements that evoke and make it possible to work with the interesting features of what is going on at the site next to the preschool where a new subway or tunnel or house is being built. Some preschools have worked more profoundly with this through engaging in cooperation with designers and architects, work that has made it possible not only to transform the already-existing environment, but also to create new furniture and material that raise possibilities of influencing and making new connections in the pedagogical environment.

Work in projects

When it comes to the work in projects, efforts have been made to challenge the logic of transmission and imitative reproduction, but also the way that projects lately seem to suffer from aiming at a certain kind of trans-disciplinary learning, where it turns out that the work often becomes quite confusing and shallow. Recently teachers and researchers have tried to challenge this through focusing on work with the *construction of problems*.

Whatever the content of knowledge, it harbours many different problems. In mathematics, for instance, there is a range of different problems; patterns, rhythm, the conception and symbolic function of numbers, the order of numbers, addition, subtraction, multiplication, etc. Each of these concerns a very specific problem within the system of mathematics and the teachers' ambition has become no longer to work with mathematics in a somewhat generalized way; but rather, through the kind of preparation, studies, observations, and cooperation with other disciplines (in this case maybe mathematicians) described above, to try to define a problem that could be worked upon together with the children during a period of time. Within such work teachers and researchers need to study carefully the content of knowledge at stake and they can be helped in widening the perspectives on the content of knowledge through cooperating with other disciplines.

Moreover, recently it has become clear that, whilst they no longer work through defining preset goals for the children to attain, it is still of the highest importance for the teachers to try to define early in the project why one should work with the children on this specific content of knowledge, as well as to define what kind of theoretical ideas of knowledge and learning one wants to try to put into work with the children in relation to the chosen content or problem. These choices, made at the beginning of the project, must be done in relation to ontological, but also ethical and political features. Teachers must decide how to treat the content of knowledge from a value-based perspective: What kind of learning are we talking about? How do we understand knowledge about this specific subject? Why is it important to work with this? For instance, in some ongoing projects on children's relation to language, one such choice has been to listen carefully to and encourage children's investigations and reinventions of language, that is, to work with the creative dimension of language that children use by rhyming, singing, exchanging and inventing letters and words. When taking into account how language in contemporary society is transforming due to an increase in multicultural encounters and technological communication channels, as well as children's ways of using language creatively, it seems important to acknowledge the creative and pragmatic aspect of language. These choices must be made both in relation to the children and in relation to how the content of knowledge plays a role and is valued in contemporary society. In this way the choices made serve as a starting point as well as a continuous pedagogical tool when proceeding with the children.

A possible problem to work upon must be defined taking into account all the different perspectives and choices that the teachers and researchers can collect and make, but most importantly it must take into account what kind of problem the children seem *to be closest to*. However it is not only the already established problem that is important. Through their experiences in the participating communes over the course of several years, it has become clear to teachers and researchers that children very often not only want to learn through approaching an already established problem within different contents of knowledge, but also they are capable of and seem to find themselves in a constant quest to go beyond established problems, to reinvent them and add new ways of understanding them. It seems that the important thing for children is to *construct* the problem they are working upon. They rarely seem to be interested in already defined problems that have predetermined solutions. An example of

what do children seem to be the closest to?

this is the above described use of language: rhyming, singing, inventing words, exchanging letters, inventing letters, etc. Children seem to use the creative potential of language rather than imitating it as an already predefined and set system. Another example is how children can work for a long time on a problem and, even though they know about the given solution, they seem to choose not to accept this straightaway. It seems that they are enjoying this process of construction and production so much, and that they know that accepting the given solution would inevitably end the process.

It also seems that children quite often construct problems through approaching the content of knowledge from a wide range of different perspectives. For instance, young children quite often approach mathematics from the point of view of its aesthetic features; they seem to get almost enamoured by the aesthetic beauty of the mathematical system. This implies that, although attempts have been made to somewhat deepen and limit the work in projects to focus on a specific problem, many different ways of approaching this problem can be used: aesthetic, technical, ethical, poetic, or other perspectives. But this is not the same thing as trans-disciplinary work which often turns out to treat the different disciplines in a quite shallow and confusing way. The focus is on the *construction* of the specific problem. The problem is not set from the beginning, it is constructed with the help of the different disciplinary perspectives and each of these serves to deepen the approach to the problem. This is a way of working that, rather than working with trivial universals, harbours a more complex, deep and creative approach to learning.

The experiences over the course of the years also show that young children treat mathematics or any other content of knowledge from a very pragmatic point of view. It has to be something that can be used and it has to serve some purpose. This has been accentuated in recent projects and careful work has been undertaken to try to situate the investigations and constructions of a problem in what is for the children a meaningful context, where it can be further worked upon. This involves arranging a situation in which children are motivated to continue their efforts.

A very simple example comes from when one group of children had an established interest in reading and writing letters. The children often chose the writing corner and they would spend many hours there reading and writing letters. The teachers prepared themselves through studying different aspects of language, reading and writing and they carefully observed the children during a period of time. They detected a problem that seemed close to the children: the children were struggling with how to understand and read each others' writings. The problem in this case was defined as the communicative aspect of reading and writing. The teachers then decided to make letter boxes for each child and provide them with a lot of material for fabricating letters, so as to create a situation where the children could feel motivated to continue their efforts in a collective process. This led to a long period of constructing the problem of communication through the written and spoken word where children pushed and constructed the problem in many complex and interesting ways.

Pedagogical documentation

Pedagogical documentation has also been affected by these efforts. The problem with pedagogical documentation was, as described above, that it seemed to have got stuck in telling the obvious or telling the truth about children. To challenge this, teachers and researchers have been trying to work with pedagogical documentation as a place where the problem one is currently working upon with the children can be visualized. In that sense pedagogical documentation does not refer to the recognizing and representative aspects of the word documentation at all. An ambition has been to challenge the recognizing and representative aspects of the photos, observations, and recordings; not to focus in these on 'what really took place', but rather to *use* the pedagogical documentation together as teachers and researchers, and most importantly, together with the children in the ongoing process of constructing a problem. Pedagogical documentation has been used by teachers and researchers in the quest for a problem to construct together with the children. Therefore, when revisiting the documentation together with the children, the question has not been about helping the children to remember what they did last time, so as to establish some kind of linear and chronological learning process; rather, it has been a question of focusing, with the help of the documentation, on what kind of problem is under construction, what questions have been produced so far, what kind of tools and materials have been tried out and most importantly, to find where the potentials for continuing the construction of the problem are located.

Subjectivity and learning as a relational field

All these recent efforts have led teachers and researchers to start talking about, and putting into practice, an idea of *subjectivity and learning as a relational field*.[3] From this perspective, children, teachers and researchers, and also the content and form of learning processes, take on the features of being in a relational and continuously moving field. Everything is involved in such a field, not only human subjects, but also the content of knowledge of different subjects as we know it, as well as the entire milieu. These are all in relation, but not as fixed entities encountering each other, rather it is the relation itself that is in movement. One needs to consider the different problems as not fixed and set. One must also see the different human subjects involved as not fixed and set once and for all; it is a completely relational situation where human subjects as much as the content of learning and the actual process are intertwined and continuously moving.

Obviously each child and each teacher or researcher has in these processes their own unique ways of thinking, speaking, acting, and feeling but these individual contributions are caught up in the collective process creating a collective culture of knowledge and values. For instance, individual children will, during explorations of drawing, use singular strategies: a certain way of drawing a perspective or a figure. When confronted with each others' strategies, without any one of these being considered the right one, the entire group of children will eventually pick up and use some of these individual strategies as a group. Learning here takes place in between everybody involved.

Or there might be a conflict of some sort at stake in a group where an individual solution to the conflict can become part of a collective value culture. In one class the youngest children who have a sleep at midday would be woken up by the older ones playing in the room next door. When confronted with this situation and asked together to find a way of handling it, one child proposed drawing maps with suggestions of how you could walk past the room where the youngest sleep so as to not wake them up. Many children adopted this proposal and started to draw maps and write suggestions of how to move through the room. These maps and suggestions became part of a collective value culture in the entire preschool and it worked since it had been produced between everybody involved.

This idea of subjectivity and learning presents an addition to the formalized school system and its attempts to predict, control, supervise and evaluate subjectivities and learning processes against predetermined goals. This does not mean that the idea of subjectivity and learning as a relational field requires neglect of the content of knowledge. On the contrary, and as seen above, it is the content of knowledge that is the centre of attention, but with a deeper and more creative and complex approach to it as consisting of many specific and different problems and that each needs to be approached through working with the *construction of problems*. The content of knowledge finds itself in the middle of the relational field and it is around a problem within the content of knowledge that children and teachers meet. But the important thing is that one must allow for the problem and the content of knowledge to continuously be on the move.

Moreover, this is not an 'anything goes pedagogy'. It is a rigorous approach where careful preparations are being made, but where, due to the idea of the content of knowledge as part of a relational field, one avoids nailing down specific knowledge goals to serve as departure points for the learning process and to be used to evaluate each child. Instead, and as seen above, teachers are carefully defining the importance of working with a specific problem, related to ontological, political and ethical features, but once they meet with the children they are left with nothing but experimenting.

The first results of this work in process are quite astonishing. From the documented material, it seems that children, through their own singularities, have connected to each other in a cooperative way of working, getting a chance to be creative in mind, speech and action and to add things to the content of knowledge as we know it. But at the same time they also learn already existing facts and codes; it is just being done in a different way. In these projects children perpetually act in surprising and somewhat untameable ways, but they still learn what they are supposed to learn from a traditional educational perspective with its logic of transmission and reproductive imitation of pre-established content of knowledge. Moreover, in addition to new features of the content of knowledge that the children bring in, new kinds of relationships grow in between children; new ways of being at the same time more singularized and absolutely unique and still united. Each child contributes to the process in his or her specific and absolutely singular way, but the contribution is caught up in the group's process, thus creating a very particular culture where knowledge as well as values are collectively negotiated, constructed and continuously on the move.

The preschools that have been working in this way are of interest for the purpose of this book, since the idea of subjectivity and learning as a relational field and their recent efforts to regain vitality in their practice involve a struggle and an ambition to regain movement and experimentation in a setting that sometimes has cemented into new maps and positions, and that has lost the vitality and intensity that can be generated in a somewhat unpredictable experimentation. These preschools and their recent efforts have therefore seemed well worth looking further into when constructing the problem of how to work with movement and experimentation in early childhood education practice and research.

Chapter 2

Theoretical resources

A Deleuzian/Guattarian philosophy of relations, creations and experimental empiricism

Introduction

To theoretically approach preschools, such as the ones described above, and join in their efforts to regain movement and experimentation in practice, some theoretical resources found in the philosophy of Gilles Deleuze (1925–1995) and Félix Guattari (1930–1992) have proved to be of great value. These two French thinkers were at their most active during the 1970s and 1980s in France. Deleuze was a trained philosopher and he published his thesis *Différence et Répétition* in 1968 (Deleuze, 1968a). The thesis was published after he had already written and published a number of important texts on different philosophers, such as David Hume (1711–1776) (1953), Friedrich Nietzsche (1844–1900) (1962), Henri Bergson (1859–1941) (1966), and Baruch de Spinoza (1632–1677) (1968b). Guattari was a psychoanalyst at the La Borde clinic outside Paris and engaged in the militant political struggle during the 1960s and 1970s in France (Sauvagnargues, 2005). Deleuze talks about the encounter with Guattari as having changed a lot. Through Guattari's experience and political engagement in the field of psychiatry, the philosophy they created together not only became directed to and engaged even more in political practices, but also created a working relationship that functioned in between the two of them, without the need to define an original author (Deleuze and Parnet, 1987).

Deleuze and Guattari were part of a generation of thinkers that also included Michel Foucault (1926–1984), Jacques Derrida (1930–2004), Louis Althusser (1918–1990) and Jean-François Lyotard (1924–1998) amongst others; their ideas were all formed in the aftermaths of the Second World War and the Liberation of France. The 1960s in France was dominated by structuralist thought in philosophy and social sciences, but the works of Deleuze and Guattari clearly point, from the very beginning, in a different direction. Structuralism, associated with linguistics, anthropology and psychoanalysis, is challenged by Deleuze and Guattari through redefining structures as open-ended and unstable assemblages (Patton and Protevi, 2003).

An important idea is that a first condition of any structure is that it is leaking; there is always something that deviates from and escapes a structure or a system. This goes for linguistic structures but also for society as a whole and even for the history of philosophy (Deleuze and Guattari, 1984, 2004). Deleuze, already in his first philosophical works, struggled to bring forward a philosophy capable of harbouring the non-discursive; that which does not fit within and escapes structure. This struggle develops and culminates in the encounter with Guattari, with an intense critique of the status of interpretation, as well as offering an alternative to post-structural attempts of deconstructing signifying regimes. A theory of the non-discursive makes it possible to detach the sign from its linguistic imprisonment and through the notion of unstable and open-ended assemblages it is possible to give the sign a status of being *a-signifying*. Its status as bearer of meaning and signification has been replaced by function, the only important thing being how it works. The sign is no longer open for interpretation but for experimentation, and creation and pragmatism have moved within language itself as abundant and producing forces (Sauvagnargues, 2005; Deleuze and Guattari, 1984, 2004).

As a consequence, and in relation to the social field, the work of Deleuze and Guattari consistently focuses on that which is not yet known. It attempts to go beyond the taken for granted and the already defined, the predetermined positions and habitual ways of thinking, talking and doing. It is a philosophy that focuses upon the ongoing creation of leakages and considers these as non-discursive, non-interpretative potentialities inherent in any structure or system that do not need to be deconstructed but rather to be activated.

Deleuze and Guattari present us with a philosophy capable of challenging the thought of recognition and representation in which the child already has its fixed position and predetermined development, and where learning is seen as a question of transmission and reproductive imitation (Deleuze, 1994a; Dahlberg and Moss, 2005). Moreover, Deleuze and Guattari's philosophy seems to offer access to ways of working with movement and experimentation that may be helpful to preschools' ongoing struggle with vitalizing their practice. The philosophy of Deleuze and Guattari is indeed peculiar. Not that there is anything mystical about it, on the contrary, as argued below, it is one of the few philosophies capable of being used in many different ways and in direct relation to practices and events in everyday life.

Still, it is enormously complex and not always an easily accessible philosophy, as it rethinks not only subjectivity and learning, but also such seemingly different features as film, the earth and the brain, not forgetting philosophy itself (Deleuze, 1989, 1992a, 1994a; Deleuze and Guattari, 1994, 2004). Deleuze and Guattari were never interested in the question of the eventual death of philosophy and the subject that has engaged many other philosophers and researchers, for whom both philosophy and the subject are dead in the sense that they are trapped within structural closure. For instance, linguistic structures are seen as closed systems, there is nothing outside discourse and one is then forced to deconstruct the discourse from within (Patton and Protevi, 2003).

But, as already stated, for Deleuze and Guattari, the first condition of a structure or a system is that it is leaking. Therefore, for them, if one is not content with the present metaphysics one needs to start producing a different one and the task of the philosopher is to create concepts. In such a creation and production the history of philosophy serves as a tool box, where old themes can always be reawakened and put to work in relation to contemporary society and the problems proper to the contemporary situation (Deleuze and Guattari, 1994).

A thought created through encounters

Deleuze and Guattari's philosophy presents a thought with the peculiar role of creating itself as it goes on. This contrasts with the way the history of philosophy has treated thought. According to Spindler (2006), all great philosophical systems start out from the idea of needing to define the grounding principles for thought, and despite the idea of thought as non-material and as interiority, these grounding principles have throughout the history of philosophy been described in spatial terms: to ground, to build, to construct, to manifest, etc. The task of philosophers has consisted in organizing a place for systematic thinking. This place is described as a sedentary and fixed place capable of harbouring human thinking. Thinking then, under these conditions, is marked by stability, systematic construction, linearity, and categorization. This thinking produces life as organized, systemized, and marked by habits.

Against such thinking, Deleuze and Guattari put forward nomadic thinking, a thinking that has no sedentary and stable place within which to perform its activity. This thinking not only deconstructs codes and habits but actually connects them together in new and unexpected ways.

However, nomadic thinking is not presented as the simple opposite of sedentary thinking. Rather nomadic thinking recognizes that the act of organizing a place for thinking is a necessity, but this act of laying out the ground or organizing the place where thinking thinks, is seen as a very bold and dangerous act of creation that never stops taking place. It is dangerous since it literally exposes thinking to a continuous loss of its own ground and conditions. The ground and conditions for thinking, as well as the act of thinking, are here considered as fragile, temporary and continuously moving features. Nomadic thinking presents a thought that embraces the courage to create, at each moment, the conditions of thinking at the same time as thinking proceeds (Spindler, 2006).

This somewhat odd thought that creates itself, is not performing this self-creation in a vacuum. According to Deleuze, and in contrast to the thought of interiority that has marked the history of philosophy, this thought is constructed through encounters and relations:

> Something in the world forces us to think. This something is an object not of recognition but of a fundamental *encounter*.
> (Deleuze, 1994a: 139; original emphasis)

These encounters are particularly violent affairs since they open up thinking to the forces of chaos. When we really think it is like being struck to the ground only to find that you are falling through it, since it does not exist any more. It concerns a kind of vertiginous feeling of losing one's references. But at the same time it is a very joyful and affirmative affair, since it can give us access to universes we did not know anything about.

Experimental empiricism

This thought differs from the thought of recognition and representation, in that it is created, and always and continuously created, through relations and encounters. Thought, in this way, also has the features of experimentation, but an idea of experimentation that is something totally different from the idea of experimentation as the lifeless controlling of all parameters as well as working with an expected outcome (Deleuze, 1994a). Experimentation here concerns that which is not yet known, it concerns that which comes about, that which is new and that demands more than recognizing or representing truth. Thought as experimentation concerns the new, the interesting and the remarkable: [1]

> To think is to experiment, but experimentation is always that which is in the process of coming about – the new, remarkable, and interesting that replace the appearance of truth and are more demanding than it is.
>
> (Deleuze and Guattari, 1994: 111)

But maybe the most striking thing about this philosophy is that it invites so many different and varied fields to use its thinking. The corpus of work in the spirit of Deleuze and Guattari is growing at quite a speed and touches all sorts of different fields; to take just two examples, Wenzer (2007) has worked with these theories in relation to music and the indie scene in the Swedish city of Gothenburg, and Damkjaer (2005) has performed an interdisciplinary study of the aesthetics of movement in Gilles Deleuze's writings and in Merce Cunningham's choreographies. The reason for this extensive and varied use might lie, bizarrely enough, in precisely the abstractedness and complexity of their ideas. It is not a question of being abstract for the sake of abstractedness itself; it is a question of being abstract enough so as to be able to treat concrete everyday life in new and different ways. Although nomadic thinking might seem highly abstract and complex, it is precisely because it creates its condition for thinking as it proceeds that it is no longer forced to rely on the codes and habits of everyday life.

When the conditions for thinking are changed in this way, there are possibilities to think, speak and live in ways that are not already known. The complexity of Deleuze and Guattari's philosophy makes it hard to use it with any ambition of nailing down or systemizing living practices. It is a philosophy capable of accounting for what seems to be contradictions, but that really are complex and continuously changing relations that are part of everyday life on all levels (Deleuze and Guattari, 2004).

This brings philosophy very close to what takes place in everyday practices. It is not a philosophical system that constructs a theory of knowledge about the world and its inhabitants that you can apply to a practice in order to critique it. In short, it is not an epistemology (Deleuze, 2001; Deleuze and Guattari, 2004). But it is an ontology that admits that it takes part in producing reality and even producing itself as it goes on. And since this philosophy is constructed through encountering thought with examples, it is what takes place in everyday life practices that makes it function.[2]

This implies a specific kind of empiricism that is different from the one referred to as an epistemological tradition. It concerns a wild kind of empiricism that accounts for the unstableness and continuous production in thought and practice. Empiricism has, according to Deleuze (2001), always harboured more interesting features than the history of philosophy has accounted for, and he urges that the question – whether there is something in the senses that needs to be organized and systemized by abstract thought – is badly posed. What we consider to be atomistic sensations in need of being systemized and organized through abstract logical thinking, are really already products of our living in the world. Before thought there is life, and life can never be totally identified or systemized. Thought here never functions as a highest organizing or systemizing principle of experience.

Empiricism in the philosophical thinking of Deleuze and Guattari is, therefore, a pluralist empiricism that accounts for thought as created through encounters. This is why it is of interest for a practice of any kind to approach this philosophy by using its concepts in relation to examples from practice. It is the encounter between examples from practice and the philosophical concepts that is capable of bringing forward something new, interesting and remarkable (Deleuze, 1989, 2001).[3]

This philosophy, with a thought that creates itself as it goes on through encounters and relations and with its experimental and empiricist features, has been of interest for preschools interested in regaining vitality, movement and experimentation into their practices. A thought that creates itself as it goes on has seemed to be a thought capable of accounting for movement. This has been useful in relation to the preschools' struggle with introducing movement in practice. Moreover this thought is described as created through encounters and relations and this has been of interest in relation to the idea of subjectivity and learning as a relational field. And the same thought defined as experimentation where the focus is on the new, the interesting and the remarkable, instead of the controlling of parameters as well as the expected outcome, fitted well with the preschools' ambition to regain an intense and somewhat unpredictable experimentation. Finally, due to the particular empiricist features described above, this has seemed to be a theoretical perspective particularly well suited to account for the close working relationship between research and practice that is taking place in the settings described above. Deleuze and Guattari's philosophy, then, has seemed well worth using when constructing the problem of how to work with movement and experimentation in early childhood education practice and research.

Important and useful texts and concepts by Deleuze and Guattari

In the study described in this book it is the texts and concepts, collectively produced by Deleuze and Guattari, that have been of most importance. Although these texts and concepts have an important history and background in philosophical sources such as Nietzsche, Bergson and Spinoza, amongst others, these philosophers are referred to in the present study only through the way Deleuze and Guattari have used them in their own work.[4]

The Logic of Sense (2004b) and *Difference and Repetition* (1994a), sole-authored works by Deleuze, have been particularly useful in the present study for developing the methodological approach presented in Chapter 5 through the use of the concept of the 'event'. *Pure Immanence: Essays on A Life* (2001) has been a source for developing the ideas presented in Chapter 4 of a relationship marked by collective, intense and unpredictable experimentation in between theory and practice. Sole-authored works by Guattari that have been especially useful for this study include *Chaosmosis, an ethico-aesthetic paradigm* (1995) and *Ecrits pour L'Anti-Oedipe* (2004). In both these, but especially the former, a political perspective on ethical questions is drawn up and this perspective has been useful for the formulation of the aesthetic-ethical framing in this study.

Guattari and Deleuze wrote together, as co-authors, refusing to identify their individual contributions and apparently finding it amusing to present their joint authorship in a confusing manner. They begin *A Thousand Plateaus* (2004) by stating: 'The two of us wrote *Anti-Oedipus* together. Since each of us was several, there was already quite a crowd' (p.3). Because of this very close collaboration, the philosophy is presented and referred to as 'their philosophy', apart from the texts that were produced as sole-authored work.

For the present study and its purpose of constructing the problem of how to work with movement and experimentation in early childhood education practice and research, a few concepts have been chosen out of Deleuze and Guattari's vast philosophy.

These concepts are:

- micro-politics and segmentarity
- transcendental empiricism
- event
- assemblages of desire.

These concepts are discussed in more detail in what follows.

Although it is quite clear that if trying to theoretically regain movement and experimentation through Deleuze and Guattari, you sooner or later need to confront their theories of time and space, a choice has been to take a slightly different starting point on the theoretical path. Since the study builds on the encounter *in between* examples from practice and theoretical concepts, the ambition has been to not apply the concepts to the practices. Rather, the concepts have been chosen on the basis of their functioning together with practices. In this study, therefore, it seemed more important to begin with the four concepts listed above, as they seemed to be the ones that function best in relation to the preschools' struggle with regaining movement and experimentation in their practice.[5] Even though writing this book has implied a lot of reading from many different texts by Deleuze and Guattari, for the chosen concepts the most useful texts have been: *Anti-Oedipus: Capitalism and Schizophrenia* (1984), *A Thousand Plateaus: Capitalism and Schizophrenia 2* (2004), *The Logic of Sense* (2004b), *Pure Immanence Essays on A Life* (2001) and *What is philosophy?* (1994).[6]

In what follows, some previous research is presented that has proved relevant to the study in this book, and provides useful connections to working with Deleuze and Guattari. Thereafter three decisive points are identified in relation to these practical and theoretical resources. These decisive points function as research questions that will guide the construction of the problem throughout the study. When identifying these decisive points, it will be described in more detail how the texts and concepts of Deleuze and Guattari have been used in the study.

Related research on Deleuze and Guattari

In the present study an effort has been made to stick as much as possible to the original texts by Deleuze and Guattari. But, as will be seen, some resources have also been found in work referring to Deleuze and Guattari and in Deleuzian and Guattarian inspired studies within the field of early childhood education. As stated earlier, many scholars from different fields pick up Deleuze and Guattari's work and use it in different ways. In addition to Deleuze and Guattari's original texts, Brian Massumi's recent work (2002, 2003) has been of particular use for the present study. Massumi has used Deleuze and Guattari's work in the field of cultural studies in order to work upon (amongst other problems) the problem of movement. Even though cultural studies is a different field than early childhood education, Massumi identifies and makes today's problems of his field speak together with Deleuze and Guattari in a way that is very close to what this study is trying to do in the field of early childhood education. Massumi's way of treating the field of cultural studies, through identifying some decisive points to further work on with the help of Deleuze and Guattari (amongst others), in order to account for movement, has turned out to be very helpful. Some of the decisive points identified by Massumi, as well as his views on political and ethical features in contemporary society have been useful so as to be able to theoretically and politically situate the research problem in this study in relation to the specific contemporary situation in the field of early childhood education.

These decisive points concern a different conception of positions, of science's critical thinking, and of the dualism individual/society. Thus, to be able to account for movement and experimentation one needs to focus on process rather than position. Moreover, one needs to admit science's inventiveness and engagement in production, rather than being confined to its critical agenda. And finally, one needs to find a way whereby the dualism individual/society is no longer treated as a cause–effect relationship, but rather find another logic for how to treat what takes place *in between* constructed and imagined entities such as individuals and societies.

Massumi treats these points in relation to contemporary society where he shows how governing has changed face and works through modulating our desires to expand our bodies and life styles. Inspired by Spinoza, he uses the term 'affect' to account for this new kind of governing. Affect is, according to Massumi, put forward by Spinoza to account for bodily potential. 'What can a body do?' is, according to him, a Spinozian question that today has become part of our lives to a greater extent than before. Governing today works through modulating our desire to expand our bodies and life styles; to expand our affective potential. In this way he describes how governing no longer disciplines us from the outside but has rather installed itself within the features of affect. In the light of this, Massumi calls for research that, rather than fighting against this modulation of affect, starts engaging in its own desiring production and modulation of affect within an ethics and politics of belonging. This implies collectively experimenting with the potentialities at hand in each singular moment.

These decisive points and the features of ethics and politics seem fruitful also for working upon the problem of movement and experimentation in the field of early childhood education practice and research. Massumi's recent work is therefore used as the most important resource apart from the original texts by Deleuze and Guattari.

For entering Deleuze and Guattari's philosophy, François Zourabichvili (2003) has also been of great help and value. He has created a 'Deleuzian vocabulary', in alphabetical order, insisting on the need to give his concepts their proper logic. It is an attempt to do away with some misunderstandings of Deleuzian concepts as metaphors, and instead giving a sort of logical consistency to the theme of immanence prevailing in the creation of concepts that Deleuze insisted upon. According to Zourabichvili, Deleuze's attempts to create a different metaphysics must be understood from a different logic than that which the history of philosophy embraces. According to him, Deleuze presents new and different conditions for thinking that nevertheless have their own stringently defined logic.

Anne Sauvagnargues (2005) has functioned somewhat in the same way as Zourabichvili: a very trustworthy and reliable source for approaching Deleuze's thinking.[7] Her work has been an inspiration for future work with some of the more complicated concepts of Deleuze and Guattari and their origins, e.g. the concept of the eternal return presented by Nietzsche, the concept of time treated by Bergson, and the concept of affect at a deeper level in Spinoza, as well as his way of drawing up a plane of immanence.

Manuel de Landa (2002) has been valuable for this study through his work on the intersection of science and philosophy, where the mathematical sources of Deleuze's thinking are focused upon and explained, giving access from a different angle to some of the more complex concepts.

Bonta and Protevi (2004) connect Deleuze and Guattari's thinking to geophilosophy, insisting on Deleuze and Guattari's politically informed use of complexity theory in social sciences. Complexity theory can be described as investigations on how systems of different kinds – organic, inorganic and social – can consist, at the same time, of levels of internal complexity and systematic behaviour, but without relying on external factors or organizing agents. Systems, in this view, are self-organizing and self-producing, though not in a homeostatic way, or according to any established order. Rather they randomly produce and organize, freely and openly. Bonta and Protevi suggest that Deleuze and Guattari's politically informed use of complexity theory in the field of social science has made it possible to undo, and add something to, one of the most important dilemmas of social science research, namely the debate on structure/agency.

This was useful to understand some of the mechanisms at stake in the preschools of this study, especially concerning the work with understanding how change comes about. In the preschools involved in this study, change has sometimes appeared to happen within complex, self-organizing and self-producing systems, where neither surrounding linguistic, social, historical, political or economic structures, nor individual contributions within the system, completely decide how change comes about. Rather, changes in practice have sneaked up behind one's back, have come about unexpectedly and are not easily explained through any cause–effect relationship.

Related research in early childhood education

Deleuze and Guattari are not the only thinkers making possible work challenging change and the thought of recognition and representation. As stated earlier, much work has already been done in the field of early childhood education. One particularly strong contribution is research carried out within a post-structural and deconstructive framework (cf. Hultqvist, 1990; Dahlberg and Lenz-Taguchi, 1994; Cannella, 1997; Dahlberg and Moss, 2005; Dahlberg, Moss and Pence, 2007). Through discourse analysis and deconstructive work, inspired by Foucault, taken for granted truths about children, childhood, preschool and preschool teachers have been analysed and deconstructed as the products of particular truth regimes, or discursive regimes, prevailing at particular times and places in history. These researchers challenge the kind of thinking taking place in what has come to be called the modern époque. As described by Foucault (1973, 1977), at this time the human subject, formerly a feudal subject in a patrimonial model of governing through the king and private property, is now governed through the nation state and centralized state apparatuses where the human subject becomes citizen. The nation-state fosters the human subject as culturally, biologically and essentially defined according to class, sex and race. The particular kind of governing at stake in society at this time expresses itself through how the centralized state apparatus functions as the all- and ever-seeing eye, from whose gaze the subject can never escape. Institutions function in resonance with the state apparatus in fostering a particular subject – the free, individual and rational citizen – as well as driving society forward along an imagined line of progression and growth towards the Good, the True and the Beautiful. Through processes of industrialization and urbanization, life is spatially divided into different compartments or procedures on a life-line that each citizen has to pass through: family, school and work life.

The researchers mentioned above have associated these ideas with the field of early childhood education, locating it as part of a wider context of governing and subjectification. Through their research efforts, they show how this particular time in history influences childhood, children and preschool. In line with Foucault's analyses, they have complicated governing in the name of the good and the true and made visible how scientific knowledge, especially the corpus of knowledge within developmental psychology, and power are intertwined and functioning in producing subjectivities of the 'normal' child. The normalization of the child entails representing, classifying and measuring of the child, through the concept of 'developmentality', which has led to the inclusion and exclusion of certain ways of being a child.

Two particularly strong images of the learning preschool child have been identified: 'the child as nature' and 'the child as reproducer of culture, identity and knowledge' (Dahlberg, et al., 2007). 'The child as nature' is a biologically determined child; its development and learning processes are considered to be inherent, natural and biological phenomena that follow predetermined stages. Through scientific theories of developmental psychology, the child's development is possible to predict, prepare, supervise and evaluate according to predefined standards. This is a child that learns in a completely de-contextualized way, its development is set from the very beginning and when the child does not develop according to the predefined schema there is something essentially wrong with the child.

'The child as reproducer of culture, identity and knowledge' is the empty child, a 'tabula rasa'. This child is always 'not ready', it is a lacking child that needs to be filled up with culture, identity and knowledge. This child is supposed to receive the fixed and predetermined content of culture, identities and knowledge brought forward by the adults and to adapt itself to it, to internalize it, to develop in a certain order, in well-defined universal stages, to later be able to reproduce it as exactly as possible. The naturally developing child is also an *individual* child. Within the logic of measuring a child that is supposed to have inherent, natural capacities that need to be expressed to a predetermined curve of development, the focus will be on each child. It becomes important to see where each individual is, in its natural state and then find out how this corresponds to the predetermined curve of development.

The two images, the natural and the reproducing child, therefore coexist, are at work at the same time. Together with the focus on the individual child, they form a predominant notion of the identity of the learning preschool child, as an individual, natural, developing child.

The pedagogical challenge lies in giving the right support at the right moment for the child to develop properly. The child's response to this developmental help then indicates whether the child is following the normal curve of development or not. What the teacher is looking for is the lack of proper development; she/he is functioning as a detector of lack, an observer of error (Dahlberg and Lenz-Taguchi, 1994). That a child develops seems unquestionably true, and to help the child develop properly seems unquestionably right. The above-mentioned research efforts have also shown how the field of early childhood education and the preschool during this period of time function as an extension of the state, a tool for governing and educating citizens. Not only the individual child but also future society as a whole is going to be governed through preschool. In this way, the preschool in modern society gets a very specific form, content and purpose.

Lately, post-structural and deconstructive researchers have faced new challenges in relation to ongoing changes in contemporary society. According to these changes, as they are described for instance by Nikolas Rose (1999) and Michael Hardt and Antonio Negri (2002), we no longer live in a world defined by separated nation-states; we live in a post-modern and global information society, where people, money and goods perpetually cross boundaries through new technologies and communication channels in network systems. We are no longer governed by centralized state apparatuses; we are individual, autonomous and flexible subjects that on account of our border-crossing and liberty of choice of lifestyles take on multiple, fractioned and hybrid identities. Accordingly government in post-modern society no longer functions through centralized state apparatuses. Society's institutions are getting more and more privatized – you can choose and buy services according to your own taste and governing takes place in a smaller local way. Life is no longer divided into different, spatially determined compartments; we work at a distance through networking structures, home is where you can rest your head for the moment and learning takes place at various locations and throughout the entire life line.

Taking these changes into account, post-structural and deconstructive early childhood researchers have detected how a new kind of subjectivity for the child has begun to emerge: 'the competent, autonomous and flexible child' (Fendler, 2001; Dahlberg, 2003; Popkewitz and Bloch, 2001; Dahlberg and Hultqvist, 2001; Bloch, Holmlund, Moqvist and Popkewitz, 2003; Brembeck, Johansson and Kampman, 2004; Dahlberg and Moss, 2005). 'The competent, autonomous and flexible child' is a child that is independent, problem-solving and responsible for its own learning processes through self-reflection. This child is presumed to have a desire and capability to learn and is encouraged to ask questions, resolve problems and seek answers. This image of the child could be seen as a challenge to the individual, natural and developing child, since the ambition is no longer to map the child with the help of developmental psychology.

But as the above-mentioned researchers have shown, it seems that the ongoing changes in society are mirrored in this image of the child and they warn that there is no question of less governing, only a different kind of governing. It is no longer only the child's body or mind or moral behaviour that are supposed to be influenced by our pedagogical endeavours; now it is a question of getting at the child's very inner desires. It concerns an ambition to get children to want to learn and willingly adapt to the new logic of continuous learning through autonomous and flexible problem solving. The focus on each individual is very explicit and obvious in the image of 'the competent, autonomous and flexible child'.

It seems that a new map to measure the child against has been drawn. Each child is supposed to have its own competencies to bring forward. These competencies are then being measured against a new set of predetermined goals and standards. Instead of being measured against the scheme of development established by developmental psychology, the child is now being measured against what is defined as competency in local as well as global contexts, including grades of autonomous and flexible behaviour.

The early childhood researchers referred to above have also pointed out that, in accordance with ongoing changes, it turns out that preschool is no longer seen as the extension of the state apparatus. There is a rise of privatization of preschools and each preschool can, to a greater extent than before, develop its own profile. People can choose which preschool to put their child in, according to their own individual taste and irrespective of geographical location. Preschools, as many other institutions in contemporary society, have started to formulate their task differently, no longer as the extension of a centralized state apparatus, but more in accordance with what works in local contexts and networks. The researchers have also demonstrated how the tendency towards autonomous and flexible behaviour is spreading into every corner of our society.

In this new kind of governing, where the state no longer figures as a central governor, individuals, through choices and actions, design their own life. Not only is the pupil in school supposed to be 'competent, autonomous and flexible' but everybody in today's society is supposed to take responsibility for his or her own life in a continuous process of learning. It is from this logic and image of the subject that the term 'life-long learning' is born. Preschool, school and work life are no longer talked about as separate units. Instead we have life-long learning, an introduction of learning along the entire life-line of a person and throughout all of society's institutions.

Some feminist scholars in the field of early childhood education (Walkerdine, 1997; Lenz-Taguchi, 2000; Blackman and Walkerdine, 2001) have tried to argue against the theoretical approach, as it seemed to do away with the possibilities of the subject's agency and sometimes reduced the subject to being simply a mirror of discourse. Feminist scholars have insisted on the multiplicity of discourses that are in play all the time and the possibility for research to not only deconstruct but also reconstruct subjectivities. For instance, Lenz-Taguchi (2000) has, through Derrida-inspired deconstructive work, experimented with three preschool teachers with a form of cooperative work, using pedagogical documentation. Through deconstructive talks as well as collective biography work and storyline deconstructions, her study investigates the possibility not only to deconstruct, but also to reconstruct subjectivities of the child and teacher and thereby, through a practice of pedagogical documentation, empower children as well as teachers.

Elisabeth Nordin-Hultman (2004) has also followed up recent efforts within post-structural research. Her study deconstructs the discursive regimes of subjectivities and learning as they express themselves through the pedagogical environments in Swedish and English classrooms. She returns to Foucault's way of treating the event as never being predictable, but rather constructing itself in the moment. Consequently, she proposes that children, when encountering a pedagogical environment or material, find themselves engaged in an encounter where both parts are simultaneously changing. In a pedagogical environment as event children, teachers and even the rooms and the furniture find themselves in a continuous process of becoming. The way in which she puts forward the pedagogical environment as possible event is also quite close to the Deleuzian/Guattarian concept of event.

All the research just outlined has been important for this study in that it highlights the struggles over subjectivity and learning going on in the field of early childhood education. This research was also an important starting point in trying to work out the theoretical tools needed for this study's specific purpose.

Related research on Deleuze and Guattari in early childhood education[8]

One of the earliest and strongest contributions to the field of Deleuze and Guattari in early childhood education is the work of Liane Mozère, who worked closely together with Deleuze and Guattari during the 1970s in Paris. She has done, and continues doing, ground-breaking and very important work. In her thesis *Le Printemps des Crèches: histoire et analyse d'un mouvement* (1992), Mozère analyses the field of early childhood education in France during a ten-year period (1970–1980), and especially in the aftermath of May 1968, through the Deleuzian/Guattarian concept 'micro-politics' and the Guattarian concept 'groupe-sujet' (subject-group). Through collective experimentation and a network structure between the research group CERFI[9] and preschools in a Parisian suburb, changes were brought about in the image of the child, the role of the teacher as well as the task of the preschool. These changes concerned ways of thinking, talking and acting with the children that went from a paradigm of hygiene and hierarchy, where children as well as teachers were positioned as lacking in competence as well as having little possibility to influence their lives in preschools, towards a practice of collective experimentation and magical moments, where children were listened to and given the possibility to influence their lives in new ways, as well as having a new relationship to adults. Adults no longer looked at children as objects for their own interventions, but took instead the position of learning from the children and being willing to experiment together with them. Both children and teachers engaged in and experimented with their collective desires in totally new ways. Preschools opened up and became public places where important and vital life processes took place, and also, where parents could have a much more active role.

Mozère describes how these changes can be understood from a Deleuzian/Guattarian micro-political perspective as a certain kind of positive local logic of activity and creativity:

> During a number of years spent in the field, in several different places and according to each preschool's specific time, we have noticed the emergence of new organisations, no longer based in functions and status, but more in accordance with local logics, capable of replacing passivity – due to the feeling of incompetence – with activity, creativity, the invention and use of new rules and new "local laws". In fact, a micro-politics reflecting and materialising, finally, a positive work.
>
> (Mozère, 1992: 15; my translation)

Mozère uses Guattari's concept of 'groupe-sujet' to account for these changes as something created partly by the encounter of the preschools with local politics and especially in the political climate after May 1968. But, according to her, most importantly, these changes took place through the logic that the Guattarian concept 'groupe-sujet' proposes; a group driven by a project and that proceeds through encounter and collective experimentation in the moment, with possible and not predefined becomings. When analysing one particular preschool from the point of view of the Deleuzian/Guattarian concepts micro-politics and segmentarity, Mozère shows how the preschool contained both rigid and supple segments. Rigid segments function as predetermined positions and habits and are seen through the prevailing hierarchy and a dogmatic view on education. Supple segments are observed through the arrival of a nomad, such as a preschool teacher who refuses the established power relations and sets off a certain kind of 'bricolage' in the educational processes. Mozère insists upon showing how these rigid and supple segments are never separated but intertwined and caught up in each other. But she also shows how, in the middle of this, lines of flight – a concept discussed and illustrated below – are traced that open up the entire school system for new forms of expression (Mozère, 1992: 193–7).

Mozère describes the role of the researcher in terms of 'le chercheur collectif' (the collective researcher), who cooperates with practices and is affected and part of the micro-political transformations, as well as the 'groupe-sujet'. It is not a question about research being implemented or the researcher intervening in practices. Rather Mozère describes how teachers decide to take the opportunity presented by the researchers to rearticulate and activate their practical environment differently, possibly liberating themselves from what have become habits and restraints in the immediate environment:

> Researchers are far from being the only ones to bring energy or willingness to change. The experiences show that at a certain moment, in a singular context – and each time singular – groups and individuals full of institutionalized and repressed energy, capture the occasion offered by the intrusion of such an exteriority to draw out of this the potential liberty that will suit them.
>
> (Mozère, 1992: 205; my translation)

This is also, according to Mozère, what characterizes a 'groupe-sujet': the process of picking up and using whatever the group needs in what is offered to them through the researchers' presence, so as to be able to continue their process. In recent works (2006, 2007a, 2007b, 2007c), Mozère has worked anew, still in close cooperation with practices, with the concept of micro-politics and desire in relation to what Deleuze has called the control society, where we are no longer governed through discipline but through control mechanisms built into our minds, bodies and desires. She has also worked on the concept 'becoming-child', showing how the Deleuzian/Guattarian concept of becoming concerns a becoming as process, freed from becoming into any fixed identity.

Mozère's work is of importance for the present study since it touches on questions of movement and experimentation in subjectivity and learning by using micro-politics and segmentarity. This is being done also in this study, but in its own particular time and space. The concept 'groupe-sujet' seems to function a bit like the concept 'assemblage of desire' does in this study; driven by a different logic to rational thinking. The way that collective experimentation is described by Mozère is of importance for the purpose of this study and its efforts to account for a similar relation between research and practice. Furthermore her recent works have been of importance for the contemporary articulation of the concepts of desire, micro-politics and becoming, all of which figure prominently in this study.

Another strong contribution to the field is the work put forward by Dahlberg (2003), Dahlberg and Moss (2005) and Dahlberg and Bloch (2006). Dahlberg (2003) departs from a Foucault-inspired deconstruction of the image of a 'competent, autonomous and flexible child'. This image contains, according to her, a specific kind of governing in the name of ethics. But this is an ethics that, following the logic of the above-mentioned control society, is of a particularly universalized and stereotyped sort. Competent, autonomous and flexible behaviour is, according to Dahlberg, part of a new way of governing subjects in contemporary society. She proposes a turn to Emmanuel Levinas (1906–1995), Derrida and the pedagogical practice in Reggio Emilia to be able to revitalize ethics and create a space for alterity and radical dialogue. Through Levinas's notion of absolute alterity – an alterity which is based on the responsibility for the other, as well as Derrida's ideas of a dissociating relation characterized by inevitable and endless uncertainty, dissensus, and ambiguity – Dahlberg puts forward the idea of a 'deconstructive pragmatism'. Dahlberg then connects this to the pedagogical practice in Reggio Emilia and their notion of a 'pedagogy of listening' and describes this as concerning 'an ethics of an encounter':

So the pedagogy of listening turns to what is to come, by inviting yes, yes, yes and the pedagogues are trying hard to listen to the child from its own position and experience and not to make the child into the same. This is not so much a processes of labeling, identification, recognition and judgement – it is more about *an ethics of an encounter*.

(Dahlberg 2003: 277–278; original emphasis)

Dahlberg also connects the work in projects that are taking place in Reggio Emilia with Deleuze and Guattari's notion of the 'rhizome'. The projects in Reggio Emilia, according to Dahlberg, are driven through this different logic of knowledge where there is no predefined progression. And the pedagogical documentation that accompanies the work in projects is described by Dahlberg as a form of construction rather than a controlling or supervising device:

Visualizing then can be seen as a form of construction – as an emotional engagement and participation rooted in the body of experience ... Seen from this perspective pedagogical documentation becomes a form of visualization, which brings *forces* and *energies* into a project work, forces and energies that can open us up to new possibilities, to the possibility of transformations.

(Dahlberg, 2003: 283–284; original emphasis)

Dahlberg's work is important in relation to the present study because it opens up for further investigations concerning the ethics of pedagogical practices and indicates the possibility of using Deleuze and Guattari's concepts in relation to phenomenon in pedagogical practices such as project work and pedagogical documentation.

Dahlberg and Moss (2005) propose that, in contrast to, and as a challenge to a universal and technical view of early childhood education, preschools could be seen as a potential place for political practice. With the help of the Deleuzian/Guattarian concept of 'micro' or 'minor politics', they propose that preschools in this way would be a stage for political actors rather than being simply objects for political interventions. They also question the seemingly unitary story told about modernity as a single movement or mentality, and bring forward examples that complicate such a story and open up possibilities to recreate political and ethical practices from another framework. other than that of control, discipline and rationalism. By connecting work in different practices, for instance the schools of Reggio Emilia, with Deleuze and Guattari's minor politics, the vitality of thought and the event, and also Levinas's ethics of an encounter, they put forward the theoretical and practical features of a pedagogy of listening and radical dialogue. This pedagogy consists of the continuous co-production of knowledge and values in between children, teachers and parents. Work in projects, and with pedagogical documentation, visualizes processes of construction of values and knowledge that are open ended and continuously transforming. Rather than any predefined programme, it is the events here and now that become important for preschool as a site for democratic politics. The work of Dahlberg and Moss is important for the present study because it also works with minor politics, the vitality of thought and the event. Also in this study the possibilities for ethical and political work in preschools are drawn out, through identifying the need for an ethico-aesthetic paradigm.

In their article 'Is the power to see and visualize always the power to control?' (2006), Dahlberg and Bloch take as a starting point the findings of Foucault-inspired post-structural, deconstructive and feminist research, telling us that the power to see and visualize is equal to the power to control. Through Deleuze's thinking and examples from a pedagogical practice of experimentation and affirmation, they turn the proposition around by putting to work some of Deleuze's most important concepts, in order to understand pedagogy and especially pedagogical documentation as a possible way to move away from the domain of recognition, representation and regulation expressed in practice through observing, assessing and normalizing children. Using the Deleuzian concept of 'rhizome' they state that they want to struggle with the possibilities of pedagogical practices as open, multiple and becoming spaces.

They discuss how Deleuze's transcendental empiricism can be considered as something quite different to the classical definition of empiricism within the logic of representation, where atomistic sensations need to be organized and systemized by abstract thought. According to Dahlberg and Bloch, Deleuze's empiricism was coupled to the ambition of bringing forward a new conception of subjectivity, a certain kind of pre-individual singularity, where the self is no longer attached to a specific identity, but rather subjectivity is considered a process of becoming. This requires a different sort of empiricism, a more 'wild' kind of empiricism that is interested only in that which is new and under creation. According to Dahlberg and Bloch, Deleuze introduced this into his very image of thought – a thought without an image that no longer functions through recognition and representation but rather through encounters, connections and assemblages. A thinking that, rather than judging, constructs and experiments through making new connections in a pragmatic way.

From this point of view, society as well as pedagogy is seen as a process of experimentation rather than a contract. This pedagogy is of a different style than the one where the teacher functions as a transmitter of knowledge. Rather, it is an affirmative pedagogy where the teacher is a listener, installed in the here and now with the children:

> To construct a community of inquirers with an experimental spirit requires listening and a radical dialogue. In "real" listening children become partners in a process of experimentation and research by inventing problems and by listening to and negotiating what other children, as well as the teacher, are saying and doing. In this process the co-constructing pedagogue has to open her/ him self to the unexpected and experiment together with the children – in the here and now event. S/he challenges the children by augmenting connections through enlarging the number of concepts, hypotheses and theories, as well as through new material and through challenging children's more technical work. Besides getting a responsible relation to other children by listening, they also are negotiating in between each other, enlarging the choices that can be made, instead of bringing choice down to universal trivializations.
>
> (Dahlberg and Bloch, 2006: 114)

Visualization in such a pedagogy, no longer concerns individuals organized hierarchically, rather there is a group of learners that functions as 'a constant generator of depersonalization and collective production and creation' (Dahlberg and Bloch, 2006: 115). Moreover, this pedagogy creates the possibility for strategies of visualization, such as pedagogical documentation, to vitalize both thought and practice:

> [...] in a pedagogy of experimentation pedagogical relationships, listening to children, documentation of learning processes – all become a form of visualization which brings different forces and energies into pedagogical work. It makes visible what is "unattributable" and new. Visualizing processes in preschools and schools might then help to gain vitality and power through connecting up to new forces, constructing new combinations and new assemblages, e.g. open us up to new transformations – to difference – to lines of flight. The visualizations being made through these ways

of imagining new rhizomatic, nomadic pedagogical approaches not only allow for seeing ready made products and processes, but open ourselves up to the leakages that are always there.

(Dahlberg and Bloch, 2006: 114–115)

Dahlberg and Bloch's work is of importance to this study in identifying the need for a new kind of empiricism to approach preschool practices and the possible use of Deleuze's empiricism in such a process. This is tried out in this study through the Deleuzian/Guattarian concept 'transcendental empiricism'. Also their way of connecting Deleuze's empiricism to pedagogical documentation as being processes of visualization beyond control is used in this study, coupled with the Deleuzian/Guattarian concept event.

Jakob Wenzer (2004), inspired by Deleuze and Guattari, has worked with deterritorializing the ideas of the being and the becoming child in relation to the notion of 'the competent child'. 'Territorialization' is described as a process where beings are ordered in strictly determined hierarchies, and where the child has its defined place and function. Becoming is here made invisible. 'Deterritorialization' concerns an ambition to make visible becoming and, therefore, to consider being to be only a temporary effect of becoming. Through describing how 'the competent child' is created through an abstract machine producing this specific subjectivity for the child, Wenzer foregrounds his argument of the need to use the Nietzschean concepts active and reactive in relation to 'the competent child', so as to be able to distinguish a becoming child free from intentions.

The abstract machine turns out to consist of several machines (an economic machine, an academic machine, a pedagogic machine, and an ITC-political machine) working in a machinic assemblage, that both creates the need for the specific subjectivity and makes it happen. The different machines operate simultaneously. Because of this specific characteristic of machinic assemblages, Wenzer argues that the notion of 'the competent child' benefits from being approached and deterritorialized with the help of the two Nietzschean concepts, 'active' and 'reactive'. A reactive use of the notion of 'the competent child' would be (as the above post-structural and deconstructive researchers have showed), the predefined definition of competency against which the child is measured; 'the competent child' is one who conforms closely to the definition. An active use of the notion of 'the competent child' would be when one takes into consideration that the assemblages every subject is caught up in are multiple, connective and in continuous change. In this case, the child would be a subject without a predefined self, a subject that is not the sum of the parts of its assemblages but rather an effect of the assemblage that is not separated from the world. This assembled subject is in continuous and continuously transforming relation with the world in a process of becoming. This becoming differs from becoming as it has been treated in relation to the child becoming adult, or becoming competent in the way wished for. It concerns instead a becoming that is free from intentions: a becoming in itself. Accordingly Wenzer says:

> [...] the active use of the term allows the child (or whoever to which the competence is attributed) to be whatever it is, bilingual or non-speaking, happy or sad, socially skilled or uninterested thereof – the child is allowed its "becoming-world", and the doubleness of the "becoming-child" of the "world" – the emergence of personhood / subjectivity and the conditions required – is not separated from this becoming, that is double by necessity.
>
> (Wenzer, 2004: 329)

Wenzer also highlights, with the help of the work of Hardt and Negri (2002), how academic institutions and research efforts must take into account the fact that capitalism and the market today function as active forces and are therefore successful in governing people's lives through their desires. If academic institutions and research efforts do not start to account for and use their own production of desire they will be condemned to work within reactive forces and will consequently always be one step behind.

> As long as academic or pedagogical institutions are confined to a solely *critical* agenda, they are locked inside of a dialectic world view when they are always chasing after the market, trying to unveil what is hidden underneath the desirable surface of the commercial messages or technologies, but always from one step behind. What is missing is the institutions' *own* desiring-production – that the institutions themselves are equally partaking in the production of subjectivities. Because what I believe is that all "criticism" is not actually revealing hidden truths or attacking some kind of Marxian "false consciousness", but instead *adding new dimensions* to what is already there, thereby producing *entirely new fields of vision* multiplying what is there already, and thereby making things visible that did not use to be. Constructions are added to the world, they are not

subtracted from it. [...] This is exactly why humanist critical studies are always one step behind – they fail to see that their own action is actually often reactive, and the one criticized is active.

(Wenzer, 2004: 333; original emphasis)

Wenzer's work is important in relation both to the deterritorialization of the notion of 'the competent child' and to the definition of the self as assembled, since these are being worked with also in the present study through the concepts of micro-politics and segmentarity as well as assemblage of desire. But it is also important because of how Wenzer identifies the need for institutions – whether preschools or universities – to acknowledge and use their own desiring production. This is what the present study attempts to do through defining research as a practice engaging in collective, intense and unpredictable experimentation together with pedagogical practices.

Glenda MacNaughton (2005) develops post-structuralist and feminist deconstructive work in early childhood education by introducing and elaborating on the Deleuzian/Guattarian concept 'rhizome'. With the ambition of deliberately practising for freedom, she draws up and uses a tactic of rhizoanalysis in relation to child observations. Rhizoanalysis, according to MacNaughton, both deconstructs and reconstructs a text. Through connecting the text in the observation with other texts coming from different sources, as well as questioning one's own influence in closing or opening up for diverse meanings, one can explore how the text organizes meaning and power and thereby create new understandings of it. She is arguing that working from a rhizomatic perspective can give gender stereotypes in young children more complex explanations than through a simple cause–effect relation. Kylie Smith, an early childhood teacher and researcher, states in MacNaughton (2005) that:

I came to exploring the place of rhizomatic patterns in my understandings of the child, parent and early childhood professional in a search for a tool that supported the exploration of the child within a gaze that recognized the complexity, multiplicity, contradictory, contingent and shifting ways that the child, the parent and the early childhood professional learn, develop, relearn and change how they understand themselves, the world and others. Further, I wanted to recognise that identities are socially, historically and politically constructed.

(Smith, 2005: 135)

She puts rhizoanalysis to work by using an observation from a play scene together with purposely chosen texts from different sources. Theoretically she uses texts from diverse feminist researchers, such as Glenda MacNaughton, Judith Butler, Bronwyn Davies, bell hooks and Valerie Walkerdine. She also chooses texts from popular culture such as the feminist story 'The Paper Bag Princess', Harry Potter and Buffy the Vampire Slayer. Smith argues that texts used in rhizoanalysis must be chosen with political intent and also that the researcher must be vigilant not to introduce his or her own gendered stereotypes into the material. MacNaugthon's and Smith's work is important for this study in that they break with the logic of knowledge encapsulated in the tree metaphor where knowledge is stable and systematically built and they attempt, both theoretically and practically, to use the different rhizomatic logic in relation to child observations. Also in this study attempts are made to use a different logic of knowledge through treating the empirical material in relation to the concept event.

In relation to Swedish preschools, Ulla Lind (forthcoming) has also followed up post-structural, deconstructive and feminist research work by using (amongst others) Elisabeth Grosz's Deleuze-inspired thinking. Lind puts forward the idea of children's bodies as assemblages, rather than organic, essentialist bodies with well-defined selves. Children's bodies as assemblages consist of organs, but also of loads of processes, desires and behaviours coming from all sorts of directions and sources. Lind has demonstrated in the preschools where she works how children's bodies as assemblages connect to other assemblages in an environment where everything interacts and connects: desires, passions, behaviours, thoughts, materials etc. Lind also insists on the importance of seeing the interplay of visual, verbal and linguistic signs and demonstrates how pedagogical documentation is part of both a negotiating practice and the research material.

In her article 'Identity and Power, "Meaning", Gender and Age: children's creative work as a signifying practice' (Lind 2005), the Deleuzian/Guattarian concept of 'rhizome' is put to work with children's play and construction in a project on creations. The project is read as a collective process of the simultaneous creation of lines of flight in between children and teachers; lines of flight that permit not only a creative approach to the material and subject worked with (different kinds of creations with the body, with clay, through drawing, etc.) but also to the existing social and gendered order. The pedagogical documentation functioned in between teachers and children, not in identifying each self's particular investment, but rather as a social memory of the collective process, where children and teachers were simultaneously and collectively directors and actors in negotiating meaning of the project's content as well as their subjectivities and learning processes.

Lind's work is important for this study in that it uses the possibility of thinking of children and preschools as assemblages. In the present study this is also done through using the concept assemblage of desire and all its components when analysing the empirical material. That implies accounting for bodies and language caught up in a rhythmic act of re- and deterritorialization, as an alternative to progressive and linear ideas of subjectivity and learning, as well as accounting for a bodily logic of potentiality through affect, rather than imagining all learning to take place through conscious thinking.

Use of Deleuze and Guattari in this study and how it contributes to the field

Through all the research work described above, many important issues have been evoked and deconstructions as well as reconstructions of subjectivity and learning have been made. In addition to these efforts, the present study will try to contribute to the field by having constructed the specific problem: *how to work with movement and experimentation in subjectivity and learning in early childhood education practice and research.*

Below, with the help of Massumi (2002, 2003), three decisive points are identified in the ongoing work of the preschools in which this study has taken place and of the related research. These decisive points function as research questions guiding the construction of the problem throughout the study. To each point is added a description of how the texts and concepts of Deleuze and Guattari, chosen as being of especial relevance for this present study, can contribute both practically and theoretically, to the efforts of all concerned, to work with movement and experimentation in subjectivity and learning in the field of early childhood education. It will also be indicated where the different concepts will be treated in the account of the study. [10]

> *1. In the preschools there is an ongoing struggle to regain movement and experimentation in subjectivity and learning through putting into practice the idea of a relational field and through experimenting with new tools. For this to be theoretically workable, there is a need to work out how to turn the focus on positions and change as moving from one position to another, into a focus on movement as something that foregoes positions and thereby open up possibilities for collective and intense experimentation.*

Starting from the struggle in preschool practices to regain movement and experimentation through the idea of subjectivity and learning as a relational field, and their recent efforts to work out and experiment with new tools, a way is needed to theoretically regain movement and experimentation. This concerns a rethinking of positioning. Positions are capable of accounting for change in terms of moving from one position to another, but not for movement and experimentation as a first principle. Any time positioning comes first, one is allowed to see movement only as intermediate stops on the way towards the goal. In other words, the focus on positions does not allow for movement preceding positions. It creates a grid that permits only the stop-over moments to be seen:

> The aim of the positionality model was to open a window on local resistance in the name of change. But the problem of change returned with a vengeance. Because every body-subject was so determinately local, it was boxed into its site on the culture map. Gridlock. The idea of positionality begins by subtracting movement from the picture. This catches the body in cultural freeze-frame. The point of explanatory departure is a pinpointing, a zero-point of stasis. *When positioning of any kind comes a determining first, movement comes a problematic second.* After all is signified and sited, there is the nagging problem of how to add movement back into the picture.
>
> (Massumi, 2002: 3; emphasis added)

In Deleuze and Guattari's *A Thousand Plateaus* (2004) there are texts and concepts that make it possible to draw up a political perspective that can account for movement as preceding positions and experimentation as a way of working for teachers in relation to children and researchers in relation to practices. The concepts 'micro-politics' and 'segmentarity' can be used through treating movement as flows or quanta of belief and desire and as that which precedes positions (Chapter 3). Deleuze and Guattari acknowledge that positions have a real impact on our lives and they talk about how we are segmented in different ways. But, the main point for them is that these segments are not stable; a first condition of a society is that it is leaking and producing lines of flight in between segments. Before positions or segments there exist forces that they call quanta or flows of belief and desire. In relation to this one can understand all change in subjectivity and learning as starting out from flows of belief and desire and it is these flows that could be described as movements preceding positions in subjectivity and learning.

These flows of belief and desire are from a micro-political perspective seen as untameable and never really possible to predict, control, supervise or evaluate against predefined goals. This makes governing more a question of 'hit and miss', and introduces the idea of an alternative to governing through experimentation, as trying to hook on to these flows of belief and desire and work with them rather than against them. This seems to function well with how preschools try to regain movement and experimentation through seeing subjectivity and learning as a relational field where everything interacts and continuously changes. And how they therefore try to develop new tools for planning where long preparations are being done, but, once acting with the children, it is all a question of experimenting through trying to connect their own problems and desires with the children's, rather than insisting on taming them. Micro-politics and segmentarity can also be used by research to see practices as consisting first and foremost of movements of belief and desire rather than positions. These movements can be worked with through research trying to experiment by hooking on to practices' flows of belief and desire.

2. In the preschools teachers and researchers work together through collective, intense and unpredictable experimentation. In this process teachers as well as researchers are caught up in a relational field. For this to be theoretically workable, the reliance on the transcendent principle of conscious critique needs to be rethought and reinforced by other possible and alternative scientific methods.

To be able to account for how practices and research can work together through collective experimentation marked by intensity and unpredictability, as well as accounting for teachers and researchers as part of a relational field, research efforts must find other means to engage with practice than through conscious critique. As long as this transcendent principle is at stake, production processes of subjectivity and learning are treated as taking place separately from the undertaking of research, which can only register them, and thereby also immobilize them as effects and not as ongoing and continuously changing processes. Critical thinking seems to lock up movement and experimentation in subjectivity and learning through a transcendent principle, where critique is undertaken from above or beyond the empirical features. Empirical features are consequently always immobilized by abstract logical thinking. Critical thinking, even though twisted and turned in different methodological approaches, is always in trouble by the end. How to account for, or how to avoid, the researcher and the research perspective influencing the empirical material? It is a self-imposed problem that has its origin in the research's claim of being apart from the reality investigated and capable of revealing and subtracting hidden features from the world:

> Critical thinking disavows its own inventiveness as much as possible. Because it sees itself as uncovering something it claims was hidden or as debunking something it desires to subtract from the world, it clings to a basically descriptive and justificatory modus operandi. However strenuously it might debunk concepts like "representation", it carries on as if it mirrored something outside itself with which it had no complicity, no unmediated processual involvement, and thus could justifiably oppose.
>
> (Massumi, 2002: 12)

Collective experimentation, intensity and unpredictability cannot be accounted for through critical thinking of any kind, but it might be through switching to methods that recognize and account for their own productiveness and inventiveness. In *Pure Immanence: Essays on A Life* (2001) and *What is philosophy?* (1994), there are writings on the concept 'transcendental empiricism', that make it possible to draw up the ideas of an affirmative scientific method possibly capable of accounting for collective experimentation in between theory and practice (Chapter 4). Transcendental empiricism concerns Deleuze and Guattari's efforts to make more of empiricism than the history of philosophy has accounted for. Instead of empiricism as an epistemological tradition functioning through transcendent logic, where atomistic sensations are seen as in need of being organized and systemized by abstract thought, they propose what they call a transcendental empiricism.

Transcendental is not the same thing as transcendent; transcendence is that which attempts to go beyond or above, a highest grounding principle such as thought and consciousness. The transcendental is drawn up by Deleuze and Guattari as a field that they also call 'the plane of immanence'. The plane of immanence is the horizon against which the thinking that creates itself thinks. Without any stable and sedentary ground thinking proceeds by laying out its ground at the same time as it thinks. This happens in a place that might not even any longer be a place. There is no longer any stable ground and there is no longer a subject capable of thinking of itself and the world as objects. This plane is in itself transforming and connective and on this plane there are only different speeds and slowness and forces and bodies encountering each other. Transcendental empiricism involves a certain devaluation of the capacity and aspirations of consciousness to account for the world, in favour of the acknowledging of a thought that creates itself on a plane of immanence as it goes on. This thought is also an experimenting thought; it experiments with that which is coming about, that which is new, interesting or remarkable.

A transcendental empiricism tries not to create conditions of thinking greater than that which is thought about. It acknowledges that everything adds to the world and therefore puts forward the need not to reduce the world through conscious critique of any sort. It proposes an alternative through theory conceived as a practice speaking with another practice, through engaging in experimentation with the new, the interesting and the remarkable. In relation to this there is no longer any need to place research above or beyond events in practices. It is a question of fully recognizing the productive aspects of the world and ourselves. It is to admit to the fullest that we all partake all the time in producing, inventing and augmenting the world. Through everything we do we add something to the world. Transcendental empiricism could possibly be an alternative, affirmative scientific method that accounts for its own inventiveness and co-production with practices and this seems to function well with how preschools, and research in this study, try to work within a relationship of collective, intense and unpredictable experimentation.

Through *The Logic of Sense* (Deleuze, 2004b) and *Difference and Repetition* (Deleuze, 1994a) it is possible to draw up the ideas of how to put to work the concept 'event' as another alternative and affirmative scientific method capable of accounting for movement when working with the empirical material (Chapter 5). According to Deleuze, the event is related to language; events are expressed by linguistic propositions. Furthermore, linguistic propositions are normally thought of as that which gives us access to what is true or false in the events in which we take part. In Chapter 5 it is argued that this could also be understood and used in relation to doing research and different methodological approaches. When doing research, one chooses a way of treating the events in one's empirical material starting out from a specific way of viewing language or linguistic propositions and their relation to claims of truth in the events.

Deleuze relates the event to language through introducing sense as a fourth dimension in language, in addition to denotation, manifestation and signification. 'Denotation' is the dimension in language that points out or designs things and the world. 'Manifestation' concerns the subjective interpretations of things and the world, and 'signification' is the dimension of language where signs are connected together in signifying chains that give meaning to things and the world. If using these dimensions in relation to the empirical material in this study, it would imply commenting upon them as if they were facts, interpreting them from a subjective point of view or reflecting upon them in order to deconstruct signifying regimes. But according to Deleuze, all these dimensions in language close the event down within claims of truth specific to each of these linguistic dimensions. With denotation the event is closed down when truth is looked for in things and the world's inner essence. With manifestation, truth is claimed within the subject itself. With signification it is said that one is looking for the conditions of truth, but Deleuze argues that this leaves truth itself unquestioned (these dimensions are discussed and illustrated further in Chapter 5).

But sense, defined by Deleuze as the unconditioned production of truth in the event, as well as being located on the border of language and things, seems capable of keeping the event complex, open-ended and in movement. Sense is related to problems, learning, and culture, in that all of these are seen as processes of production and constructions that come before solutions, knowledge and methods. This offers a methodological approach where one can do research as well as pedagogy through looking for and engaging in the ongoing construction and production of sense, problems, learning and culture in the empirical material. Starting out from the event, the focus will be on how all participants construct and produce sense and problems in processes of learning where methods have to give way for the entire culture surrounding the problem. The event thus defined seems capable of establishing a focus on movement as a first principle when approaching subjectivity and learning in the empirical material.

3. In the preschools all participants – children, teachers, teacher students, teacher educators and researchers – are caught up in the desire to experiment with subjectivity and learning. They are acting in a relational field through collective, intense and unpredictable experimentation. To work with this theoretically, the relation individual/society needs to be rethought. It needs a twist and a turn that no longer puts any importance on one or the other side; the whole dualism needs to take on another meaning.

In relation to how all participants are caught up in the desire to experiment with subjectivity and learning, the idea of subjectivity and learning as a relational field, and the features of collective, intense and unpredictable experimentation, a twist and turn is needed concerning the relation individual/society. As long as this dualism is still at work, movement and experimentation finds itself trapped in a cause–effect relationship that immobilizes subjectivity and learning, and hinders experimentation. As seen in the related research efforts, there has been a turn away from claims of the biological, natural and innate essence in individual subjects. What has been focused on instead is society's impact on individuals through notions such as history, structure, culture, and semiotic systems. Through this it became possible to treat the individual as shaped by historical, structural, cultural, or semiotic discursive regimes prevailing in society. But what needs to be highlighted is the risk that the same logic is still present – only now the essentialist claim is being made in relation to society instead of the individual. It is now society that comes first as a founding principle. As an answer to this, more recent efforts speak of the multiplicity of discourses, hybridism and border crossing, in an attempt to inscribe a certain kind of movement in between positions. It is an attempt to valorize the in-between. The problem is, again, that the borders crossed can only be so by first defining the positions establishing the borders. The hybrid becomes only a mix of already set entities, already fixed positions:

> But to the extent that the in-between is conceived as a space of interaction of already-constituted individuals and societies, middle-feeders end up back on the positional map. The tendency is to describe the in-between as a blending or parody of the always-already positioned. [...] Erase the progenitors and the hybrid vanishes: no terms have been provided with which to understand it in its own right.
>
> (Massumi, 2002: 69)

In *Anti-Oedipus* (Deleuze, 1984) and in the sequel *A Thousand Plateaus* (Deleuze and Guattari, 2004), there are writings that provide terms that seem capable of working, theoretically and practically, with the individual and the society no longer as entities caught up in a cause–effect relationship. Through the concept 'assemblages of desire' it seems possible to treat individuals and societies as variations of assemblages that can account for both movement and experimentation in subjectivity and learning in both practice and theory (Chapter 6). Assemblages of desire are multiple, within individuals as well as within society. It is impossible to say where an assemblage in an individual stops and where society's assemblage takes over. It doesn't work this way. Assemblages work in society and the individual simultaneously; it is really only a question of extension and variation; an assemblage extends itself to many levels, to an individual, to a group, to an entire society, and it varies both on a social and an individual level. We are made of many assemblages. We desire, never alone or in relation to a particular object; we desire in a network of relations. Assemblages of desire concern how desire sets off as a little machinery and takes place in between people. The distinction between individual and the society no longer becomes meaningful. We are all assembled, society is assembled, and the distinction individual/society has to give way for assemblages where the relation between individual/society finds itself in continuous movement and thereby open for intense and unpredictable experimentation.

Assemblages of desire contain several components that seem important in relation to what takes place in the preschools and in relation to the purpose of the study. In *Anti-Oedipus* (Deleuze, 1984), the definition of desire by psychoanalysis as lack is challenged and desire is given a definition as 'unconscious production of real'. This seems to work well with the preschools that more and more try not to bother about children's needs, by starting to wonder about what kind of features of reality children through their collective desires are producing. This also seems to work well with how research now tries more and more to bother not with what practices are lacking, focusing instead on how movements, consisting of flows of belief and desire, are produced in practices.

In *A Thousand Plateaus* (Deleuze and Guattari, 2004), the initial ideas of desire are given a more complex setting. Desire is there described as always assembled and it is clearly connected also to language and bodies that go through a rhythmic act of re- and deterritorialization; breaking out of and settling into habits as territories. This can be useful so as to describe how subjectivity and learning in the preschools concern both the bodies and the language involved and how these billow back and forward in a rhythmic act that cannot be accounted for through the idea of progressive and linear ideas of subjectivity and learning. Progressive and linear ideas of subjectivity and learning inevitably lock movement and experimentation up in predetermined development as well as within a cause and effect logic.

Moreover, in an assemblage of desire there is a different logic involved than in conscious thinking; there is a bodily logic. Deleuze and Guattari account for this through turning to Spinoza's concept 'affect', meaning bodily potential. Affect seems to present an alternative to treating subjectivity and learning solely through conscious thinking. The somewhat untameable subjects, learning processes and experimentations that take place in the preschools could be accounted for through this bodily logic, where everything is a question of the encounter between different bodies and forces and where it becomes important to look at each situation's particular potentiality. Assemblages of desire, containing all these components, seem capable not only to account for how desire in the preschools expresses itself through new ways of thinking, talking and acting, but also, and in relation to the purpose of the study, it seems to go beyond the cause–effect relationship inherent in the individual/society dualism, and therefore seem to manage to keep the empirical material open-ended and in movement, as well as functioning like a pedagogical and scientific analysing tool that invites one to engage in intense and unpredictable experimentation in subjectivity and learning.

Chapter 3

Micropolitics and segmentarity in early childhood education

We are segmented from all around and in every direction. The human being is a segmentary animal. Segmentarity is inherent to all the strata composing us. Dwelling, getting around, working, playing: life is spatially and socially segmented. The house is segmented according to its rooms' assigned purposes; streets, according to the order of the city; the factory, according to the nature of the work and operations performed in it. We are segmented in a *binary* fashion, following the great major dualist oppositions: social classes, but also men–women, adults–children, and so on. We are segmented in a *circular* fashion, in ever larger circles, ever wider disks or coronas, like Joyce's "letter": my affairs, my neighbourhood's affaires, my city's, my country's, the world's ... We are segmented in a *linear* fashion, along a straight line or a number of straight lines, of which each segment represents an episode or "proceeding": as soon as we finish one proceeding we begin with another, forever proceduring or procedured, in the family, in school, in the army, on the job. School tells us, "You're not at home anymore"; the army tells us, "You're not in school anymore" ...

(Deleuze and Guattari, 2004: 230; original emphasis)

Introduction

In this chapter the concepts micro-politics and segmentarity will be treated and connected to the preschools' efforts to try to regain movement and experimentation in their practices. This chapter works with the first of the three decisive points, introduced in the previous section:

1. In the preschools there is an ongoing struggle to regain movement and experimentation in subjectivity and learning through putting into practice the idea of a relational field and through experimenting with new tools. For this to be theoretically workable, there is a need to work out how to turn the focus on positions and change as moving from one position to another, into a focus on movement as something that foregoes positions and thereby open up possibilities for collective and intense experimentation.

In relation to the quotation that starts this chapter – from Deleuze and Guattari on micro-politics and segmentarity in *A Thousand Plateaus* (2004) – it is possible to imagine that children, as much as adults, are segmentary animals and preschools are part of segmented life. According to Deleuze and Guattari, segmentarity takes on different shapes and functions in different ways. In the above quotation a description is given of how the human being is being segmented in a *binary, circular* and *linear* fashion. Deleuze and Guattari also show that the different segments function sometimes in a rigid way, sometimes in a more supple way (Deleuze and Guattari, 2004: 231). This is what other research within a post-structural and deconstructive framework, related to this study, has already noted, though in their particular ways. Connecting their deconstructions of subjectivity and learning in modern and post-modern society with the concept of segmentarity, it is possible to describe how subjectivity and learning in preschool are segmented, sometimes in a rigid and sometimes in a more supple way. Modern segmentarity would then seem to be of a more rigid kind and post-modern segmentarity of a more supple kind.

But, just as this related research work has acknowledged and warned, as have Deleuze and Guattari too, there are dangers with 'believing that a little suppleness is all that is needed to make things better' (Deleuze and Guattari, 2004: 237). There are dangers with the supple segments that must be acknowledged. Moreover, for Deleuze and Guattari the segments function as lines crossing through all society and all individuals, but they are not separated and they do not chronologically follow one after the other, rather they are intertwined and simultaneous. All segments or lines, rigid and supple, are at stake all the time (Deleuze and Guattari, 2004: 234).

But most important, for Deleuze and Guattari, there are more than rigid and supple lines; there is also so-called 'lines of flight', and these are most interesting, because they imply the creation of something new. A line of flight runs like a zig-zag crack in between the other lines – and it is only these lines that, from the perspective of Deleuze and Guattari, are capable of creating something new (Deleuze and Guattari, 2004: 238). This also gives a specific conception of governing. From a micro-political point of view, all change of subjectivity and learning takes place through flows of belief and desire, governing is about adapting the segments to this flow, and it can never be totally successful; it is a question of 'hit and miss' and something always escapes. The idea is that macro- and micro-political actions are at stake at the same time, but it is always the micro-political that 'makes it or breaks it' (Deleuze and Guattari, 2004: 244).

What follows is a review of how one can consider the findings from related research studies as illustrating binary, circular and linear segments, working sometimes in a rigid and sometimes in a supple way in the field of early childhood education. Then the dangers of the supple segments are identified. Through an example from a small project, lines of flight in the practices in the Stockholm preschools are distinguished and the micro-political perspective is considered. The chapter ends with evoking the contemporary situation where governing seems to have installed itself in the very flows of belief and desire. How to navigate as teachers and researchers within such a setting? A proposal is made, putting forward the idea of going with these movements rather than fighting them and connecting our efforts to an ethics and politics of listening and experimentation through modulation of affect and a care for belonging.

Rigid binary, circular and linear segmentarity in early childhood education

Starting out from the findings of post-structural and deconstructive research in early childhood education, it can be noted how binary, circular and linear segmentarity have worked in preschool, sometimes in what Deleuze and Guattari call a more rigid way (Deleuze and Guattari, 2004: 231–234). Binary segments when rigid function, according to Deleuze and Guattari, through 'duality machines' that create binary choices (Deleuze and Guattari, 2004: 232). This could be connected to how the child in the modern époque is separated from the adult through specific definitions, such as 'the child as nature' and 'the child as reproducer of culture, identity and knowledge'.

Coming with these rigid binary segments are the circular and linear ones. According to Deleuze and Guattari, the circular segments are rigidly organized when they all resonate with one single force; for example the centralized State apparatus, functioning as the surveying and disciplining Eye (Deleuze and Guattari, 2004: 231–234). Accordingly, the field of early childhood education and the preschool is during the modern époque seen as an extension of the State and as a tool for governing and educating citizens. Not only the individual child but also future society as a whole is going to be governed through preschools. According to Deleuze and Guattari, linear segments are rigid when they are over-coded, with distinct and determined positions, contents, forms and purposes set once and for all (Deleuze and Guattari, 2004: 231–234). Accordingly, preschool in modern society has its predetermined and well-defined task. Very young children in preschool are here being segmented in a linear fashion; they are no longer at home, they are in preschool and the next step on the predetermined line is becoming a young student in school; thereafter work life awaits them.

Supple binary, circular and linear segmentarity in early childhood education

Starting out again from the findings in post-structural and deconstructive research in early childhood education, segmentarity sometimes works in what Deleuze and Guattari call a more supple kind of way (Deleuze and Guattari, 2004: 231–324). This, for example, could be when the binary segments in post-modern society take on the features of the child as 'competent, autonomous and flexible'. According to Deleuze and Guattari, circular segmentarity is supple when all circles no longer resonate with the State (Deleuze and Guattari, 2004: 231–234). To this one can connect the contemporary situation in post-modern society: the rise of privatization and profiling of preschools; people can choose which school to put their child in according to their own individual taste and despite geographical location. Preschools formulate their task differently, no longer as the extension of a centralized State apparatus, but more in accordance with what works in local contexts and networks. According to Deleuze and Guattari, linear segmentarity seems to be of a more supple kind when life is no longer divided in to predefined compartments spread along the lifeline (Deleuze and Guattari, 2004: 231–234). In relation to this, preschool, school and work life are no longer talked about as separate units. Instead there is what is called 'life-long learning', an introduction of learning along the entire lifeline of a person and into all of society's institutions.

The dangers of supple segments

But, as already noted, for Deleuze and Guattari there is no guarantee that 'a little suppleness is enough to make things "better"' (Deleuze and Guattari, 2004: 237). Recent post-structural and deconstructive research studies have already made this clear by acknowledging and asking an important question: is not this new image of the child as 'competent, autonomous and flexible' just a new way of governing the child, and a mirror of the current political and economic governing of the human subject through the very same imperatives? Deleuze predicted this new kind of governing in the late 1980s, when he described what is happening as a change from a disciplinary society into a control society, and when he predicted a new way of controlling people from the inside, so to speak, instead of as earlier, disciplining them from the outside into sanctioned behaviours. According to him, we won't even need environments for shutting people in; we will no longer need factories, prisons or schools. Instead, every individual is supposed to go through life in an endless process of continuous learning. Deleuze did not at all suggest that this is a future of freedom for the individual; it is just a question of a different kind of governing affecting the individual, one of internal control instead of discipline coming from the outside (Deleuze, 1995a).

In short, there seem to be complications that need to be sorted out when talking about supple segments. According to Deleuze and Guattari (2004: 237), there are four dangers to be avoided when dealing with this type of segment. Below these are connected to the contemporary situation in early childhood education:

1   The first danger is thinking that 'a little suppleness is enough to make things "better"'. We think that with the supple segments we are freer, but finer segmentations work as much and as forcefully in governing as rigid ones (Deleuze and Guattari, 2004: 237). A pedagogy that encourages and bases itself on children's own interests and desires could, from this perspective, be considered as just as much governing as before, but through the new imperatives: 'competent, autonomous and flexible'. It may be even more governed since this kind of governing becomes somewhat more invisible, no longer touching only the child's body or moral behaviour but actually shaping its inner dispositions and desires.

2   The second danger with supple segments is of the psychological sort. It consists of a redirection of segmentation as if it took place within each individual (Deleuze and Guattari, 2004: 237). In this case, within the field of early childhood education, the focus is more and more directed towards each individual child. It becomes important to know each child's particularity, disposition and character and it becomes important to build into each individual child a desire to learn and be educated.

3   The third danger consists of the misconception that supple segments always work in smaller groups and work 'better' in smaller groups; this is an idea of 'smaller governing'. But in no way does this mean that governing takes place in a less intensive

and forceful way (Deleuze and Guattari, 2004: 237). In relation to this, it is possible to propose that in private preschools, in smaller networks and project groups, or smaller classes in school, there is as much intensity and violence in governing as within the rigid segments. Governing through supple segments coexists with the entire social field and what takes place in society at large and on the entire social field also takes place in small groups, networks or projects.

4   The fourth danger with the supple segments consists of seeing them as being separated from the rigid ones. In fact, they overlap and cut into each other, they exist in a completely proportional relation; there is never one without the other (Deleuze and Guattari, 2004: 237). In this perspective it becomes troublesome to think of rigid segments of early childhood education as belonging to another time: the modern époque. Rather, at all times rigid and supple segments coexist in the field of early childhood education.

There are three lines, rigid, supple and lines of flight and they are all at work at the same time

As the fourth point of danger illustrates, it is very important to acknowledge that there is no clear-cut distinction or shift between rigid and supple segmentarity. According to Deleuze and Guattari, the segments function as different lines crossing the entire field at the same time and in continuous variation: sometimes rigid lines, sometimes supple lines. These lines are always simultaneous and even intertwined (Deleuze and Guattari, 2004: 230). In the preschools in Stockholm and its suburbs it is clear that all of this is going on at the same time. Rigid segments, supple segments, dangers; everything takes place at the same time. In what takes place there is never a question of a simple progression from worse to better. Rather, everything happens at the same time, there's a wandering back and forth in between habitual and new ways of acting, talking and thinking. Even though there is a belief and a striving towards new ways of thinking, acting and talking, it is often found that these new ways do not necessarily mean better ways.

Sometimes these seemingly new ways of thinking, acting and talking turn out to be new versions of the same old logic. Sometimes they turn out not to function very well at all. From time to time though, there are moments where something new and different may happen, something that increases all participants' capacity to act and create interesting connections and features in between teachers and children as well as between the form and content of the practice. These are the moments of the lines of flight.

For Deleuze and Guattari, the lines of flight create a zig-zag crack going in a new direction. These lines differ from the rigid and the supple lines in that they bring on the new. This is why their efforts when engaging in any kind of political practice are directed towards that which escapes (Deleuze and Guattari, 2004: 238).

In this study this is also where the effort will be directed: towards the lines of flight. When something new and different is coming about, when the lines of flight are created and activated in the practices, it is never taking place as a rationally planned and implemented change by specific individuals. Rather, there are from time to time magic moments where something entirely new and different seems to be coming about. This is recognized only by the tremendous intensity and, very often, the physical expression of goose bumps that take possession of participants. The following example illustrates a number of lines of flight created within the practices of a preschool. The example concerns a small project that took place there. Out of this project, as well as out of the earlier description of practical resources, lines of flights will be drawn. Through these examples it is possible to see how lines of flight have sometimes been created, concerning the image of the child, the role of the teacher, the task of the preschool institution, the pedagogical environment and the organizing of content and form in learning processes.

An example: a project on 'The rhythm of the heart'

This small project started up after a 'Heart exposition' for St Valentine's Day on the public square in one of the communes of Stockholm, where all preschools in the commune participated. The children in one preschool group, all aged four or five years, had talked a lot about the heart and its rhythm, during the work of preparing for the exposition, and when they were talking and describing the rhythm of their heart to each other, they very often used drawings as a way to show each other their ideas. So shortly after the exposition the teachers ask the children if they could illustrate with paper and pen how they conceive of the rhythm of the heart. The teachers provided the children with stethoscopes, paper and pens (Figure 3.1).

The children are sitting around a table. They decide to get up and run around the table. They then sit down and listen to each other's heartbeats. They discover that their hearts are beating faster.

Figure 3.1 Measuring the rhythm

Figure 3.2 Running around the house

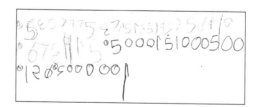

Figure 3.3 Illustration with numbers

Then the children decide that they want to try to run around the preschool to see if their hearts will beat even faster. They get up and run (Figure 3.2) and then hurry inside to measure the rhythm of the heart with the stethoscope. They then try to illustrate in various ways how they conceive of this changed rhythm of the heart. After the activity the teachers sit down with their own documentations of the children's process and they try to analyse and understand how the children have used their illustrations.

Two girls started off by sitting down measuring the rhythm of the heart with the stethoscope. They then wrote numbers like 1, 3, 5 etc (Figure 3.3). After doing this they run around the table and illustrate the faster rhythm through writing 50. Thereafter they run around the preschool and then change the numbers to 5,000, 1, 5, and 1,000. Then they sit down to have a rest and then go back and write 12; they take off again for another run around the preschool, come back, measure and write 2,000, 2,001 etc.

Two other girls work together. They immediately start off by illustrating the different rhythms of the heart through dots (Figure 3.4).

The teachers analyse and discuss several different possible directions to continue working with the children's illustrations and actions. What seems to fascinate the children is the sound of the heart through the stethoscope, but also the mathematical logic of the rhythm and the possibility to illustrate this in different ways – for example, with numbers or dots. They also register that the children seem to agree upon how to proceed when they choose their different activities and strategies,

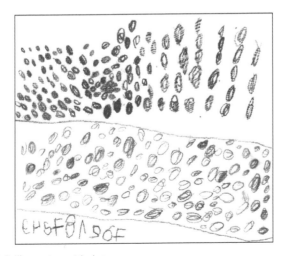

Figure 3.4 Illustration with dots

although they do not speak to each other. It seems to the teachers that these agreements and the giving and taking of different strategies take place beyond the spoken word. All this – the sound of the heart, the mathematical logic of rhythm, the different illustrations, the silent agreements and giving and taking of strategies – would be possible directions for the children and the teachers to continue working with. But the teachers, before defining a specific track along which to continue, decide to go back to the children with their documentations and discuss with them, to explore if they can get closer to a possible and interesting problem to work on together with the children.

The next day the teachers gather the children together again; they have brought the children's illustrations and their own observations and documentations. But to make these more visible they have cut down the children's images and scanned them onto one sheet so that the illustrations are easier for the children to handle. They have also brought only the parts of the observations that they, as teachers, found most interesting and so they re-read for the children only some of what the children talked about the day before. When doing this, the children react in a very surprising way; they get very upset by the fact that their images have been cut down in size and that the teachers read only parts of what they said the day before.

One girl says: 'But hello! That is actually not my whole picture!'

Her friend adds: 'But why haven't you written down everything we said?'

The teachers try to save the situation by explaining how they were thinking and they try to invite the children to continue the discussion. But the children are not interested; they turn away from the teachers, start to giggle together and show with all possible signs that they do not intend to continue this discussion. The teachers understand that they have to back away for the moment and leave the children for some time. They discuss between themselves what happened and understand that the children felt that things that they saw as important were not acknowledged by the teachers.

The teachers start discussing whether to hook onto children's desires, questions and problems in such a way that the children want to continue the process is the most difficult part of their job. Very often they feel that they miss what the children are actually doing; it is hard to identify what kind of desires, questions and problems are actually important in children's thinking, talking and actions and it is difficult to arrange situations where they can meet with the children in collective experimentation and construction of problems. However, they decide to arrange for a new discussion to take place a few days later. They then sit down with the children, this time with the children's original illustrations and all observations present and they explain once again to the children how they were thinking and discuss with them what in the material interests the children the most. This time the children join the teachers in the discussion and they quickly decide that they want to look for more sounds, but they want to do this outside in the garden of the preschool.

The next day the teachers provide the children with the material and tools needed for exploring sounds outside. The children are intensively engaged in the activity and they find many different sounds that they start illustrating by drawing.

The girl who on the first occasion used numbers to illustrate the heartbeats, now changes strategy and uses her friend's technique for illustration through dots (Figure 3.5). She also borrows the technique of zig-zag lines of another friend in the group.

The girl who on the first occasion illustrated through dots starts illustrating the sounds with symbols of different kinds (Figure 3.6). The teachers now register that there is an established and intense interest in between the children around sounds and that they are eager to illustrate these sounds in different ways. They are fascinated and curious about the flow of ideas, strategies and activities that are exchanged in between the children, but they have a hard time observing how and when this happens. They decide to investigate this more closely together with the children by making it clear to the children that they have observed all the different ways the children have been using to detect and illustrate sounds and how they have cooperated in doing this.

So they gather the children together and they tell them how they have seen all their different ways of detecting and illustrating sounds and how they have noticed that the children exchange their ideas and strategies (Figure 3.7). They ask the children if they would like to continue investigating all this through working in pairs where each pair invents

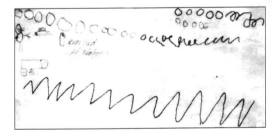

Figure 3.5 Illustration of sounds I

Figure 3.6 Illustration of sounds 2

Figure 3.7 Discussion

three sounds with their mouths that they then illustrate and play for the rest of the group as a charade.

This time the children immediately latch on to the teachers' proposition and they start working straight away (Figure 3.8). What kind of sounds to create? How to illustrate them? How to show them to the rest of the

Figure 3.8 Working together

group? Some children immediately start illustrating the sound of talking (Figure 3.9). Other examples are the sound of laughing (Figure 3.10) and whispering (Figure 3.11). The sounds are then silently played out for the rest of the group (Figure 3.12). This creates an intense atmosphere in the room with a lot of activity and laughter, followed by many other related activities over a period of time.

Lines of flight created in the preschools

This delicate negotiating, this wandering back and forward, and this continuous exchanging in between everybody, can occur in preschools that sometimes have taken off and created their lines of flights. Such

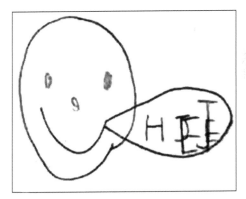

Figure 3.9 The sound of talking

Figure 3.10 The sound of laughing

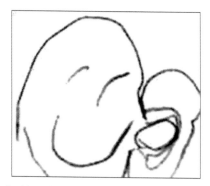

Figure 3.11 The sound of whispering

Figure 3.12 The sounds are played out

examples raise a number of important issues, illustrating which conditions favour the creation of lines of flight:

1 A line of flight seems to have been created through the way that children are no longer looked upon as identified and already represented individuals with a predetermined development or as flexible, autonomous learners. In the project described above the idea of subjectivity and learning as a relational field is put to work. Not only are the different strategies for illustrating born through cooperative work; the strategies are also being picked up, stolen, and exchanged. Also children and teachers join in their negotiations somewhat outside themselves: on a field, a playground, where they all meet around a problem. This field and the relation itself find themselves in movement; the problem to be worked upon is not clear from the beginning, children and teachers work on its construction. Through the definition of subjectivity and learning as a relational field, interests or desires and beliefs are treated as a flow that takes place in between everybody. This differs both from supple and rigid lines in that it creates a deviation, a zig-zag crack in the construction of the individual and in learning processes. Teachers no longer solely define children as individuals according to rigid lines created by theories of children's predetermined development and children's interests or desires and beliefs are in these moments no longer tamed and controlled. Teachers rather look for what took place in between children, their interests are treated like contagious trends and they do not reside in each individual. This is exactly where lines of flight are born. This gives an image of the child and of learning as a relational field which is something totally different than both rigid and supple binary segmentarity.

2 A line of flight seems to have been created by the way the teachers now start to prepare themselves even more than when they were planning work that was predefined for the entire semester or the year. They prepare carefully only to find that something always escapes in the actual encounter with the children. This way of acting as teachers in relation to planning the activity can be seen as a line of flight because it differs from the rigid line of organizing and planning content and method a long time beforehand, thereafter to control and supervise, to ensure that the planning is being implemented in the right way, and then finally evaluating what took place against predetermined outcomes. But it also

differs from the supple line where children are asked to become responsible and flexible in relation to content and method and to take care of the planning themselves. Rather, what happens, in for instance the meeting with the curtailed images, is that not only the children but also the teachers and the content and method are set in motion, demanding a delicate but intense act of collective negotiation and experimentation.

3   A line of flight seems to have been created through the preschool being defined as a place for the collective construction of knowledge and values. This differs from rigid lines that see learning as a question of simple transmission of an already set and defined content of knowledge and values. It also differs from the supple line of governing through autonomy and flexibility. In both these modes of segmentarity the content of knowledge and values are still treated in an essentialist way. The difference with the preschool as a place for collective construction of knowledge and values lies in the actual content of knowledge and values being questioned, assuming the status of a continuously transforming feature in a relational field. In the above example nobody fully knows the problem under construction; is it going to be about rhythm, mathematics, illustrations of sounds, exchanging of strategies? The problem is formulated collectively as the process goes on. Teachers and children struggle with the ethical features of the situation to reach a way of acting in singular and unique ways, while still being united. This can only happen when knowledge and values are treated from the point of view of continuous production and creation.

4   A line of flight seems to have been created in relation to the pedagogical environment. The event above takes place in an environment where children participate in the organization of time and space. In morning meetings the day's content and structure is negotiated in between teachers and children. Children can choose to work in groups of different sizes with different contents during a day. The furniture and the material are accessible to children and possible for them to influence and change according to their demands. Within rigid lines of pedagogical environment, the furniture is arranged once and for all, the day's content structured in the same way for everybody. Within supple lines of pedagogical environment, the day might offer more choice to each child, but still only to the extent that it serves the goal set; time, space and furniture must still serve a fixed and predetermined goal.

The architecture and the furniture have been challenged and sometimes replaced in the preschools in Stockholm and its suburbs. In some cases, collaborative work with designers and architects has led to new pieces of furniture and new materials for investigations. By so doing, the possibility of new kinds of subjectivities and learning processes for children and teachers has also been created. The furniture created by teachers and architects together presents a divergence, a zig-zag crack in the interior of a preschool. Through these new pieces of furniture the pedagogical environment is taken over by children and teachers, they influence the room and the furniture in new and unexpected ways. The furniture was built in such a way that it made possible transformation and new connections in unpredictable patterns. It is when this unpredictability and connectivity inscribed in the furniture is activated that a line of flight is born that differs from both supple and rigid lines of architecture and design.

5 A line of flight seems to have been created when projects focus on the construction of problems and when this process is considered to be more important than the outcome. This differs from rigid lines of thinking and acting in learning processes in that it does not work with transmission of a predetermined form and content of knowledge. But it also differs from the supple appeal to children to reflect upon and solve problems, but still within the logic of the problem as well as the solution being predetermined. When projects function with the construction of problems they can be considered as lines of flight, since they have given up the idea of pre-existing solutions and answers. Instead they focus on the process of constructing a problem and adapt the methods as the process goes on. This is precisely what is happening in the project on the rhythm of the heart, where there is a circulating around what is maybe going to become a fully constructed problem, but answers or solutions are not what are focused on or highlighted. This differs from both rigid and supple lines that still consider problems, solutions and methods as a predefined set of relations.

6 A line of flight seems to have been created through pedagogical documentation used as a visualization of the problem under construction. Above we can see how children and teachers meet around the pedagogical documentation and how it functions as a place where the problem worked upon can be visualized. Through the documentation new ideas and actions may take form. This differs from the rigid line of observing children through the lens of

normality or spying on them with the ambition to check that they are following a normal trajectory. It also differs from the supple line that would use documentation to domesticate children's desire and learning processes and make of them flexible and autonomous learners. When pedagogical documentation is used as a meeting point in the relational field where the visualization of the problem worked upon can take place, it does not rely on any conscious or taming logic; it is a line of flight in that it is unpredictably experimenting.

These are a few of the line of flights created in these preschools. They do not exist alone. Rather they find themselves on a field of combat where, together with rigid lines and supple lines, they fight for space to survive. This makes the preschools quite a messy place to be in. Everything takes place at the same time and there is a constant struggle with creating favourable conditions for lines of flight to be created.

Micro-politics: 'it is the molecular and its assessments that makes it or breaks it'

In this messy and struggling atmosphere, there seems to exist a kind of mobile system where the logic of a higher organizing principle – such as, for example, a driven leader or the amount of money or time available – no longer functions. Change sneaks up behind one's back. It is not a question of teachers, researchers and children reaching a higher level of awareness, there is not a conscious subject thinking about and consciously and rationally changing itself or somebody else as an object. This is a micro-political practice. This is what the micro-political perspective says: everything is *at the same time* of a micro/molecular and macro/molar politics, but it is 'the molecular and its assessments that makes it or breaks it' (Deleuze and Guattari, 2004: 244).

Even the most rigid of governing systems is built upon a whole set-up of micro movements. 'Hierarchy is not simply pyramidal; the boss's office is as much at the end of the hall as on the top of the tower' (Deleuze and Guattari, 2004: 231). Hierarchy is not functioning without the inventiveness and creation of a flow of micro-political movements. Even the most totalitarian and bureaucratic of organizations exhibits examples of suppleness and creativeness when facing administrative regulations (Deleuze and Guattari, 2004: 237). In this respect, a curriculum for instance is to be seen as a macro-political decision; but when it encounters preschool practices, an enormous creativity is released that completely and continuously transforms and defines the curriculum and its accompanying practices in a reciprocal relationship.

But not only macro-political decisions of an administrative character are involved; everything is involved in the micro-political. In the particular situation of the truncated images, the children refused to go along with the teachers' suggestions since they were not content with how the material and their questions and problems were handled. They were engaged in other problems than the teachers in the first instance were able to acknowledge. A little micro-political gesture from the children overturned the macro-political situation of the teachers' attempt to continue the investigations on their own terms.

But what, then, are these molecular/micro-political movements? According to Deleuze and Guattari (2004: 241), micro-political movements can be described as flow or quanta of belief and desire. Flow, or quanta, is all about belief and desire, they are quantities constructing the very beginning of all change. Accordingly, all change in society and in individuals start in flow or quanta of belief and desire. All governing is about adjusting the segments to the flow or quanta that runs through all societies and each individual and all attempts to predict, supervise, control or evaluate according to preset standards, anything or anyone, is simply a question of trying to adjust the segments to this continuous flow.

Governing, from this perspective, is not at all about transcendent, rational conscious choice. Governing is simply a question of 'hit-and-miss' in the adjustment of segments to quanta. Great molar organizations or decisions, whether they seem to take place in an individual or in a group, are built on a myriad of molecular movements, of flows of belief and desire (Deleuze and Guattari, 2004: 238–241).

This is what very often happens in the preschools in Stockholm and its suburbs; what is being picked up and realized is in no way predictable, it is molecular movements of belief and desire that decide this. This goes for the entire group and its movements, as well as every individual detail of the process, like for instance the moment with the children's illustrations; it is always the micro-political that decides the making or breaking of the process. The same thing goes for all the dualisms that we handle in society; for sure, they have real impact on our lives but from a micro-political perspective they are always and continuously in movement. This creativity can be picked up and made use of through struggling with creating the most favourable conditions possible for lines of flights and leakages to appear.

In this manner we could for instance consider children in preschools as the opposite of adults through a molar and macro-political definition.

But the notion of 'the child' would be recognized as built on a massive molecular movement of 'a thousand little childhoods and children' (Deleuze and Guattari, 2004: 235).[1] From a micro-political perspective these would be activated and made use of.

This is what sometimes takes place in the preschools. Teachers, who many times figure as the macro-organizers and decision makers, may develop an attitude to governing as taking place through 'hit and miss' in adjustments of segments. From the example above, we have seen how teachers activate and use this idea by trying to latch on to children's desires. A great example of 'hit and miss' is the children refusing to continue and connect with the teachers. Everything is involved and everything is capable of completely overturning the situation. This is how the micro-political perspective considers change through movements as flows of belief and desire; even within the most tamed setting, change lives its own life. Movements of belief and desire are impossible to predict, control, supervise or evaluate according to preset standards.

What to do when contemporary governing takes place through desire and affect?

Maybe these ideas of change rather as movements or flows of belief and desire and not as predictable, controllable, or possible to supervise or evaluate against predetermined standards, are more applicable in contemporary society than they have ever been. Governing in Western societies indeed has changed its face. We have already heard about it through recent post-structural and deconstructive research; governing today takes place through desire. Massumi (2003) takes this even further in describing how contemporary governing has installed itself in and hi-jacked affect. Affect is a concept that Massumi picks up from the work of Spinoza, and it concerns a different logic than the conscious logic of taming through predicting, controlling, supervising or evaluating according to predetermined standards.

Affect concerns a body's potential and the Spinozian idea of the fact that we do not yet know what a body can do. It is a logic that surpasses the knowledge we have of a body as well as the consciousness we have of it. When this logic is activated, as it is in the practices in preschools described above, it gives rise to collective experimenting, intensity and unpredictability. The logic of affect also concerns a question of the encounter of bodies and forces; these encounters can never be predictable, they are marked by intensity, and they can only be recognized as effects: when we can account for them through feelings.

In this case, feelings are not the same thing as affect; they are the actualization of affect. Affect is thereby separated from feelings in that it concerns only bodily potential. Feelings are the registration of intensive affect; they are effects of affect. Encounters that increase a body's capacity to act bring joyful passions and encounters that decrease a body's capacity to act bring sad passions, (Deleuze, 1988a; Massumi, 2003).

According to Massumi (2003), contemporary governing has now installed itself right in the heart of the features of affect. For instance, we are now defined as consumers, not merely in relation to goods, for what we buy is the right to extend our lives and adapt to different kinds of life styles. We buy and are governed through our own desire to expand and take on different subjectivities and lifestyles; to increase affect or to increase our bodily potential. In relation to marketing on the Internet, Massumi shows how it has gone beyond niche marketing, where attempts were made to hit specific target groups, to a kind of relational marketing that works through contagion rather than convincing. The affect has been hi-jacked by governing in a way that when events take place in the world, politics and mass media treat them not through analysis but through the direct exposure of affect. This is, according to Massumi, what took place on and after 9/11 in the United States; media no longer mediates but exposes the events directly and appeals to the sensitive registers of the spectators. What we see is a political modulation of the affective (Massumi, 2003, 2005).

What to do then? How to navigate as teachers and researchers in this situation? It seems that all attempts at critique and resistance are condemned to fight only remnants of past enemies.[2] If contemporary governing today has installed itself in movement, the weapons of critique and resistance practices might not even be effective any more as they detract movement from the picture by focusing immobilized positions. These practices run the risk of inevitably always being one step behind, reacting upon what has already taken place, but not working to influence and act in that which takes place. So what to do? There seems to be no point in trying to work against movement. One must, probably, go with it and answer with the same modulation of desire and affect.

Meet modulation of affect with modulation of affect – a politics of listening and experimentation

> It seems to me that alternative political action does not have to fight against the idea that power has become affective, but rather has to learn to function itself on that same level – meet affective modulation with affective modulation. That requires, in some ways, a performative, theatrical or aesthetic approach to politics.
>
> (Massumi, 2003: 19)

After the riots in the suburbs of Paris in November 2005, a very interesting and different analysis of what took place was put forward in the journal *Multitude*. Yann Moulier Boutang (2005) and Anne Querrien (2005) propose to see the riots as an expression of a defence of the society, not just a violation. They show how racism today in western European countries functions as a naturalized feature and effectively cuts off all kinds of experimentation by installing itself at the very core of affect and through this cutting off possible lines of flights. In such a situation the only way left to experiment might be by violence. Even though Moulier Boutang and Querrien do not give the riots in Paris the status of a political action, they are prepared to see what took place in Paris also as a defence of the society.

We could maybe understand this by thinking of what Rajchman (2001) talks about, referring to Deleuze, in relation to a certain kind of violence that exists outside the State and that it is not capable of controlling or predicting. It is a case of a violent evocation of problems that do not seem to fit into our settled way of thinking or our agreed-upon definition of the right way to comprehend politics. These are most often posed by exactly such environments as suburbs (banlieus), environments considered to be the negative side of a city. Accordingly such forces are capable of making us think differently and there is no governing capable of completely silencing these forces (Rajchman, 2001: 104).

This implies that governing on all levels could benefit from listening to and valuing such protests as a production of something new. This is of course not the same as proposing that violence is the way to experiment, but it is an acknowledgement of the fact that contemporary conditions very often force experimentation to take the shape of violence. Instead, maybe what is needed is an approach to governing on all levels, where one needs to prepare oneself for an act of true listening. This would be listening to what kind of desiring production is at stake, for instance, amongst children, but also in larger local contexts such as a suburb. What kinds of desires are people preoccupied with?

Such listening would also need to be followed by preparation to go into a process of collective, intense and unpredictable experimentation. This would of course be a politics that does not rely on violence, but attempts to create exactly the space needed for affect, the space needed for bodies to do things and that permits the exploring of the potentiality of every situation.

> The crucial political question for me is whether there are ways of practising a politics that takes stock of the affective way power operates now, but doesn't rely on violence and the hardening of divisions along identity lines that it usually brings. I'm not exactly sure what that kind of politics would look like, but it would still be performative. In some basic way it would be an aesthetic politics, because its aim would be to expand the range of affective potential – which is what aesthetic practice has always been about.
>
> (Massumi, 2003: 20)

A politics of listening and experimentation might be a politics capable of taking into account the way affect functions. Rather than fighting against modulation of affect, condemning it from one step behind, it would engage in and meet this modulation with the same kind of modulation through focusing on each singular situation's potential. This implies first of all the act of listening to beliefs, desires and production processes already at stake, and engaging in collective, intense and unpredictable experimentation, where one can explore unknown and unexpected ways of thinking, talking and doing. But this also means to engage in a particular kind of ethics.

An ethics and politics of belonging instead of a universalized ethics

To engage in a politics of listening and collective, intense and unpredictable experimentation through modulation of affect also implies a specific kind of ethics. Massumi shows how Spinoza uses ethics and morality in a specific way. According to Massumi's reading of Spinoza, 'morality' concerns the idea that it is possible to judge, on the basis of a pre-determined system, or code, what are positive or negative values in any action. 'Ethics', by contrast, is about focusing on the question of what a body can do and looking for the potentiality in every action. This could, for example, imply questioning the taken-for-granted value system in a preschool that says that teachers are the ones to set the rules for moral behaviour, and instead being prepared to join with the children in a collective construction of new values that are connected to that particular situation and the singular people involved. In relation to this Spinozian differentiation between morality and ethics Massumi says:

> So it's hard for me to put positive or negative connotations on affect. That would be to judge it from the outside. It would be going in a moralising direction. Spinoza makes a distinction between a morality and an ethics. To move in an ethical direction, from a Spinozan point of view, is not to attach positive or negative values to actions based on a characterisation or classification of them according to a pre-set system of judgement. It means assessing what kind of potential they tap into and express. [...] Ethics in this sense is completely situational. It's completely pragmatic. And it happens in between people, in the social gaps. There is no intrinsic good or evil. The ethical value of an action is what it brings out in the situation, for its transformation, how it breaks sociality open. Ethics is about how we inhabit uncertainty together.
>
> (Massumi, 2003: 7)

From the above we can see how affect works as a relational feature. Liberating oneself from existing structures is not about breaking constraints, it is a question of 'flipping them over' and this needs to be done in a relational kind of way. To look at it this way implies a different kind of ethics and politics, it implies an 'ethics and politics of belonging' (Massumi, 2003: 10–11), instead of a politics of identity. A politics of identity works with the way the structures are already functioning whilst a politics of belonging relies on affect's way of collectively using the potentiality in every situation; 'in affect we are never alone' (Massumi, 2003: 4). Nobody can know beforehand how this is to be done or what might be the consequences. But one thing is sure; this demands a totally different idea of ethics than one composed of universalized moral codes and laws:

> In our view, the preschool is never outside ethics, even if technological practice masks the ethics' presence. But what ethics? When we speak of preschools (or other provisions) as sites for ethical and political practice, the issue is not simply one of quantity, of how much ethics

and politics there should be. We are not talking just about 'more ethics' or 'more politics'. Nor are we speaking of ethics and politics as subjects for the curriculum, for example the need to have more time allotted to learning the difference between right and wrong or the workings of democracy, or the need for more codes of ethics to regulate behaviour. For us, the critical questions are 'What ethics?', 'What politics?', 'What sort of practice? and 'What would it mean to understand preschools as, first and foremost, loci of ethical practice and minor politics?'

(Dahlberg and Moss, 2005: 12)

According to Dahlberg and Moss, we live in a time when it becomes of highest importance to raise questions of the possibilities of social institutions for young people. We find ourselves in a time when the institutionalisation of childhood is accelerating: expansion of preschools, a longer period of schooling and longer days within the institution. It then becomes even more necessary to take responsibility for what kind of conditions of childhood we are creating. They see a tendency of treating questions of ethics and politics in preschools today as if the institution is:

first and foremost a site for technical practice, seeking the best methods and procedures for delivering predetermined outcomes – a stable, defined and transmittable body of knowledge, but also implicitly a particular subject, today the autonomous and flexible child.

(Dahlberg and Moss, 2005: 2)

They see this tendency as a social construction that now has become a naturalized feature – and as a naturalized feature it seems almost impossible to contest the idea that we can judge what is good and bad and ensure a way of reaching a 'good' practice. This construction of preschool as a technical practice is built around three conditions; a particular kind of cognitive-instrumental-performative-utilitarian rationality that justifies ethical and political actions in a systematic and structured manner; it contains a desire to order the world and to tame nature. Within this rationality we measure and calculate in a rational manner and try to find the most effective way for reaching our ends. A specific kind of scientific and objective knowledge complements this rationality by giving access to generally formulated laws that describes the order of the world. This is a knowledge that works by defining the wished for outcomes and the goals to reach. Finally, related to this knowledge, there are technologies that will ensure the process of accessing these outcomes in the most effective way. Examples of such technologies are different tools for evaluation, developmentally appropriate curricula and different instruments for measuring quality, for instance the Early Childhood Environmental Rating Scale (ECERS) a universal standard for evaluation spread over the world (Dahlberg and Moss, 2005: 5–9).

What seems to be happening in these technical practices is what Deleuze has called 'orthodox thought' (Deleuze, 1994a: chapter 3). According to Deleuze, most of the time we do not really think at all, thought is often just a question of going in circles, where we rarely see anything new.

> "Everybody" knows very well that in fact men think rarely, and more often under the impulse of a shock than in the excitement of a taste for thinking.
>
> (Deleuze, 1994a: 132)

The reason for this is, as earlier said, that the thinking that creates itself often turns out to be a very violent and unpleasant affair. Since real thinking is such an unpleasant affair we do everything we can in our everyday lives to tame the chaos constantly waiting for us, by installing thought in a safe place where we can rely on its true nature, where the thinker thinks with the best intentions and where thought functions in a steady pattern of recognition and representation. In this safe place of thought it is possible to know what is wrong and right without violence, here we find a taken-for-granted sense that harbours given solutions that correspond to given problems and given answers that correspond to given questions. In this place learning is a relatively safe process guided by the knowledge that will come out of the learning process. In this place it is relatively easy to find the most effective method for learning, despite the complexity of local cultures surrounding the learning process.

This thought and this safe way of thinking in circles is what Deleuze names 'orthodox thought'. It seems that it is this thought that is functioning in the above-described features of 'good practice'. The orthodox thought contains an image of a true nature of thought and the best intentions of the thinker. In relation to this it is possible to define 'good practice' on the basis of what is true, right or wrong. This is done with good intentions and supposedly in the best interest of everyone. Orthodox thought also embraces a common sense; seeing questions of ethics and politics as a matter of technical practice is a naturalized feature, it is common sense. An orthodox thought implies that we can recognize what is 'good practice' and fit it into the map, the representation that is being drawn up of 'good practice'. We can judge when practice is wrong, lacking, not fitting into the map of 'good practice'. Since there is never a question of the construction of the sense of 'good practice', but rather the sense of 'good practice' is predetermined, the problem of establishing 'good practice' has preformed and corresponding solutions. The point is then, under these conditions, to arrive as quickly and effectively at the predetermined outcome, the process is subordinated to the outcome and the focus will be on the most effective method, subordinating the culture surrounding the problem of 'good practice'.[3]

An ethico-aesthetic paradigm

To engage in a politics of listening and collective, intense and unpredictable experimentation through modulation of affect implies a shift of paradigm in relation to ethics and politics. Instead of a universalized ethics offering predetermined solutions that is easily reduced to a technical practice, there seems to be the need for an ethics that can stand to live in the moment. This can be described as an ethics that is all about a certain kind of case-by-case logic, where the focus is on the actual process of formulating law, not applying the already set laws and codes, and that can account for listening, and collective, intense and unpredictable experimentation and modulation of affect.

One possibility here is to engage in what Guattari has called an ethico-aesthetic paradigm. For him, to be able to address many of the problems on earth today, we need to work with, for instance, environmental problems, and engage in a total reinvention of our ways of thinking, not only about the environment, but also about the individual and the social. To accomplish this he proposes that we approach all these areas at the same time, but this must be done through adapting an *aesthetic* approach to life as a creation.[4]

> Our survival on this planet is not only threatened by environmental damage but by a degeneration in the fabric of social solidarity and in the modes of physical life, which must literally be re-invented. The refoundation of politics will have to pass through the aesthetic and analytical dimensions implied in the three ecologies – the environment, the socius and the psyche. We cannot conceive of solutions to the poisoning of the atmosphere and to global warming due to the greenhouse effect, or to the problem of population

control, without a mutation of mentality, without promoting a new art of living in society.

(Guattari, 1995: 20)

This ethico-aesthetic paradigm confronts and challenges the ontological presuppositions of orthodox thought. It could be seen as a different kind of ontology that gives a different kind of ethics. This is an ethics that tries to experiment with and move away from orthodox thought by looking at the world and ourselves from the angle of creative production and ongoing process without predetermined outcomes and rational and effective methods. This can be seen as a pragmatic and tentative approach that includes the necessity of making choices and thereby also includes a certain kind of political responsibility:

> The new aesthetic paradigm has ethico-political implications because to speak of creation is to speak of the responsibility of the creative instance with regard to the thing created, inflection of the state of things, bifurcation beyond pre-established schemas, once again taking into account the fate of alterity in its extreme modalities. But this ethical choice no longer emanates from a transcendent enunciation, a code of law or a unique and all-powerful god. The genesis of enunciation is itself caught up in the movement of processual creation.

(Guattari, 1995: 107)

To try to put into practice a kind of ethico-aesthetic paradigm is a question of political responsibility since it implies a kind of creation and thereby the need to be responsible for that which is being created. To choose to try to work in this way is an ethical and political choice. But this choice can never be made by relying on any great or predetermined structures or laws or conscious transcendent critical thought. Going back to the events in the preschools in Stockholm and its suburbs, these events are ongoing processes where teachers and researchers struggle with questions of subjectivity and learning. They all ask the questions: what ethics, what politics and what sort of practice? These practices have more use for collective, intense and unpredictable experimentation with various ways of talking, thinking and acting than for technical instrumentality. They not only contest what we know of young learning children, but they also create new ways of understanding this, for which they continuously need to take responsibility.

In this matter these preschools are not solely a place of internal affairs, as these new constructions, these new understandings, could also possibly stretch out and influence and be influenced by other fields. Through this they become political in a larger sense than solely limiting themselves to the life of a particular preschool, as they try to complicate the idea of a predetermined outcome and enter into an ethico-aesthetic and political practice where knowledge and values are continuously created. The ethico-aesthetic political approach that is here being practised concerns the political and ethical life of preschools where people engage in listening and experimentation through affective potential. It concerns a care for belonging and collective experimenting without really knowing where one is heading. It goes without saying that this is a quite unsafe and vague place to be, and a place where you have to carefully work to be able to take responsibility for the choices made.

To accomplish this we probably need to focus less on the imagined future and have more trust in the moment and its potentiality. This actually gives us a lot to do; even more than if the outcome had been set already. It is from here, the moment with all its constraints and potentialities that we could work.

There are dangers with every line

However we cannot be careful enough, as according to Deleuze and Guattari, there are dangers connected to each of the segments or lines (Deleuze and Guattari, 2004: 250–255). Due to this we have to go into listening and collective, intense and unpredictable experimentation with the moment's potentiality, never forgetting about these dangers but always keeping them with us, and being prepared to interrupt or reconstruct our experimentation at any moment. Below, the dangers of the rigid and the supple segments or lines as well as the lines of flight, as described by Deleuze and Guattari, are connected to the contemporary situation in early childhood education.

Fear

Fear is the danger of the rigid line. It concerns our fear of losing the rigid segments or lines. As we are comfortable with our definitions and positions it is worrying when they are not functioning or not available. This makes us stick to what we already know, as when we meet something unexpected we get scared and fall back into using the segments we already know about (Deleuze and Guattari, 2004: 250–

251). For example, you might be extremely enlightened, but still, racist thoughts sometimes hit you coming from behind as a reflex, there's nothing you can do, as it is your habit of rigid segments at work. It is your fear of losing and it makes you cling to the rigid segments. In relation to this, it can be proposed that we want to know what a child is; a child that does not behave like a child scares us, so we use our rigid segments to tame the child. Everything is involved in this, the way we think, speak and act with children.

Clarity

Clarity is the danger of the supple line. It seems less obvious because it concerns the molecular. It seemingly frees itself from the rigid segments, it appears as more supple, but Deleuze and Guattari show how the supple lines imitates the rigid ones but in a miniature scale (Deleuze and Guattari, 2004: 251–252). In relation to this, the idea of a child as competent, autonomous and flexible runs the risk of being exposed to the danger of the supple line. It seems self-evident that it is good for a child to be judged no longer from its lack but from its competencies; the child, however, is still judged.

There is a new mission, a new truth; the child is competent, and teachers and researchers are supposed to bring forward the child, to give the child a voice. But what is this definition of competency? Who are the children considered not so competent today? Might not the definition of being competent still function within the same logic as the individual, natural and developing child? The supple segments seem to be at stake when teachers and researchers sometimes believe that they have switched from one image of the child to another one, a better one. This can make everyone busy keeping this new image intact, sometimes even through controlling and judging each other; do the others have the right image of the child or not?

> Instead of the great paranoid fear, we are trapped in a thousands little monomanias, self-evident truths, and clarities that gush from every black hole and no longer form a system, but are only rumble and buzz, blinding lights giving any and everybody the mission of self-appointed judge, dispenser of justice, policeman, neighbourhood SS man. We have overcome fear, we have sailed from the shores of security, only to enter a system that is no less organized: the system of petty insecurities that leads everyone to their own black hole in which to turn dangerous, possessing a clarity on their situation, role,

and mission even more disturbing than the certitudes of the first
line.

(Deleuze and Guattari, 2004: 252)

Power

Power is a danger that works on both lines simultaneously, on both the
rigid and the supple line. The danger of power is its betraying suppleness
that disguises its will to stop every line of flight that tries to break through.
This is, according to Deleuze and Guattari, the woman/man of power
changing faces all the time (Deleuze and Guattari, 2004: 252). In relation
to this one can, for instance, think about the contemporary situation and
the political debates concerning the field of early childhood education. At
one moment the woman/man of power will speak with a supple tongue
of the individual: her or his rights, choices and independence. But in the
next moment, her or his speech will turn hard and rigid, and s/he will
assure us that it is for our own good that we need more law and order,
more tools for measuring quality and the right input/output relationship
to be able to guarantee the expected outcome.

In the field of early childhood education there is an enormous increase
in attempts to control, supervise and evaluate even very young children.
Tools for predicting, controlling, supervising and evaluating these young
children often lay claim to function in the best interest of the child,
and they are being put forward with an insistence on the importance
of producing autonomous and flexible learners and as a guarantee for
personal freedom (Elfström, forthcoming). But the question is not only
what happens with a child when being judged at an early age; it is also if
these tools are actually functioning within the logic of wanting to stop at
all costs every line of flight that tries to break through.

'The great disgust and the passion for abolition'

The danger of the great disgust and the passion for abolition concerns
the lines of flight themselves. The lines of flight not only run the risk of
being captured and segmented, they also 'emanate a strange despair, like
an odour of death and immolation' (Deleuze and Guattari, 2004: 252).
This happens when a line of flight is not connected to any other line;
it then runs the risk of turning into disgust, destruction and abolition
(Deleuze and Guattari, 2004: 252–255). This could be connected to
Moulier Boutang's and Querrien's analysis of the riots in Paris mentioned
earlier in this chapter. What happens when all ways of experimenting are

cut off and what happens when there is no space for lines of flight to be created and connected to other lines? Moulier Boutang and Querrien give one answer: violence.

Maybe it is of importance then to think about how children today pass through both the rigid and the supple segments. They are defined and segmented in a rigid way at the same time as they are talked to by supple tongues as free, independent and flexible individuals. Through the way power functions by wanting to stop and cut off the lines of flight, a great focus is put on each individual. For instance, today very young children are asked more and more frequently to reflect upon themselves, to evaluate themselves and their competencies and at the same time they are being evaluated, measured and controlled according to both national and international standards, sometimes very far removed from the child's context (Elfström, forthcoming).

The autonomous, flexible individual was maybe thought to present a certain kind of liberty and uniqueness in contrast to essentially defined subjects, but the point is not only that the same mechanisms still seem to be at work, but also that this individual might now be the loneliest person on earth. We might need to ask ourselves questions about what happens to young children's possibilities to experiment in a setting where the lines of flight cannot connect to other lines. There might be a risk that if a young child does not find ways to connect her or his lines of flights with other lines, this might force the lines of flight available for the young child to turn into abolition and destruction. And according to Deleuze and Guattari this is the danger we should take most seriously since, 'All the dangers of the other lines pale by comparison' (Deleuze and Guattari, 2004: 255).

Part 2

Methodological approach

Chapter 4

Pedagogical work and transcendental empiricism

Introduction

In the previous chapter the concepts of micro-politics and segmentarity were presented and put to work in order to account for movement as preceding positions. In this chapter, we turn to the concept 'transcendental empiricism'. The concept is presented and put to work as a way of trying to account for the ongoing work of collective, intense and unpredictable experimentation that is taking place in between practice and research in the preschools in Stockholm and its suburbs. This chapter makes a first attempt to work with the second decisive point:

> 2. In the preschools teachers and researchers work together through collective, intense and unpredictable experimentation. In this process teachers as well as researchers are caught up in a relational field. For this to be theoretically workable, the reliance on the transcendent principle of conscious critique needs to be rethought and reinforced by other possible and alternative scientific methods.

The research being undertaken in the present study is situated within the discipline of pedagogical work. Pedagogical work is a fairly new discipline in Sweden with a particular history and specific aims.[1] The birth of this new discipline may be seen against the background of an identified need for development in teacher education and in classroom practices. Pedagogical work as a discipline is supposed to address questions concerning the scientific basis of teacher education as well as the need for new knowledge in classroom practices; the ambition is a development of both scientific theories and teacher education and classroom practices and especially the relationship in between research and practice, in relation to the political, economic and social context of contemporary society. According to Ahlström and Kallós (1996), Carlgren (1996a, 1996b) and Erixon Arreman (2002) these questions have formerly been addressed through the discipline of pedagogy. But within this discipline, they argue, there has not been sufficient growth in new knowledge, concerning neither research nor practices. Even though didactic research has been conducted within other research fields and in other departments, such as linguistics and history, researchers working on questions related to teacher education and classroom practices have been very few and the critical mass has not been sufficient for constructing creative working environments.

Part of the background and one of the reasons for the development of a new discipline is that in the classroom there are few people with postgraduate education. There has been a great need to create a research field that permits a closer working relationship between research and practice. One aim of the new discipline of pedagogical work is to make possible a working relationship between practice and research where teachers can be given the possibility to formulate questions and problems and to conduct research that is closely connected to their practices. A way of making this possible has been to give the opportunity to teachers with more than two years of field experience and a teacher education to enter so-called 'research schools'. These research schools are full time and courses and seminars are regularly organized. They offer many opportunities for PhD students to develop their research capabilities and collaborate in preparatory work for dissertations. Through building up a research school functioning as an extension of the basic teacher education, it is hoped to create a research environment that will engage in different ways in questions that concern the life of teacher education and classroom practices. In the curriculum for the research school in pedagogical work, it is pointed out that research needs to take into consideration, and grow out of, pedagogical practice and theory with the purpose of:

> ... contributing to an increased base of scientific knowledge and theory about the construction of knowledge, the work of pedagogical practitioners, students' learning and socialisation, as well as about how these processes are shaped by economic, political, and social contexts of which they are part.
>
> (Umeå Universitet, 2005: 1; my translation)

This study builds on experiences made in preschools as well as in in-service training courses at the Stockholm Institute of Education. But for these experiences and for the discipline pedagogical work to be effective in existing research environments and fields, there is a need for theory capable of encompassing the complexity of the relation between theory and practice. The discipline and the experiences that cannot do this run a double risk. On the one hand they risk being invaded by already existing theory that suffocates these unique experiences by shaping them to fit into existing moulds of scientific procedures and results. And on the other hand they run the risk of not being theorized enough, that is, they will be glorified as true events from practice and described no differently to the way that every teacher can already describe them.

Throughout the development of the new discipline pedagogical work we can see an insistence on practice being put at the centre of the research efforts. Considering this and taking into account the above definition of the discipline – a discipline just being born, finding itself in its early stages of formation, running this double risk of suffocation by existing theory as well as flattening out by practice glorification – there is supposed to be room for experimentation and exploring new theoretical perspectives. Under these conditions it seems quite legitimate to try out a new theoretical perspective such as Deleuze and Guattari's in the research field of pedagogical work.

Deleuze and Guattari seem to offer important concepts, capable of loosening a few long-established knots within research in social sciences. One such scientific knot that seems hard to overcome, and which is of central importance for the development of the discipline, is that of the relationship between research and practice. This relationship might benefit from having a closer look at Deleuze and Guattari's way of treating empiricism through the concept transcendental empiricism.[2] What will be argued below is that Deleuze and Guattari's concept of transcendental empiricism could, through its accounting for the collective, intense and unpredictable experimentation in which teachers and researchers engage in the preschools, present a valuable contribution to the question of the relation of research to practice.

Transcendental empiricism is an empiricism that has gone wild

According to Deleuze, the history of philosophy has absorbed empiricism by defining it as the reverse of rationalism (Deleuze, 2001: 35). Empiricism has been forced to account for something that supposedly should not exist in thought: atomistic sensations. Through the history of philosophy, these have been seen as needing to be organized and systemized by rational thinking. Through Deleuze and Guattari's presentation of a transcendental empiricism, empiricism is shown to harbour much more interesting features. Empiricism here breaks away from an epistemological tradition, no longer treating thought as the great organizer of sensations.

Before thought there is life, and life can never be totally organized or systemized. Thought is here a producer, not a discoverer or an organizer. Thought happens through encounters. It is an effect of life, not a cause (Deleuze, 1994a, 2001; Deleuze and Guattari, 1994). In this way Deleuze and Guattari are immanent thinkers, since all transcendence implies thought as cause and organizer. Transcendence is that which attempts to go beyond or above, a highest grounding principle such as thought and consciousness. But, still, in Deleuze and Guattari's thinking we hear of a 'transcendental' empiricism; how come?

There is a difference between the words transcendence and transcendental. Philosophers working in the transcendental tradition are challenging transcendence and instead following an immanent way of thinking.[3] An immanent way of thinking insists that all transcendence must be considered empirical and that philosophy should not create conditions of thinking greater than that which is thought about.

> What is a transcendental field? It can be distinguished from experience in that it doesn't refer to an object or belong to a subject (empirical representation). It appears therefore as a pure stream of a-subjective consciousness, a pre-reflexive impersonal consciousness, a qualitative duration of consciousness without a self.
>
> (Deleuze, 2001: 25)

From this quotation it becomes clear that the question of a transcendental empiricism, transcendence and immanence has got something to do with consciousness and the status and capacity of the human subject to use her or his consciousness to comprehend and act in the world. Transcendental empiricism concerns a certain devaluation of consciousness's capacity and aspirations to account for the world.[4] Consciousness somewhat invades the transcendental field, takes possession of it and makes possible the subject capable of thinking of itself and the world as objects. This is being done through the taking for granted capacity of consciousness to account for experience.

What is proposed instead is a field, a transcendental field, where consciousness no longer functions so as to establish the essential thinking subject. This field is also called the plane of immanence (Deleuze and Guattari, 1994: chapter 2; Deleuze, 2001). Before consciousness there is a plane of immanence where the dualism subject/object no longer functions and where empirical representation is abolished:

> The transcendent is not the transcendental. Were it not for consciousness, the transcendental field would be defined as a pure plane of immanence, because it eludes all transcendence of the subject and of the object.
>
> (Deleuze, 2001: 26)

The plane of immanence concerns the self-creation of thought mentioned in Chapter 2. Without any stable and sedentary ground thinking proceeds by laying out its ground at the same time as it thinks. This happens in a place that might no longer even be a place. There is no longer any stable ground and there is no longer a subject capable of thinking of itself and the world as objects. This plane is in itself transforming and connective and on this plane there are only different speeds and slowness and forces and bodies encountering each other (Deleuze and Guattari, 1994: 36–37).[5] In line with this it is possible to understand that it implies that all transcendence must be considered empirical and why an immanent thought does not create conditions of thinking that are greater than that which is thought about.

In a world where consciousness no longer invades the transcendental field, everything becomes immanent; the subject is already immanent with the world and the subject/object dualism ceases to function. Thereby, the empirical representation also ceases to function; what we have is a plane of immanence where no representation is possible. Empirical representation is challenged by a much more 'wild' kind of empiricism that can account for the unstableness and continuous production of the world.[6]

Transcendental empiricism and science/theory as a practice, speaking with another practice

But what does this imply for the relation between theory and practice? It might be fruitful to connect the concept of transcendental empiricism to this question since the relation between research and practice normally functions as a dualism where one subject explains the other, the latter functioning as object for the thinking undertaken by the subject. Research normally approaches what takes place in practice through a transcendent logic that delivers conscious critique of practice. This way of approaching practice relies upon the capacity of consciousness to account for the world and ourselves. It is a kind of research that through transcendent, conscious critique takes the position as subject, while the practice and the people in it function as objects: they are objects for the scientific thinking about them.

Going back to the description of the discipline pedagogical work, it was described above as arising from a concern to create a research environment where teachers can formulate research questions that concern them. But if this means that the questions they are supposed to ask are being asked from the already existing transcendent logic of scientific thinking (that is, thinking as the subject) this will not change anything. The only difference will be that the transcendent thinking now is to be done by the subject thinking about itself as an object. Attempts at scientific or pedagogical critical self-reflection are inevitably based upon a logic of transcendence; when for instance researchers, students or young children are asked to reflect upon their learning, they are asked to become conscious of their learning in accordance with the transcendent idea of the subject thinking about itself as an object. Self-reflection is maybe the strongest indication of a transcendent logic.

When using Deleuze and Guattari's transcendental empiricism, what seems to be needed is a reformulation and revitalization of the status of research and practice. A transcendental empiricism might be capable of such a reformulation since it implies that science and theory have to be considered as themselves being a practice. This would be a practice that does not take for granted that it needs to think or speak *about* another practice as if it was an object. Rather this practice of science and theory would speak *with* another practice:

> Science or theory is an inquiry, which is to say, a practice: a practice of the seemingly fictive world that empiricism describes; a study of the conditions of legitimacy of practices in this empirical world that is in fact our own. The result is a great conversion of theory to practice.
>
> (Deleuze, 2001: 36)

Acknowledging science's productiveness and inventiveness

This practice of science or theory would no longer approach other practices with the sole ambition to bring forward conscious critique, because when using conscious critique the empirical data is immobilized and experimentation is locked up and formalized, as the critique is based in a transcendent thought that does not account for its own production and inventiveness. Of course, it is never put this simply. Researchers in general make a great effort to handle the ontological and ethical questions that come up in every research effort. But whether one chooses to validate one's data with stringent statistics, intrinsic interpretation procedures, complex processes and methods of categorizing, or attempts at critical reflection, if, still, the idea is that what takes place needs to be represented solely through the means of critique one can only speak of an empiricism that has been swallowed and digested by rationalism and the reliance on consciousness's capacity to grasp the world and ourselves.

To use a transcendental empiricism is to create conditions of thinking not greater than that which is thought about. That means that science or theory would need to expose itself to the encounter with empirical data in a way that tries to avoid the copying of transcendent thought onto the empirical (Deleuze, 1994a). To do research would in this sense mean to collectively invent rather than discover at a distance. It would imply fully recognizing that when doing research one is also inventing and adding things to the world. If admitting this, research and practice can through collectively experimenting together produce and invent situations where it is possible to account for things that we do not yet know about.

The transcendent thought is not capable of appreciating encounters that make thinking think.[7] Deleuze and Guattari argue that it is not prepared for the not familiar and the unexpected. But a thought that creates itself as it goes on through encounters is precisely looking for that which is unfamiliar and unexpected, especially since this thought is also a thought of experimentation with the new, the interesting and the remarkable (Deleuze and Guattari, 1994: 111). This is why, from the perspective of a transcendental empiricism, theory should not be content with criticizing and reducing practice. As an addition to these scientific methods, research can acknowledge its own productiveness and inventiveness and engage in collective, intense and unpredictable experimentation with practice.

The relation between theory and practice could be an encounter of collective, intense and unpredictable experimentation

From the perspective of transcendental empiricism, as it is being treated here, you cannot put a theory onto a practice. What is needed is a kind of encounter in between the theory and the practice, where neither has the right to function as a highest organizing or defining principle. In a conversation with Foucault (Deleuze, 2004a: 206), Deleuze talks about the relationship between theory and practice as a fragmented relationship. Neither theory nor practice must totally embrace, explain, apply or be the cause of the other. You can never apply a theory to a practice but, this also goes for the other way around, you can never glorify practice and make it embrace theory, or be the origin of theory. There can never be resemblance between theory and practice, they are both practices but not of the same sort.

According to Deleuze, a theory always, sooner or later, runs into a wall. To pierce a hole in that wall, theory needs a practice. In relation to this it could be proposed that both the concept (or science and theory) and the practice (or the empirical data) need to experiment together so as to awaken something within each other, and bring forward something yet not known. A good way of putting it might be how Foucault describes it in the foreword of *Anti-Oedipus* (1984):

> Use political practice as an intensifier of thought, and analysis as a multiplier of the forms and domains for the intervention of political action.
>
> (Foucault, 1984c: xiv)

This seems to be a fruitful definition of how theory and practice can work together and a good way of describing how theory and practice have worked together in this study; within theory, concepts need to be created and intensified by the challenges that practice brings upon them, and practices need to work with displacement in the sense that theory and its concepts can bring, seeing their daily lives from different perspectives and thereby taking part in political action with a broader meaning. This kind of experimentation and encounter in between theory and practice, can, as will be shown below, be of a very concrete sort. When starting to investigate how to use theory in relation to the experiences from preschools, it seemed that Deleuze and Guattari's work would be a fruitful theory to use in order to be able to work with features of movement and experimentation in subjectivity and learning. What was found in Deleuze and Guattari was a series of concepts that seemed possible and worthwhile to try to make work together with the experiences from the practices. It seemed not that the concepts corresponded in any simplistic way to the preschools' work, but rather that something new happened both to the experiences from preschools and to the concepts when they were put into work together. They sort of transformed each other in a reciprocal relationship, sometimes in a very violent way. The experiences made in the preschools and Deleuze and Guattari's concepts working together seemed sometimes to contain an almost explosive force. The concepts had to stretch themselves out of the text they were created in, into an everyday life in a preschool and thereby sometimes completely change their function in the theoretical system. And experiences in practice when meeting certain concepts would sometimes completely change and transform into new ways of thinking, talking and doing.

One example of this is how Deleuze and Guattari's definition of desire encountered the experiences from the preschools and how they together accomplished a different way of thinking, talking and acting with the children. When the idea of desire as unconscious production of real (see further Chapter 6) encountered the new way of listening to children in preschools, this seemingly quite abstract concept all of a sudden changed its function. In relation to the preschools, desire as unconscious production of real could be seen as a way of permitting children to deploy their desires in different ways.

When desire is no longer defined as lack according to the psychoanalytical definition, but desire instead becomes entirely productive, the gaze of the teacher on children completely changes. Instead of looking for what the child is lacking or needing, the teacher can now look for what the child through desire is producing. This seemed to be an almost revolutionary turn for a preschool institution. Desire defined in this way seemed to be capable of doing away with the definition of the child in need, which has consequences for the entire practice. When desire is defined as lack and need, the teacher takes the role of an authority and a judge, supervising the children and judging them against predefined categories of normal development. Teachers will then arrange and perform activities for the children starting out from these judgements and with the ambition to help them to develop 'normally'. In this situation, children have very few opportunities to influence their lives in preschool.

But when desire is defined as production, the teacher first and foremost listens to and detects what kind of desires are at stake in the classroom. These desires are then not seen as children's needs, but rather, they are looked at as very intense forces that are the starting out point for all learning. Teachers can then arrange situations where it is possible for the children to continue to deploy their desires within everyday life in preschool. This involves the content and form of the pedagogical environment: the use made of time and space, as well as the actual content of the day. When children's desires are listened to and considered as productive, teachers can bring these into the planning of the activities in a way that make children part of producing new realities in preschool.[8]

The concept of desire was not the concept first chosen to work with. In the beginning of the research process, it had a more secondary role. But due to the discoveries made of how this concept connected to so many important features in the practice and since all concepts within Deleuze and Guattari's work seemed to have the same status in a non-hierarchical system, it was chosen as one of the best functioning and most important concepts to use, putting it to work with the field of early childhood education. So, not only did the encounter in between the concept of desire and the experiences from preschools produce a wider area for the practice to work within (what does this definition of desire imply for the role of the teacher, the task of a preschool, its architecture and pedagogical environment, its way of organizing and treating the form and content of knowledge etc.?), but also the concept itself became somewhat widened and more intense as well as changing its function in the theoretical system.

The entire research process has been like this: a wandering back and forth from theory to practice and vice versa, and it is through the encounters where something not yet known was coming about that this study was produced. During the entire process children, teachers and researchers have continuously met and all these encounters have forced the concepts to intensify themselves and change their function. Many of the preschools have shown examples of how certain of these concepts became really important to them and made them look at and work with their practice in a totally different way. For instance, many of the preschools would really latch on to the concept of desire, struggling with turning around the logic that says that a child is a child in need and lacking. They have also been struggling with the idea of desire as always assembled, by insisting on working with relational learning.

According to Deleuze and Guattari desire is always assembled; it takes place in between people. We never desire an object; we desire the object in a complex network of relations. This has been used by the preschools by turning the gaze that focused on the individual child around; teachers instead starting to look for what goes on in between the children. Which kind of assemblages of desire are at stake in the group? What are the children exploring? How do they move in the classroom? What kind of rituals have they created and how do these function? Which material attracts the children the most for the moment? What do they do with it? When they explore together do individual contributions get taken up by the group creating a collective culture? Are there words and expressions that the children use singularly and collectively at the moment and how do these words and expressions function? All these questions indicate that the focus has changed, from a focus on the individual child and her or his lack and needs, to a focus on assembled and productive desire that takes place in between children in a completely relational situation.

Another example of the relation between theory and practice comes from the in-service training courses for preschool teachers held at the Stockholm Institute of Education.[9] These courses were organized so as to create an encounter in between theory and practice. At the beginning of a course the participants are given an introductory lecture on the theoretical resources and the possibility to connect them to the field of early childhood education. In the very first session participants are given observational tasks to undertake in their classes. They come back to the course bringing with them their pedagogical documentations, which are theoretically and practically analysed. The course has no detailed pre-planned curriculum, but at the first lecture several important and decisive points and themes are pointed out as possible and important problems to work upon during the year. Participants work in their classes with the children in between the course meetings and they always bring their pedagogical documentations back to the course.

This gives an excellent opportunity to create an encounter in between theory and practice, where the concepts presented in the course need to stretch themselves out and into the practice, often with the result that they change their function in the theoretical system, and where practices need to broaden their perspectives and widen their possibilities to work in class. The strongest example of this might be how desire, as described above, totally changed its function both as a theoretical concept and in the everyday life in preschool. This encounter in between theory and practice was possible only through collective experimenting. During the course nobody knows exactly what is going to happen from one course meeting to another, but instead there is in each group a construction throughout the year of a collective culture of knowledge.

The concepts that seem to have been of most importance for participants in the courses are desire, micro-politics and the event. Desire was used by participants in the way already described: as a complete overturning of the gaze so as to be able to embrace and work with the notion of production in relation to very young children and in preschool. Micro-politics was often used as a way to inscribe in one's practice the possibility of a different role as a teacher, questioning the governing of children through judgements and assumed authority. But also, as a consequence of discovering how repressing desire functions, the concept was used as a way to avoid intimidation by the power normally ascribed to the teacher. So micro-politics as a concept and as it is being presented by Deleuze and Guattari, in relation to changes on a different level and in larger systems, was all of a sudden being used in relation to the role of the teacher in a classroom. It seems that micro-politics is capable of permitting teachers to engage in collective experimentation not only with the children but also together as teachers.

The event seemed to make it possible to focus on the way children use language in a different way. Teachers were already accustomed to the use of the term 'meaning-making'. But it turned out that the use of this term very often indicated language as signifying and representing. When used by the teachers, 'meaning' was already somewhat implied in language and still trapped within a certain claim of truth. This made it hard to access young children's 'meaning-making', since this quite often was very far away from the 'meaning' adults would acknowledge. When teachers discovered sense as an alternative to meaning and how sense can be considered as continuously produced, as well as intimately connected to nonsense, this made them re-evaluate children's speech. Many teachers became very skilled at detecting what kind of sense children were producing through their speech. They were on the look out, even with the very youngest children who express themselves through other means than language, for what kind of sense and problems the children were constructing and producing.

This completely changed the idea of the very young child. There have been many moments of surprise and astonishment in the courses once the children's production of sense through language was accessed through the event. To many teachers it has become clear that children are always after something. When looking at it from the point of view of not already given, but continuously produced sense, even children's oddest expressions are never random. It has become clear to many teachers that children produce sense all the time. The event, which is a complex concept and which might seem very abstract, was at these moments filled with life, and what seemed to be an abstract concept proved to be really about the events we pass through in our daily lives, although these were now somewhat twisted and turned.

The role of the researcher

From the above perspective of a transcendental empiricism, theory is converted into a practice speaking *with* another practice. This also implies a specific role for the researcher. In the conversation already mentioned between Deleuze and Foucault (Deleuze, 2004a), the role of the intellectual is being discussed.[10] Foucault suggests that the role of the intellectual should no longer be to position him or herself outside or above practice:

> The role of the intellectual is no longer to situate himself "slightly ahead" or "slightly to one side" so he may speak the silent truth of each and all; it is rather to struggle against those forms of power where he is both instrument and object: in the order of "knowledge," "truth," "consciousness," and "discourse". So it is that theory does not express, translate, or apply a praxis; it is a praxis – but local and regional, as you say: non-totalizing.
>
> (Foucault, 2004: 207)

Deleuze answers to this that:

> Yes, that's what a theory is, exactly like a tool box. It has nothing to do with the signifier ... A theory has to be used, it has to work [...] In my opinion, you were the first to teach us a fundamental lesson, both in your books and in the practical domain: the indignity of speaking for others. What I mean is, we laughed at representation, saying it was over, but we didn't follow this "theoretical" conversion through – namely, theory demanded that those involved finally have their say from a practical standpoint.
>
> (Deleuze, 2004a: 208)

'The indignity of speaking for others', within such a statement there is no longer room for giving voice, or making people aware of their own ignorance. It is a matter of working together to produce new constructions of what we are all part of. The way in which the theoretical concepts met the practices involved in the present study could possibly be a way of not getting enamoured of, nor intimidated by, the power normally included in the role of the researcher and the intellectual. The relation between theory and practice as well as the relation between researchers and teachers has in this study taken on the features of co-production of research as well as practice. In this respect, ethical questions in research also take on another light. As a researcher you have no inherent right to know better than teachers their own problems and questions, but at the same time teachers might benefit from the encounter with researchers in the ways described above.

Doubtless there is (and probably always has been) a co-production of research and practice at stake. Maybe this is the first thing to be acknowledged; we all add to and invent the world. But maybe it is also important to see that this adding to the world, these contributions take their specific and different shapes in different practices. In the encounter between research and practice each has its own distinct role. But encounters between these practices marked by collective, intense and unpredictable experimentation might be capable of letting new things be born.

Chapter 5

Pedagogical documentation treated as events, a culture, a use, a style

Introduction

In Chapter 3 the concepts micro-politics and segmentarity were presented and put to work in order to work with the first decisive point. Chapter 4 presented and worked with the concept of transcendental empiricism as a first attempt to work with the second decisive point. In this chapter the concept of the event[1] is presented and used as yet another attempt to work with the second decisive point, this time to be able to account for movement in the empirical material. The empirical material in the present study consists of pedagogical documentations: in this case photographs accompanied by written observations of learning processes. The concept, the event, is drawn up as an alternative scientific and pedagogical methodological approach, capable of treating the pedagogical documentations as complex and open-ended events in movement.

To remind the reader, the second decisive point proposed that:

> 2. In the preschools teachers and researchers work together through collective, intense and unpredictable experimentation. Also researchers are caught up in a relational field. For this to be theoretically workable, the reliance on the transcendent principle of conscious critique needs to be rethought and reinforced by other possible and alternative scientific methods.

According to Deleuze, events are usually related to language in three general ways: through denotation, manifestation and signification. However, for Deleuze, these ways of relating the event to language close the event down within claims of truth specific to each way of using and approaching language and events (Deleuze, 2004b: 16–18). These three general ways are below connected to the work with pedagogical documentations, and it is argued how they would probably imply commenting, interpreting or reflecting upon these documentations, thereby immobilizing them and the event through closing them down within truth claims.

In addition to the three general ways of relating events to linguistic propositions, Deleuze inserts sense as a fourth dimension in language. Through defining sense as the unconditioned production of truth in a proposition, as well as locating it on the border of linguistic propositions and the state of things, the event seems to escape the closing down within claims of truth. According to this we always have as much truth as we deserve in relation to the specific sense under production (Deleuze, 2004b: 22–25, 83; 1994a: 154). Below it is shown how sense, according to Deleuze, relates to nonsense, problems, learning, and culture as ongoing production processes (Deleuze, 2004b: 63–65, 78–83; 1994a: 155–166). This is tried out as a methodological approach that focuses on the ongoing production of sense in between all participants when approaching the pedagogical documentations. This implies taking into account how sense is expressed through nonsense, focusing on the construction of problems rather than on solutions, on processes of learning rather than on the outcome, and finally on the entire culture in the pedagogical documentations rather than looking for how methods are used.

It is argued that although it is inevitable to use the first three dimensions in language – denotation, manifestation and signification – when approaching pedagogical documentations, the introduction of sense as a fourth dimension can contribute and function as an addition to these in that it is possibly capable of doing something else with pedagogical documentations. At the end of the chapter, these ideas of the event are related to the research process and there is a discussion of how they relate to questions of the framing of the present study, as well as to questions of validity and the possibility of generalizing the research efforts carried out in the present study. Finally, it is described how the collection of the empirical material proceeded and how ethical questions concerning the research process have been handled.

The event is connected to language – three general ways of treating language and the methodological implications

According to Deleuze, the event is in close connection to language; events are expressed by linguistic propositions. Linguistic propositions are normally thought of as that which gives us access to what is true or false in the events in which we take part (Deleuze, 2004b: 16–18).[2] This could also be understood and used in relation to doing research and different methodological approaches. When doing research, one chooses a way of treating the events in one's empirical material starting out from a specific way of viewing language or linguistic propositions and their relation to claims of truth in the events. Deleuze distinguishes three common ways of relating the event to linguistic propositions. The three common ways of treating language and linguistic propositions are:

1 by 'denotation'
2 by 'manifestation'
3 by 'signification'.

'Denotation' is the way by which a proposition relates to an exterior state of things. Denotation is the function within language that creates images that correspond to or represent the words. Examples of such words are: 'this', 'that', 'it', 'here', 'now'. Denotation works within language so as to point out what is true and what is false. True implies that denotation is filled up with the pointed out thing, true is when the right image is selected. False is when denotation is not filled up, when the wrong image is chosen or when there is no corresponding image at all (Deleuze, 2004b: 16–17).

Maybe one could say that the truth claim when using language as denotation resides in the denoted object itself. Things have an inner essence and language is directly corresponding (or not, in the case of false) to this essence. Considering pedagogical documentations, this way of relating linguistic propositions to the event would probably connect with the way of documenting events in preschool that was already being challenged by the preschools in the mid-1990s. In this case, the events as well as the children and teachers in the photos and other observations were *commented* upon on the basis of the findings of developmental psychology. The events, as well as the children and the teachers, were objects in the photos and the observations and it was thought possible to judge if the events and the children corresponded to the linguistic propositions expressed by developmental psychology. Put another way, truth was found in the judgement of how well the events, the children and the teachers corresponded to the linguistic propositions put forward by developmental theory.

'Manifestation' is the way in which a proposition refers to the one who is speaking. It is the personal utterance of desires and beliefs that corresponds to the proposition. Examples of such words are: 'I', 'you', 'always', 'everywhere'. The manifesting I has here a special role, since all the other manifesting words relate to it or rather are expressed by it. It is the grounding manifesting word. Manifestation works so as to point out not what is true or false – as with denotation – but whether or not the I is correct in its desires and beliefs (Deleuze, 2004b: 17).[3]

Maybe one could say that the truth claim when using language as manifestation no longer resides in the object but has moved within the subject itself. Considering pedagogical documentations, this way of relating linguistic propositions to the event would probably approach documentations through putting forward and using one's own or others' subjective point of view. The events as well as children and teachers in the photos and observations would be *interpreted* by one or several subjects (for instance by me as a researcher, or by several researchers, or the teachers, or the children or by a combination of all these). Truth would here be found in each interpreting subject.

'Signification' is the way by which a proposition relates words and universal concepts. It is the way that we consider words within a proposition to signify something. Signification works by connecting words or signifiers within one proposition with those within another proposition in so-called signifying chains. In these chains the signifiers either have the role of being each other's presumptions or each other's conclusions; one word depending upon another's way of conditioning it. Examples of such words are: 'imply' and 'therefore'. Signification does not work to point out what is true or false, nor whether or not the I is correct in its beliefs and desires; rather, it points out the conditions under which truth comes about (Deleuze, 2004b: 18).

Maybe one could say that truth, when using language as signification, is no longer looked for either in the object or the subject but within structures in language that are shaping truth regimes. If we again consider pedagogical documentations, this way of relating linguistic propositions to the event would probably use documentations in line with the efforts already made in preschools where teachers and researchers have deconstructed their linguistically shaped truth regimes. The photos and observations would be *reflected* upon to look for the conditions of truth that they express. This has been done in preschools both on the level of teachers reflecting upon their own signifying truth regimes to make them visible and possible to change and also in relation to children making visible and reflecting upon their own learning processes as a way of proceeding.

But, according to Deleuze, all of the three linguistic approaches in their respective ways close the event down within truth claims. This is because they all ground truth in presuppositions, that define the event as a closed system. The presupposition that closes the system within designation is the assumption that truth can be found when there is a correspondence between linguistic propositions and things – as if truth resided in the inner essence of things. The presupposition that closes the system within manifestation is the assumption that the manifesting I is correct in its beliefs and desires – as if truth was to be found within each person and as if truth was a personal question.

When it comes to the presupposition within signification it gets more complicated. With signification we are no longer looking for truth, but for the conditions of truth. We are finding ourselves on a level where we condition truth as being possible in a proposition. But, according to Deleuze, by elevating ourselves from the already conditioned to the level of conditioning, where we look at the conditioned as a simple possibility, we focus a grounding principle but leave the grounded as it was. It is sort of a false movement where we move truth to the field of the possible, but still leave it as it was. In short, truth is never questioned in itself (Deleuze, 2004b: 20–22).

Taking into account what is said above about the closing down of the event, it seems that it will be difficult to keep the event in the pedagogical documentations complex and open ended in order to be able to account for movement when using them. A possible way here might be to follow Deleuze's argument about the importance of introducing sense as a fourth dimension in language and as unconditioned production of truth in the event.

The introduction of sense as the unconditioned production of truth

What Deleuze is after is a way of treating truth that starts with something *unconditioned* in a proposition. Something unconditioned that does not mix itself up with the proposition and something that escapes designed things, subjective representation and signifying concepts:

> The question is as follows: is there something, *aliquid*, which merges neither with the proposition or with the terms of the proposition, nor with the object or with the state of affairs which the proposition denotes, neither with the "lived", or representation or the mental activity of the person who expresses herself in the proposition, nor with the concepts or even signified essences?
>
> (Deleuze, 2004b: 23; original emphasis)

When seeing truth as being an 'unconditioned production' within a proposition, the event could be connected to language in a way where it is freed from being caught up and closed down within claims of truth. Deleuze tries to establish this by introducing a fourth dimension in the proposition: that of sense. It is through seeing language and propositions as producing truth in a proportional relation to sense that the event can avoid closing down within claims of truth:

> For the condition of truth to avoid this defect, it ought to have an element of its own, distinct from the form of the conditioned. It ought to have *something unconditioned* capable of assuring a real genesis of denotation and of the other dimensions of the proposition. [...] Sense is the fourth dimension of a proposition.
>
> (Deleuze, 2004b: 22; original emphasis)

According to Deleuze, truth is never a question of simple denotation, manifestation or signification. Truth always relates to sense in a completely proportional relation. *We always have as much truth as we deserve in relation to the sense we start from.* Sense is the production of truth. Truth is only the effect, the result of sense. Sense, then, might be a way of getting out of the circle of presuppositions, whether they are posed within denotation, manifestation or signification (Deleuze, 1994a: 154).

In relation to the pedagogical documentations, they can be treated as events by adding something to the commenting upon them as if they were already made facts, to the interpretation of them based on one's own subjectivity, or finally, to the reflecting upon them or deconstruction of them looking for signifying regimes. That something, the addition to these ways of treating the relation of linguistic propositions to events, consists of a focus on the sense in the events. Truth needs to be considered as something that is continuously produced in the events, intimately and proportionally related to sense. The focus will be on what sense is at stake in the empirical material and truth will be considered to be only a proportional effect. An example of how to do this can be the following analysis of a documented project that took place several years ago.

In one class the children explored the measuring of time and speed within the context of a car race between two cars. The children had built a racing track that started with a narrow tube. When they let the two cars start at the same time the cars got stuck in the narrow tube. The children were asked to discuss the problem together. During the discussion it becomes clear that it is important for the children that both cars start at the same time and that they use their eyes to judge which one is the fastest car; the car that first comes down the tube and finishes the track is the fastest one. By the end of the discussion the children come up with the idea to put wings on one of the cars. This slightly incomprehensible and seemingly incorrect way of measuring time and speed had its own perfect rationality when considering that the children used their eyes to measure time and speed. The sense of measuring time and speed for these children at that point was using the eyes to see which car came first. The solution with the wings then deserves its own truth; if one car can fly outside the tube, then both cars can start at the same time and it is still possible to use the eyes to see which one is the winning car. The solution and the truth here find themselves in a proportional relation to the sense they start from.

To use the concept event in relation to pedagogical documentations seems a promising methodological way of accounting for movement in subjectivity and learning in the empirical material. If the focus is no longer solely to comment, interpret or reflect upon the empirical material, but instead on the production of sense in children's and teachers' thinking, talking and doing, then maybe this could be a way of keeping the events in the pedagogical documentations complex, open ended and in movement.

Of course this can be no more than an addition. It is inevitable to use all of the first three dimensions when speaking or writing. But the addition of sense might be capable of doing other things with the events in the pedagogical documentations; it could possibly add something to them that could not be produced through commentary, interpretation or reflection.

But what then is sense?

'To look for sense in the events': how does one go about such a seemingly abstract mission? Deleuze says that to try to look for sense, to join the fourth dimension in a proposition, might be a bit like going on a hunt for Lewis Carroll's Snark. And maybe, he adds, maybe this fourth dimension is the hunting act itself and the sense is nothing more or less than the Snark (Deleuze, 2004b: 23). Sense and events, then, must be seen as ongoing activity. In relation to this, Deleuze takes as an example 'green' as a quality and exchanges it for 'greening'. This active greening is called 'the attribute of the thing or the state of things' (Deleuze, 2004b: 24–25).

What, then, is this 'attribute of the thing or the state of things'? Well, according to Deleuze, sense has a peculiar and complex status in that it does not exist outside the proposition that expresses it. Rather than existing it *insists* in a proposition.[4] But, at the same time, sense has its very own 'objectivity', in that it is not confounded with the proposition. The sense is distinct from the proposition. It attributes itself, but is not the attribute of the proposition; it is the attribute of the things or of the state of things (Deleuze, 2004b: 25). And being the attribute of the thing is not really being, since it concerns only the verb form, only the becoming. The attribute of the thing is 'the event expressed by the verb':

> But the attribute of the thing is the verb: to green, for example, or rather the event expressed by this verb.
>
> (Deleuze, 2004b: 25)

We then have to consider sense as containing two sides; on the one side it is insisting in the proposition, on the other side it is the attribute of the thing or the state of the thing:

> *Sense is both the expressible or the expressed of the proposition, and the attribute of the state of affairs.*
>
> (Deleuze, 2004b: 25; original emphasis)

But in neither case is the sense confounded with the proposition or the state of things. Sense is the very border of things and propositions. Sense is the very moment of becoming. This is how sense is considered to be the event itself, but on one condition; that we do not mix up the event with what appears to be self-evident in its way of being actualized in time and space:

> It is in this sense that it is an "event": *on the condition that the event is not confused with its spatio-temporal realization in a state of affairs.*
>
> (Deleuze, 2004b: 25; original emphasis)

In relation to pedagogical documentations, they need to be treated, not from the point of view of their qualities as they express themselves in time and space. The focus must be on the verb form in the pedagogical documentations, the ongoing event. The notion of sense as continuously produced on the border of linguistic propositions and things is quite a complex notion. Maybe it can help here to consider what the preschools in Reggio Emilia talk about in relation to the work with pedagogical documentation; the importance of the invisible (Reggio Children, 1997). What takes place in everyday life in time and space is so familiar to us that we take it for granted. When working with pedagogical documentation there is a great risk of just retelling and nailing down the story of the already obvious. There is a risk that we document that which we already know about children and learning and that by doing that we immobilize and close down the event.

But another way of working with documentation is established if one is considering that which is not immediately obvious as important. The focus then concerns that which is in the process of coming about. Documentation here loses its representative aspect; it no longer concerns the manifestation of 'what really took place'. It becomes a vital material that can be used as a tool in the process of learning. Maybe the pedagogical documentations in this study, if treated as events where sense is continuously produced on the border of language and things, could be kept complex and open ended, in their process of coming about. But this can only happen on one condition: that an effort is made to try to not mix up what seemingly takes place, what can be seen or heard in the pictures and the observations – 'the spatial-temporal effectuation' – with the ongoing event itself.

On nonsense

According to Deleuze, there exists a habit of making an opposition of sense and nonsense. Normally sense is that which corresponds to the ability through a chosen way (commenting, interpreting or reflecting), to decide what is true and what is false. Nonsense is thought about as that which is neither true nor false; it is the opposite of sense. But Deleuze shows that sense and nonsense find themselves in a much more complex relation than being each other's opposites. In fact, nonsense is the very means by which we reach sense. In Deleuze's perspective, a nonsense word is a word that says its own sense. It is the only word that is not easily denoted, manifested or depending on its place and function as presumption or conclusion in a signifying chain. A nonsense word such as 'Snark' refers to nothing else but itself, it has a certain kind of self-presence. But, the important thing is that not only nonsense words have this kind of self-presence; all words, also the ones we consider make sense, must pass through a moment of self-referring and self-presence. There is a presence of nonsense within sense (Deleuze, 2004b: 78–83; 1994a: 155).

In contrast to the perspective on language where each word in a proposition depends upon other words to make sense, from Deleuze's perspective, each word must momentarily enjoy a nonsense status – self-presence – to be able to *produce* sense together with the others. We can understand now the importance of introducing nonsense in sense. It can make us no longer take for granted that sense is predetermined, already defined. When installing sense and nonsense in an intimate relation of creation and production, it becomes possible to escape sense as already determined. Language, linguistic propositions and events can now take on a truly complex, open-ended and becoming character:

> It is thus pleasing that there resounds today the news that sense is never a principle or an origin, but that it is produced. It is not something to discover, to restore, and to re-employ; it is something to produce by a new machinery.
>
> (Deleuze, 2004b: 83)

In relation to pedagogical documentations, an effort must be made to look for and construct sense, from the point of view of the *production* of sense. And what appears to be nonsense must be considered as important as that which appears to be sense in this process of production. This seems to be a promising way of approaching young children and their learning processes, since the experiences from practices show that young children very often use language without making sense and nonsense into each other's opposites.

As said, young children play with language through inventing it again. They exchange the first letter in a word, they rhyme and sing words and letters and they invent new languages never before heard of. In short, children seem to be using the above idea that all sense words momentarily enjoy a nonsense status. This is often the approach that children have not only towards language but towards most things they learn; everything is potentially otherwise and not static. It seems then, that treating pedagogical documentations as events in which sense is produced through nonsense might be a fruitful way of accessing children's learning without closing down the events in which they are taking part.

On problems and solutions

According to Deleuze, the event concerns problems: 'The mode of the event is the problematic' (Deleuze, 2004b: 64). For Deleuze, problems are usually treated as givens and ready-made and once they have found their solution they will disappear as problems. He says that very often the importance of problems is highlighted in educational as well as research contexts, but it seems that this is just a very common way of talking.

The problem is always somewhat subordinated to the solution, the actual outcome. Problems seem to be considered only as preparatory movements that will disappear once the solution has been settled (Deleuze, 1994a: 159). Rather than this generalized way of presenting problems, Deleuze describes how events function through problems and he defines these problems as consisting of the points of singularities that express their conditions:

> The event by itself is problematic and problematizing. A problem is determined only by the singular points which express its conditions.
> (Deleuze, 2004b: 64–65)

But what are these singular points? Well, they seem to range from ways of being, speaking, feeling and thinking, as well as to physical phenomena in the world, but the most important thing is that they are not possible to ascribe to denoted things, neither manifesting subjects nor signifying concepts; they are 'pre-individual, non-personal, a-conceptual':

> Singularities are turning points and points of inflection; bottlenecks, knots, foyers, and centers; points of fusion, condensation, and boiling; points of tears and joy, sickness and health, hope and anxiety, "sensitive" points. Such singularities, however, should not be confused either with the personality of the one expressing herself in discourse, or with the individuality of a state of affairs designated by a proposition, or even with the generality or universality of a concept signified by a figure or a curve. The singularity belongs to another dimension than that of denotation, manifestation, or signification. It is essentially pre-individual, non-personal, and a-conceptual.
> (Deleuze, 2004b: 63)

This is something different than imagining a problem that is already set and waits for its corresponding solution. Problems treated as points of singularities can never be givens and they will not disappear with the solution. Rather, once the solution is formulated, only then will the problem be fully constructed (Deleuze, 1994a: 158). Moreover, not only is the event working through problems as determined by singular points; also and very importantly, a problem always relates to sense.

Actually, sense is located in the problem itself (Deleuze, 1994a: 157). But, as said before, sense when insisting, rather than existing, in the proposition is not to be confounded with the proposition. Rather, sense is continuously produced on the border of language and the state of things. It follows then that the problem, where the sense is located, must not be treated as a given. And solutions are neither waiting for nor corresponding to pre-formed problems. Solutions will be an effect and will have the degree of truth and falseness in a proportional relation to the sense of the problem:

> Far from being concerned with solutions, truth and falsehood primarily affect problems. A solution always has the truth it deserves according to the problem to which it is a response, and the problem always has the solution it deserves in proportion to *its own* truth or falsity – in other words, in proportion to its sense.
>
> (Deleuze, 1994a: 159; original emphasis)

In relation to the pedagogical documentations, then, it is necessary to look at and engage in the events, starting with the ongoing construction of problems, not solutions. From previous experiences in the preschools, this seems to be a promising way of approaching young children's learning since children very often seem to enjoy the process of constructing a problem. Preschool teachers, too, have begun to work more and more with the construction of problems, rather than the solving of predetermined problems.

The experiences show that children, if allowed, choose not to accept already given problems and solutions. It is as if they suspect that the whole process of creating and inventing things will then be closed down. Children also seem to work very often with truth as an effect of sense and not a cause. They sometimes engage in a production of sense that leads to truths that we as adults can have a very hard time understanding. Therefore it is necessary to approach the pedagogical documentations by focusing on how the children's construction of a problem relates to the sense under production. It is not of value to judge the truth or falseness in the event, unless an effort is made to connect truth and falseness to the problem under construction and in relation to the sense being produced.

On learning and knowledge

Problems and their solutions concern the domain of learning and knowledge. Depending upon how we define problems and solutions, we will define learning and knowledge in specific ways. From the above definition of problems as never givens, but as points of singularities and as derived from sense and thereby deserving their solutions as well as their proper degree of truth and falseness, a specific view on learning and knowledge can be drawn up. From this perspective, learning is to enter into the problematic field of singularities that constitutes a problem. Deleuze takes as an example to learn to swim. To learn to swim is to join the distinctive points of our body with the singular points of the sea to form a problematic field (Deleuze, 1994a: 165).

This is different than adapting oneself to an already set sense or solving a predetermined problem with a corresponding solution. This latter learning is really nothing more than a question of imitation and reproduction. Learning defined by Deleuze is about entering the production of sense and problems; it is to join a problematic field. According to him, in educational and research contexts, not only the problem but also the process of learning is frequently highlighted. But again, this seems to be said a lot because it is the fashion. Learning processes seem very often to be judged and evaluated from an already set outcome, from the point of view of the content of knowledge to be attained. Again learning, just like the problem, seems to be only a preparatory movement that will disappear in the result (Deleuze, 1994a: 166).

The learning that Deleuze refers to, by the example of how to learn to swim, can never beforehand be predicted, planned, supervised or evaluated according to predefined standards. Moreover this is a kind of learning that, since it is not tameable, always takes place in the unconscious. Nobody can completely decide how the sea should move its waves and nobody can completely control the body in the water. It is an encounter in between nature and mind that takes place in the unconscious:

> As a result, "learning" always takes place in and through the unconscious, thereby establishing the bond of a profound complicity between nature and mind.
>
> (Deleuze, 1994a: 165)

The focus of work with pedagogical documentations must be on the processes of learning, not knowledge or goals to attain. Moreover learning must be treated as impossible to predict, plan, supervise or evaluate according to predefined standards. This presents a real challenge today, as we have seen throughout this study how much importance is put on the achievement of predetermined goals.

What is presented with the event is a re-conceptualization of learning and knowledge. As was seen in Chapter 3, there is an increase of different tools for evaluating subjectivities and learning and also tools for self-reflection and self-evaluation already at an early age. These tools are all based on the idea of subjectivity and learning as tameable: predictable, and possible to plan, supervise and evaluate against predetermined standards. But above we have seen, within the setting of the concept the event, a different definition of learning; learning takes place in the unconscious and it is not a process of achievement. Learning concerns the entering into a problematic field. What to look for and construct in the empirical material is therefore how the involved bodies enter the production of sense and problems; how they join a problematic field.

On culture and method

The general subordination of problems to solutions, and learning to knowledge, can also be seen when it comes to method. In this case what is subordinated is the culture surrounding a problem. In a learning that is about imitation and reproduction, sense and problems are givens, solutions wait for them ready made, so the process of learning is just a preparatory movement to attain the goal, the knowledge. In such a situation it becomes important to find the most effective method to achieve the solutions, reach knowledge and attain the goal. Culture, on the contrary is that which surrounds a learning of entering problematic fields. To proceed in learning by, allowing the culture surrounding the problem to decide how to proceed, is something totally different then deciding beforehand the most effective method (Deleuze, 1994a: 165–166).

In relation to pedagogical documentations, what is needed is to focus not on the methods of learning. As could be seen in relation to the question of 'good practice' in Chapter 3, this is the most common focus when it comes to subjectivity and learning; to find the most effective method in order to achieve the goal as quickly as possible. Method is here universalized and trivialized and does not take into account the complexity of the events in everyday life. But from the point of view of the event as it is described here, when approaching the pedagogical documentations, one must take into account the entire culture that surrounds the problems being constructed. What is the sense that the construction of problems departs from, how is the entering into the problematic field happening? Everything plays a role here, the persons involved and their different thoughts, speech and actions, the material, the environment. What needs to be looked for and constructed in the pedagogical documentations, is how the entire culture surrounding the entering of a problematic field takes shape.

How to methodologically treat the empirical material, the pedagogical documentations, as events

As has been said, it is of course inevitable that all the dimensions of the linguistic proposition are used when approaching pedagogical documentations as events; this is the way we usually use language. Therefore there will certainly be elements of commentary, of interpretation as well as of reflection in the analysis of pedagogical documentations as events in the present study. But it still seems worth trying to add something to the commentary, the interpretation and the reflection. Maybe the fourth dimension of sense as unconditioned production of truth is capable of doing something else with the pedagogical documentations. From the above description of how sense is introduced as a fourth dimension in linguistic propositions and what that does with the relation of the proposition to the event, it is possible to formulate what kind of approach to use when analysing pedagogical documentations as events:

Take into account the three general ways of approaching language and linguistic propositions, as well as their relation to events, and try to avoid falling into only commenting, interpreting or reflecting. Add instead sense as a fourth dimension of language and go for a hunt/experiment with the pedagogical documentations, so as to find and construct what sense is being produced in the events. Do not be blinded by what seems to be obvious truth but leave truth to be produced by sense.

Look for and construct sense in the pedagogical documentations, as that in the events which is not the taken-for-granted qualities of things and persons in time and space. Look instead for and construct the verb-form in the events; focus on that which is coming about.

Look for and construct the production of sense through nonsense. Do not look for solutions; look for and engage in the construction of problems and how this relates to the sense under production. Do not look for knowledge, look at learning processes, that is, look for and construct how the involved bodies join a problematic field. Do not look for methods, look for and construct how the entire culture surrounding the entering of a problematic field proceeds; take into account thoughts, speech, actions, but also material and environments.

Analysing tools

The perspective that has hitherto been put forward on desire, lines of flight and affect as part of segmentarity and micro-politics, as well as the perspective on language put forward above on the event, is in the next chapter reassembled in the concept 'assemblage of desire', which will function as an analysing tool in relation to the project on the overhead projector machine. The assemblage of desire consists of the four components referred to above: desire, lines of flight, affect and language. They are reassembled in the concept assemblage of desire in the following way: desire creates the first component, 'machinic assemblage'; language creates the second component, 'collective assemblage of enunciation'; lines of flight are part of the third component, 're- and deterritorialization'; and finally, 'affect' is treated as the fourth component. These components are further elaborated and explained in Chapter 6, where they are used in the analysis of the featured project.

A culture

When starting up the research process there was a lot of empirical material to deal with. More precisely, almost ten years of collected pedagogical documentations from practices that teachers, teacher students, teacher educators and researchers had made. Parts of this enormous collection of empirical material have been chosen and used in contextualizing the research problem in Chapter 1 and served as examples in Chapter 3. It seemed important, when introducing the theoretical perspective, to connect it with practice, as this was how the research process proceeded: as an encounter in between theory and practice. Throughout the research process new material has come in from in-service training courses at the Stockholm Institute of Education. This is very rich and absolutely new and 'hot' empirical material from different preschools. One documented project has been chosen out of this material to be analysed in the following chapter. The reason for choosing one example concerns the ambition to try to really draw as much as possible out of what seems to be a tiny little event. This is how one needs to work if choosing to work from the point of view of the event, since:

> Underneath the large noisy events lie the small events of silence[.]
> (Deleuze, 1994a: 163)[5]

By choosing one documented project there is a chance to really get into the event's complex relation to sense and problems. Choosing a limited piece of empirical material gives one a better chance to see all the singularities as well as the entire culture involved in children's and teachers' ways of constructing problems and sense.

The principle described above of letting the culture surrounding the problem decide how to proceed was applied when it came to choosing the theoretical concepts and also the entire construction, framing and methodological approach of the present study. The purpose of the study is the construction of the problem. This is to acknowledge that problems are not givens but rather need to be constructed in relation to the sense under production. And in such a process there is no single method available; instead one must make use of the entire culture surrounding the problem as it is constructed. This implies that the method must be designed as the construction of the problem proceeds. Monica Sand (2008) states that the word 'method' has its origin in the preposition 'meta', which means 'along', and 'rodos', which means 'the road'. 'Method', then, in its origin means 'along the road', which is exactly what the methodological approach drawn up in this study tries to do; the method takes shape as the construction of the problem proceeds.[6]

The first part of the study was called 'Contextualizing the problem'. Contextualizing is here to be understood as that use of the culture surrounding the problem. It concerns accounting for all the coordinates, theoretical as well as practical that are put into relation when constructing a problem. In the present study this is done through exposing the practical and theoretical resources, as well as situating the problem in relation to the contemporary political debate, that is, to take into account the surrounding culture used when constructing the problem.[7] The concepts have been picked out on the basis that when confronting them with the empirical material 'something happened'.[8] This was described in Chapter 4 through the proposed relation between theory and practice. This choosing of concepts seems to have taken place more through the logic of what was earlier talked about as affect, than through any rational thinking or conscious choice. This has been a process of working where, as said above, the method must adapt itself to the specific culture in which the problem is formulated; it must be the culture surrounding the problem that defines by which means to proceed. And this culture does include the 'feeling' of expansion or limitation of the research body: the theoretical concepts and the empirical events. When there was a 'feeling' that something happened in the encounter in between events from the empirical data and a specific concept this would be further explored to see if it could possibly say something new or interesting about the research problem. The whole process of research has been like this, not a logical straight line where one thing comes before another in a pre-determined manner. On the contrary there has been a continuous wandering back and forth in between empirical data and theory and when choices were made they were often made more on a 'gut level' than through a conscious academically trained mind.

A use

Deleuze and Guattari's own relation to the history of philosophy is a constructive relation and their problem has not been to position themselves through commenting, interpreting, reflecting or criticizing what the history of philosophy and all its inhabitants so far have said and thought. Neither, as said in Chapter 2, has their ambition been to declare the death of metaphysics. But, rather, their ambition has been to write with the original text and use whatever is available to relate it to one's own problem of today, and possibly make these problems take on new and different features.

To be consistent with that kind of approach implies to put less effort into trying to find the 'weak spots' of a theory, or comparing and situating one's theoretical and methodological perspective in relation to other perspectives. The focus is rather on what one can *do* with this particular theory in relation to this particular practice. What is the *use* of this specific theory in relation to this specific practice? What are they capable of producing together? For this reason, in the present study connections are made to other research that is related to the problem being worked upon here. An attempt has been to draw out of previous and related research that which is needed for the construction of the problem in this study's particular context.

In this chapter some references to other possible ways of treating the empirical material have been made. But, due to the approach described above and taking into account the fact that all methods are complex constructions not easily reduced to one single idea, it was done without wanting to nail down any particular kind of scientific method. However, for anyone interested, there is a series of footnotes where some possible ways of relating Deleuze and Guattari's philosophy to other philosophical and methodological perspectives are indicated. These notes deal particularly with other philosophical perspectives as these are seen as the starting point for any kind of scientific method. Although this is not a study in philosophy but in pedagogical work, it seems important to recognize that when doing research and using different scientific methods, one stands in direct relation to ontological and epistemological questions that have already been treated in various ways throughout the history of philosophy.

Philosophy asks ontological questions about reality and what is, as well as epistemological questions about what, when and how we can know something. Scientific theories are based on certain suppositions made in relation to these ontological and epistemological questions and they ask themselves questions about the conditions for and methods of scientific research. From this perspective, scientific method is always a consequence of the ontological and epistemological choices that scientists make. To be consistent, therefore, it seemed of the utmost importance in this study to develop the methodological approach in accordance with the ontological and epistemological features of the chosen theoretical perspective. Consequently, there is less need (as well as less space and time!) for criticizing, comparing and situating this particular perspective with other possible ones.

The work carried out in this study, then, concerns the *use* of Deleuze and Guattari's philosophy in relation to the field of early childhood education. What kinds of validity can one claim for such a research effort? Well, this question must be seen in relation to the reasoning outlined above on the relation between sense, problems and solutions. As seen above, a problem can only be properly defined once it has a solution, but there is no direct one-to-one correspondence between problems and solutions. The most important thing is the construction of a problem in relation to its sense. The entire research process is in this perspective about formulating a problem. This means that the conclusions or solutions that are given in this book must be evaluated from the point of view of the construction of the problem, in relation to its sense, not from the point of view of being true or false. This theoretical perspective also implies that when evaluating the construction of the research problem other categories than those of true or false must be used, such as for instance, 'Interesting, Remarkable or Important' (Deleuze and Guattari, 1994: 82).

This is not a question of doing away once and for all with criteria for good research, such as validity. But, as a consequence of a research perspective that acknowledges truth only as continuously *produced* truth, there is an attempt to slightly replace and change the definition of validity so that it no longer concerns questions of truth and falseness. When a problem is looked upon as intimately connected to sense, and thereby deserving the amount of truth and falseness that the construction permits, other criteria for good research can be of the pragmatic sort, asking if the research is 'interesting, important or remarkable'.

A style

This study is being conducted within the discipline of pedagogical work. It is not a study in philosophy. This has imposed a pragmatic treatment of the Deleuzian/Guattarian conceptual framework. The concepts have been used only exactly as much as was needed in relation to the empirical material. Choosing theoretical concepts was absolutely necessary since the thousands and thousands of pages of highly complex concepts that Deleuze and Guattari have presented cannot be included and worked within the framework of one single study. Moreover, due to the complex nature of each concept and their complicated and earlier mentioned non-hierarchical relationship, the presentation of each concept has been reduced to what was absolutely needed in relation to the empirical material. Sometimes and especially later on in the research process, this gives a feeling of just scraping the surface of certain concepts. Even though this has been one of the more complicated tasks within this study, some support can be found in the way that Deleuze and Guattari themselves propose a certain kind of pragmatism in relation to other people using their work. Liane Mozère, who has worked with Deleuze and Guattari, talks about this as a certain 'style' of doing philosophy: a style that made possible the changes in the intellectual life following 1968:

> What I would call the "revolution in the mind" radically changed the teaching patterns and curriculum. Some scholars and academics took 1968 seriously, in other words as opening new universes and possibilities unknown till then. Gilles Deleuze would lecture in a small, smoky room in the brand new University in Vincennes, near Paris, where one didn't need to have the sacrosanct *baccalauréat* (ending high school) to become a student. People would interrupt him, ask questions and never use the usual *vous*, but *tu*. As Deleuze would have said a "style". The novelty also of course was the way he *used* philosophy and how he encouraged people listening to him, not to conform but to experiment with new ways of being that would suit them.
>
> (Mozère, 2002: 4; original emphasis)

The style of doing philosophy instead of imitating thought is a style of experimentation and creation. The work presented in this book, then, tries to *do* research by *using* and *experimenting with* whatever seems to function so as to create an encounter between experiences from the chosen preschools and the Deleuzian/Guattarian philosophy. It is a style of work that is not about imitating thought or telling practices what they are lacking. It is a style that includes looking at the world and human beings without letting the perception and affection constantly turn towards the negative by focusing on lack and need. It is a question of looking at ourselves and the world from another perspective than that of lack. Rather, this style will enable us to ask the question of how desire deploys its forces in the everyday life of a preschool as well as within the academic system.

Accordingly, this study is a trying out of Deleuze and Guattari's theoretical thinking in the field of early childhood education. It as a kind of experimentation with parts of this gigantic philosophical system where an attempt has been made, with the same kind of method that the authors themselves use, to not make the authors say something that they wouldn't have said, but still to use their thinking in a new and needed way in relation to the particular empirical material available. The claims, then, of the study are not more far reaching than to gain vitality in the sense earlier mentioned: intensifying the concepts and the theory and broadening the means and domains for intervention of the preschools.

The research being undertaken here has of course nothing to do with large-scale quantitative approaches. It would be something of a paradox to claim, under these circumstances, any possibility of generalizing the research work carried out in the present study. Still, paradoxes are often the most fruitful ones when it comes to inventing new things, so let's not leave the question of generalizing behind that easily. Deleuze and Guattari's philosophy, as described and used in this study, might serve in more cases and practices than the ones presented here. They offer concepts that are well and stringently defined but that still leave the situation under investigation quite open. There is no nailing down of categories or use of predetermined outcomes. There might be room and use for this perspective, not only in relation to other events from the field of early childhood education, but also in other areas of education. Maybe even academic education and writing could benefit from adding some of these thoughts into the system?

Collection of empirical data

The empirical data in this study consists of pedagogical documentations: observations, photos, video films, and artefacts from learning processes. The empirical material presented in the previous chapters was collected by myself and by teachers during my fieldwork. As already said, this fieldwork stretched over a long period of time and it was conducted within the setting described in Chapter 1. Analyses of the empirical material were conducted collectively according to the relationship in between research and practice that is described in Chapter 4, but there also were moments when I worked with analysis on my own, trying to produce something from the encounter in between the theoretical resources and the empirical material and I then shared these analyses with the teachers.

The specific pedagogical documentation that will be analysed in the last part of this book is collected from a group of 15 children in a preschool, aged between 1 ½ and 2 years (when the project started). What is documented is a project about an overhead projector that the children, teachers and researchers were involved in during a period of two years. It has been chosen since it uses very interesting material that is very well documented in detail by the preschool teachers, and also it turned out to be material capable of finding itself in an encounter with the theoretical concepts in the way that is described in Chapter 4. One of the teachers working with the preschool group attended, during this period of time, one of the in-service training courses at the Stockholm Institute of Education. It was this preschool teacher who took the photos and wrote down her observations of what the children were doing and saying. During this period I met the teacher and the other participants in the course once a month, as a group at the Stockholm Institute of Education. During the process of the project, we analysed together in our class the documentations and proposed different ways to proceed with the children. I also met the teacher in between the classes where we continuously worked with the material and where I shared my analysis with the teacher.

Ethical considerations

I adopted the Swedish Research Council's ethical principles for research in the humanities and social sciences (Gustafsson, Hermerén and Petersson, 2006).[9] These principles include both the criterion that the research must be important and of high quality, and the criterion of the protection of the individual. The latter criterion is formulated in four important rules that concern information, consent, confidentiality as well as the use of the research. These rules were followed in this study through informing teachers and parents involved in the study at an early stage about the purpose of the research. A letter was sent out to all parents and teachers stating the purpose of the study and asking for permission to use observations and photos produced in various research contexts (see

Appendices 1 and 2). All parents whose children are in the study gave their permission to publish photos as well as the analyses. The teachers who collected the material gave their permission to use photos as well as observations and collectively produced analyses.

One particularly important ethical question that has come up during the research process concerns the third and fourth rule on confidentiality and the use of the research: should the photos of the children be published? In the research group we had discussions about whether the expressions on the children's faces are needed to understand what is happening in the processes. The photos are a very essential part of this methodological approach. But the ethical problem arises from the rule of confidentiality and also the fact that no researcher can guarantee how the material will be treated and viewed in the future. Maybe the children present in this study will feel, as they grow up, that they are not fairly represented, or maybe somebody else will use the material in a way that was not intended. In the light of this problem a solution would have been to manipulate the photos of the children's faces so that they were not recognizable.

After discussions in the research group as well as with other research colleagues, a decision was made to retain the photos of the children's faces. Although aware of the problem with confidentiality, it seemed counterproductive to mask the children's faces, both for the clarifying aspect of the photos and since throughout the study there was never any question about doing away with the subject once and for all; what is talked about is in no way whatsoever a 'dead' subject. On the contrary the ideas of subjectivity that are put forward in this study concern a subject that is more alive than ever. But it is also a subject that is constantly in the making, a becoming subject, and this subject is much more than an individual subject; it is a totally unique and singular subject that is never repeatable, not even to itself. Furthermore, subjectivity in this study is treated as caught up in a relational field, where every single person's thoughts, speech and actions really count for the creation of the field itself, but the focus is really on what takes place in between the children, and in between children and teachers. Although individual contributions count, the focus is on the way they are caught up in a collective process. This implies that what is said in this study has less to do with individual children or teachers and they are in this way protected from being exposed as data about individuals with specific characteristics that could be used in ways not intended.

In relation to the rule that stipulates how research data may be used it is important, again, to highlight that what was put forward in this study is an idea of subjectivity as being in continuous movement as well as in relation with everything and everyone around. This implies that, in relation to the children present in this study, we only know something about the singularity of the children related to the entire field they were caught up in during a period of time. But we do not know where they are heading; we do not know anything about their becomings. The children presented in this study have already moved on, they are already somewhere else, caught up in totally different things. Moreover throughout the study there was an insistence on recognizing science's inventiveness and productiveness. That implies that what is said about the children present in this study, is said in the context of the perfectly singular and chosen practical and theoretical resources at hand. It is not a true story about these children. It is a constructed story and throughout the study efforts were made to be as careful as possible in making visible how this construction has proceeded.

The ethical problem with photos also gave rise to discussions about the recent development of censorship in the name of security and risk. This seems to have become a movement that is assuming unexpected proportions. Within what Beck (1992) has called 'the risk society', it becomes more and more important to prevent anything from happening. This is a movement that is of course responding to actual and unacceptable events that do occur in contemporary society. But at the same time it is also, as Massumi (2005) shows, a new way of governing through fear. If we do not find ways to navigate within such a governing through fear we might end up being capable of doing absolutely nothing; if you touch a child in preschool you might run the risk of being accused of paedophilia, children can no longer participate in the kitchen of the preschools due to the risk from bacteria, ice cream is no longer allowed for the celebration of birthdays in preschools due to the recent debate on obesity ... the list is endless. It seems that these strategies for governing through fear and the prevention of risk now invest the field of early childhood education with an outrageous speed and they seem to find places to function almost everywhere.[10]

In the light of this discussion, the decision to retain the photos is also motivated by a wish not to abdicate to those well-constructed strategies for governing through fear, constructed to keep us all in place and prevent us from thinking, talking, doing, inventing, experimenting, in short, doing anything outside the pre-formulated correct ways. The choice to retain the photos and stick with the original message of this study, that subjectivity is not lost and is not static, is further motivated when seeing it from the perspective described above. This does not imply an ignorance of actual risks, for, as has been shown in the present study, this way of working practically and theoretically with movement and experimentation demands great vigilance and carefulness in relation to ethical and political questions.

Part 3

Analysis and conclusions

Chapter 6

Assemblages of desire in early childhood education

Introduction

In this chapter the concept assemblage of desire is put to work in order to work with the third and last decisive point. Assemblage of desire is used as an alternative way of understanding the relationship individual/society in order to account for movement and experimentation in subjectivity and learning. As already indicated, the focus here is on a project with an overhead projector (OHP) machine in which all participants act in a relational field through collective, intense and unpredictable experimentation. The project took place during two years in a preschool group, with 15 children around the age of 1½ and 2 years when the project started. The third decisive point stated that:

> *3. In the preschools all participants – children, teachers, teacher students, teacher educators and researchers – are caught up in the desire to experiment with subjectivity and learning. They are acting in a relational field through collective, intense and unpredictable experimentation. To work with this theoretically, the relation individual/society needs to be rethought. It needs a twist and a turn that no longer puts any importance on the one or the other side, the whole dualism needs to take on another meaning.*

The chapter starts with an introduction to the OHP project through giving a short description of its first year. Then Deleuze and Guattari's definition of desire is presented as 'unconscious processes of production of real' (Deleuze and Guattari, 1984: 26, 49; 2004: 19–20, 313). It is shown how this connects to the way in which teachers now look for how children, through their desires, produce new realities. After this, the logic of desire as lack is worked through and thereafter the concept assemblage of desire is defined as consisting of four components: machined desire, assembled desire, re- and deterritorialization, and affect. The components are each defined according to Deleuze and Guattari's writings, and finally they are used as an analysing tool in relation to the second year of the project.

Introduction to the overhead project – the first year

Within a preschool group, five children worked during two years with a project on an overhead projector machine.[1] It all started with the children being immensely interested in vehicles of different kinds. When they saw cars, motorbikes, buses or trains they would get very excited. The teachers decided to pick up the children's interest and give them further possibilities to investigate all sorts of different vehicles. They took photos of many sorts of vehicles: buses, cars, the instrument panel of a truck. They made these photos into overhead projector sheets and an OHP machine was placed in their group room so that the children could play with and within the photos. The children were very interested in the photos and they would bring all the vehicles from their room to play on and within the photos.

But after a while the teachers noticed that the children became more and more interested in the OHP machine itself and the features of light and shadow. So they decided to try to go into a period of investigation with the children around the OHP machine and the features of light and shadow. They started off by carefully observing what the children were doing when using the machine. At the beginning of the project they could see that the children were preoccupied, either with the light coming from the machine, the effect it had on things put on to it, or trying to cover the light with various materials on the glass surface (Figure 6.1), or they focused entirely on the shadow effect on the wall (Figure 6.2).

But surprisingly enough, they never seemed to make the connection between what took place on the machine and the effects on the wall. They were investigating each phenomenon separately: shadow, or light.

Parallel to this happening in the preschool, the teacher of the group was coming to a course at the Stockholm Institute of Education and wanted to discuss how to act in relation to this situation. The teacher and her colleagues hesitated to tell the children about the connection between what they did at the projector with the light and what happened on the wall screen with the shadow. They did not want to intervene too much in the children's process, but at the same time they felt that they somehow betrayed the children in not telling, since this discovery could open up for many more investigations of the features of light and shadow. When

Figure 6.1 Investigating light

Figure 6.2 Investigating shadow

Figure 6.3 Moves an object on the OHP

discussing this in the course, a decision was made not to intervene in this situation, as it seemed important to see what would happen if the children were left to discover in their own way the relation between the light from the projector and the shadows projected on the screen. As a result, the teacher and her colleague decided to wait and make more observations of the children's investigations.

One day when two children were sitting in front of the OHP machine, their backs turned to it, the teachers observed one of them all of a sudden turning around and moving one of the objects on the overhead machine (Figure 6.3), and then the other child made the discovery of the connection (Figure 6.4).

This got the whole group going and they all ran up towards the screen, dancing and shouting in front of it: 'The Ghost, the Ghost!' They were very excited and they would not stop running around and screaming. When the teacher brought this documentation back to the course, the discussion turned around the fact that it was a good thing to wait for the children to make the discovery on their own. The expression on the child's face that made the discovery told about the particular intensity involved in the situation (Figure 6.5). It was important to let the children discover the connection between the projector and the screen on their own.

The teachers felt a bit confused by the children's reaction after the discovery. They wondered what the children were doing when they evoked the Ghost. The teachers had seen that the children made the Ghost appear on several occasions. They had noticed that there was a very intense atmosphere in the group when the Ghost appeared. The entire group was up running, dancing and screaming: 'The Ghost, the Ghost!' (Figure 6.6).

Is the Ghost that kind of figure that we often think of in relation to children, which scares them a little bit, but that still is very exciting? And in that case, could this be a possible track to pick up and create a situation around? The discussion at the course turned around the possibility of making shadow figures in the shape of ghosts for the children to play with. But again, as the discussion went on, a decision was made to wait before proposing this to the children and instead to continue doing careful observations every time the Ghost appeared. What kind of function does the Ghost have for the children?

The teacher and her colleagues decided to wait and she came back to the course the next time with observations. The teacher brought the photos of what happened after the first time the children made the Ghost appear. It was a series of photos of investigations that the children did once

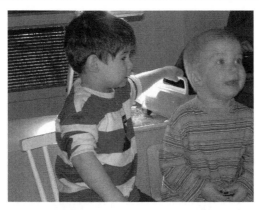

Figure 6.4 Discovers the shadow

Figure 6.5 The discovery of the Ghost

Figure 6.6 'The Ghost, the Ghost!'

they had calmed down after the Ghost had gone. The teacher explained that she and her colleagues at the preschool thought that it was possible that the children used the Ghost not at all in the way that we think of children's relation to Ghosts. They proposed that, rather than being a figure that scares and excites the children, the children used the Ghost as a ritual for celebrating when they have discovered something new, or when they stand in front of something that they do not understand but that interests them and excites them.

Through their observations, the teachers noted that the Ghost always appeared when the children had discovered something new or unexpected. Each time something new and unexpected was discovered this wild and euphoric ritual of dancing around screaming 'The Ghost, the Ghost', was taking place. In the documentation it became clear that after the discovery of the relation between what takes place with the light on the projector and what happens with the shadows on the screen, the children started asking many questions about the features of light and shadow. For instance, they organized the material in different ways to explore the effects on the screen. They organized by size (Figure 6.7) and by categories (Figure 6.8). They took a thing similar to the one placed on the projector and they approached the screen, probably asking questions about the different size of the thing and the thing's shadow (Figure 6.9). They discovered that if they dressed up in the costumes available in the classroom, they would have even more spectacular shadow effects on the screen (Figure 6.10). They also discovered that they could create stories on the screen (Figure 6.11).

The children continued to use the OHP machine throughout the year. It was placed in the centre of the room and they used it every day. The teachers observed that the children seemed to have created a kind of ritual around what they were doing with the machine. For instance, they always started off by putting the costumes on. They spent quite a while negotiating with each other and they never started working until everybody was pleased with their outfit. The children brought each other in all the time; it was important that everybody was part of the investigations. The teachers intervened through their observing and giving back the observations to the children. They gathered the children around the documentation and this created a moment for them to get together as group and continue their investigations, as well as for the teachers to understand more about what the children were doing, and thereby being better able to arrange new situations where the investigations could continue.

Figure 6.7 Organizing by size

Figure 6.8 Organizing by category

Figure 6.9 Comparing

Figure 6.10 Costume shadows

Figure 6.11 Creating stories

Figure 6.12 Gathering around the documentation on the wall

The teachers also gave the documentation back to the children by putting it up on the wall at their height. This was a place where children constantly gathered to talk about the pictures and their investigations (Figure 6.12).

During these moments gathered around the documentation, the children talked about what they were doing in the photos and they often used their bodies to repeat what they were doing when the picture was taken. They named each other and sometimes tried again.

Sooner or later, every time the children gathered around the documentation, one of them would get up to invite the others to continue with their investigations.

'Come, come work machine!'

Desire turned on its head

As we can see from this documentation, the preschools engaged in revitalizing their practice are able to turn desire on its head. Desire is normally thought of as lack of a fantasized object (Deleuze and Guattari, 1984: 25). Within this perspective a learning child is always seen as lacking and in need. Institutions working within the logic of desire as lack do all they can to tame children's desires; to predict, control, supervise and evaluate them to predefined standards.

But the preschools in and around Stockholm have turned this logic of desire upside down. In the introduction to the OHP machine project we can see that teachers carefully look for what children are after, what they desire; they take seriously and for real children's questions and problems.

These are considered as possible productions of new realities and new ways of thinking, talking and acting. These new ways of thinking, talking and acting are evaluated as being as important and real as that which we already know. These practices in the preschool acknowledged that desire is never something tameable; they anticipate intense and unpredictable experimentation taking place in between everybody. Subjectivity and learning are in these practices marked by movement and experimentation; the practices do not look for what they already know about children, but rather they put the focus on desire as the driving force involved in the children's learning, and through collectively experimenting they try to hook up to these desires.

As seen in Chapter 3, for Deleuze and Guattari all change of subjectivity and learning has its origin in desire. But as we will see, it is not desire as it is normally treated: desire as lack of a fantasized object. Deleuze and Guattari accomplished the same kind of turning desire on its head as the practices in the preschool; for them desire is 'unconscious processes of production of the real' (Deleuze and Guattari, 1984: 26, 49; 2004: 19–20, 313).

To be able to see how their definition forces this turning desire on its head, in what follows, the logic of desire as lack of a fantasized object is described.

Desire as lack

According to Deleuze and Guattari, even though psychoanalysis made a great contribution by inventing[2] the psyche and the production of desire and the unconscious, desire has been condemned by psychoanalysis to be repressed under the law of lack; you desire something because you do not have it. Desire has also been reduced by psychoanalysis to the features of fantasy; the fact that you do not have what you are missing makes it an unreal object, a fantasized object. We desire something that we do not have, so logically it does not exist apart from in our dreams and wishes:

> To a certain degree, the traditional logic of desire is all wrong from the very outset: from the very first step that the Platonic logic of desire forces us to take, making us choose between *production* and *acquisition*. From the moment that we place desire on the side of acquisition, we make desire an idealistic (dialectical, nihilistic) conception, which causes us to look upon it as primarily a lack: a lack of an object, a lack of the real object.
>
> (Deleuze and Guattari, 1984: 25; original emphasis)

Viewed like this, desire has never been given the right to freely exist as the unconscious production of the real, but has through the workings of psychology been treated as fantasies. These fantasies have been over-coded and forced to fall back on already predefined schemas, the most dominant being that of Oedipus.[3] Within psychoanalysis the figure of Oedipus is being used so that every experience is read through the formula of desire as lack. The psychoanalyst interprets the patient's actions and speech (his or her assemblages of desires) through lack and predefined schemes of interpretation. The analyst can in this way only see what he or she is already prepared and expecting to see and nothing else.[4] According to Deleuze and Guattari (1984), Oedipus is the figure of desiring-repression, it is a schema at work that reduces everything the subject says and does into a figure of lack. This Oedipal figure of lack is not only prominent within the practice of psychoanalysis, it is prominent everywhere where desiring-repression takes place.

Even though the field of early childhood education is, in many ways, a different field than the field of psychoanalysis, the features of lack are quite prevalent within the practices of early childhood education. As seen in the rigid, binary segments, images of the child are constructed on the basis of a scientific paradigm collecting its theories from developmental psychology. Within this setting, the desiring-repression is evident when we see what children do, reducing their desire to lack, talked about as children's 'needs'. From the perspective of developmental psychology[5] children act the way they do based upon inherent needs.

But we are mistaken if we take this innate heritage for granted. The needs that are attributed to very young children have been carefully constructed and defined by developmental psychology. These constructions and definitions repress and tame children's desires into already defined schemas of development. And as we could see in the supple binary segments, the new imperatives of the child as autonomous, flexible and with a constant desire to learn, could also be considered to enter the logic of taming desire, though in a different way. Desire is now the starting point, but only so as to make it possible for the institution to redirect children's desire into the attainment of predetermined goals and standards. These goals and standards define exactly what the child is still lacking.

So from both the rigid and the supple ways of treating desire, children come forward as 'needy'. Children need something because of their lack of it, or they need to get rid of something that they have too much of (over-activity, too much imagination etc.) or their particular desire needs to be redirected so as to attain a specific goal or standard. It is the institution's task to fill up what is needed, to take away what is abundant or to redirect the needs towards the wished for outcome. From Deleuze and Guattari's perspective and as seen above, need or lack is not something pre-existing within the children. Rather, it is created through social production and through the logic of desire as lack and fantasy:

> We know very well where lack – and its subjective correlative – come from. Lack [...] is created, planned, and organized in and through social production. [...] It is never primary; production is never organized on the basis of a pre-existing need or lack (*manque*). It is lack that infiltrates itself, creates empty spaces or vacuoles, and propagates itself in accordance with the organization of an already existing organization of production.
>
> (Deleuze and Guattari, 1984: 28; original emphasis)

There are no pre-existing needs or lack within children. It is lack by itself that invests the field of social production, associates itself with the repressing structures and enters the institutions and the everyday life of preschools. It transforms and tames desiring forces that try to make themselves heard, to fit them into models of very young children's behaviour and development. Institutions try to capture, mould and adapt desires to the content and form of the institution.

When it comes to children that in one way or another deviate from what is considered to be normal, it is important to see that they can be understood rather as *produced* as not normal through the introduced devices thought to help the children. The not-normal children are from this point of view to be seen as a result of the organization of content and form in the institution. This does not mean, of course, the denial of the fact that children have differently conditioned ways of managing and navigating within the system of the institution. It is not a naturalization or ignorance of certain illnesses or handicaps, but it is a questioning of how these illnesses or handicaps have been socially *produced* as such through the logic of desire as lack and fantasy. Deleuze and Guattari say: 'A schizophrenic out for a walk is a better model than a neurotic lying on the analyst's couch' (Deleuze and Guattari, 1984: 2).

It is not that Deleuze and Guattari try to make a glorified model or nature out of the schizophrenic identity by presenting her/him as the very idea and function of desiring machines (the schizophrenic as pure production that refuses to say I, and that refuses to be oedipalized). Rather, it is a way to get at the fact that the schizophrenic identity is produced within the walls of the institution. With the schizophrenic identity read as desiring production, Deleuze and Guattari contest the reduction of a life into one single story that defines an individual and that we tell over and over again. They put forward the idea that the schizophrenic is only schizophrenic when defined by psychology; away from there, for instance on a walk in the forest, other things happen to her or him. And these other things could, according to them, be seen as more advantageous than staying within the walls of the institution.

In an interview with Claire Parnet (Boutang, 2004), Deleuze says about his and Guattari's efforts to talk about desire: 'We wanted to say something really simple, we wanted to say; do not go and get analysed, never interpret, experiment with your assemblages' (my translation). To be neurotic, for instance, is in their perspective, just a consequence of a society that has produced neuroticism as a sickness to be cured. Rather than trying to cure ourselves through running into yet another schema of representation and repression, we would be, according to Deleuze and Guattari, better off experimenting with our assemblages.

Indeed, it is all very simple. The presentation of the concept of desire as unconscious processes of production of real tries to turn around the logic that says that institutions, such as psychiatric clinics, but also preschools, respond to pre-existing needs embedded within mad people and within children. By proposing that desire is production of real, lack and need can be positioned not as a cause but rather as an effect. Within the logic of desire as lack, mad people and children become 'needy' since institutions never capture their desires as production of real, but reduce them, tame them and adapt them as signs of need and lack. Since this is a prevailing logic within most of society's institutions, it is easy to see that the same kind of desiring-repression that is at stake within the walls of the psychiatric clinic also functions in preschools.

There seems to be a peculiar habit of reducing and repressing children, in the same way as the schizophrenic, into a pre-set definition of identity. Very often there seems to be an idea of the child wandering around in the world ready to imitate and repeat what family traditions, formalized school systems and cultural heritage pour into them.[6] Children's own desires are rarely considered important or valuable. The only desires taken seriously seem to be what comes from the outside: family, school and culture imposing their desires on to the children. We make of the mad person and the child examples of ignorance; we say of them that they are spontaneous, natural but lacking in experience and sense. But this is because we misunderstand the productiveness of desire. When a child is born, desiring production immediately starts. The child of course has a strong and important love relation to her or his mother and father, but the child also has, from the very moment of birth, other relations going on. We give birth to unfaithful children. They are not ours, not even from the beginning:

> The small child lives with his family around the clock; but within the bosom of his family, and from the very first days of his life, he immediately begins having an amazing nonfamilial experience that psychoanalysis has completely failed to take into account. [...] It is not a question of denying the vital importance of parents or the love attachment of children to their mothers and fathers. It is a question of knowing what the place and the function of parents are within desiring-production, rather than doing the opposite and forcing the entire interplay of desiring-machines to fit within (*rabattre tout le jeu des machines désirantes dans*) the restricted code of Oedipus.
>
> (Deleuze and Guattari, 1984: 47; original emphasis)

From the perspective of desiring-production, children are connected to and experiment with many more sorts of desire than those offered through family, school and culture. The child crosses the barriers of family traditions, formalized school systems and cultural heritage constantly. We create within the figure of desiring repression a specific environment that we call childhood but the child is constantly trespassing this place and definition and shows us that she or he is already elsewhere. Still, children live in the same world as we do. They are not a people from a foreign galaxy. That children experiment with their desires quite frequently should not be understood as a natural trait inherent in children.[7] Rather, we should understand this pragmatically and simply through the fact that they have not lived long enough to have their desiring-machines completely oedipalized and the repressive schemas completely stuffed into them:

> By boxing the life of the child up within the Oedipus complex, by making familial relations the universal mediation of childhood, we cannot help but fail to understand the production of the unconscious itself, and the collective mechanisms that have an immediate bearing on the unconscious in particular[.]
>
> (Deleuze and Guattari 1984: 49)

When we admit nothing else than the logic of lack or need to treat children's doings we completely miss out on the unconscious production of realities that can take place with desire, where children as well as teachers could be affected in totally different ways than by the predetermined figure of desiring-repression.

Desire as unconscious production of real

In the preschools in Stockholm and its suburbs, children and teachers have indeed been affected in totally new and different ways through turning desire on its head. The preschools start looking for how children's desires deploy themselves away from the institution's repression of desire. Instead of judging children from predefined schemas, the logic is now turned around and questions are asked about what the children are after; what they are interested in, that is, what they desire and what they produce. This is an important reversal for a preschool institution, or for any institution.

Subjectivities and learning processes in these practices come about through desire used as an unconscious process of production of new realities. Children and teachers act and *realize* new features of subjectivities and learning processes when desire is deployed not as lack or need, but as *production*. This takes place in such a manner that it is not possible to talk about a rationally planning conscious subject, which makes this definition of desire something different than both the rigid and the supple way of repressing and taming desire. It is different because both the rigid and the supple way of treating desire rely upon the capacity of consciousness to comprehend and rationally modulate desire. The preschools enter a new logic of desire where they actually seem to ask children the questions: 'Now, where are your desires, what kind of assemblages are you for the moment experimenting with?'

Desire as assembled

According to Deleuze and Guattari (2004) desire never comes alone, desire always comes along assembled; it comes along as assemblages of desire. *Desiring machines* work in these *assemblages*. Assemblages contain two axes. On one axis is a *machined assemblage*, that is, material processes of bodies and actions, as well as a *collective assemblage of enunciation*, that is, corresponding speech and signs. On the other axis the assemblage contains *reterritorialized lines* that stabilize it, and create territories functioning as systems of habit, as well as *points of deterritorialization*, that is, movements by which we leave the inhabited territory and break loose of habits (Deleuze and Guattari, 2004: 97–98). When something in an assemblage changes, what happens is that the bodies involved are being *affected* or are *affecting*.

Affect is a term that Deleuze and Guattari take from Spinoza and it indicates a body's capacity to act. In an assemblage the involved bodies are either expanded or restricted in their capacity to act. This is registered as 'feelings'; when a body extends its capacity to act it is registered and recognized by feelings of intensity, joy, satisfaction etc. When it is restricted in its capacity to act it is being registered and acknowledged by feelings of passivity, sadness, dissatisfaction etc. (Deleuze, 1988a).

Movement and experimentation in subjectivity and learning in the preschools are being accomplished through desiring forces working in an *assemblage*. Change does not come about through the logic of rational and conscious planning. There is no longer the sustained individual/society dualism that functions through a cause–effect relationship stopping movement and hindering experimentation.[8] Still the experiences made in the preschools show a very forceful character; forces not connected to rationally thinking individuals seem to produce and shape the movements and experimentation in subjectivity and learning (*desiring machines*). The assemblage in the preschools is about new ways of acting and talking (*machined assemblage* and *collective assemblage of enunciation*). A new kind of learning is entered into where children construct and produce their own questions and problems and where the processes of learning are not predetermined but take shape as they continue. New words enter the scene and permit new ways of talking about the child: subjectivity and learning as a relational field. Sometimes already existing schemas of bodies and signs within the practice are reproduced and imitated (*the reterritorialized lines*) – like when the preschools run in to stereotyped images of the individual, natural and developing child, or the autonomous, flexible child.

But sometimes there are experiences of new and different ways of conceiving of the very young learning child (*the points of deterritorialization* or *the lines of flight*) – like when children are seen as acting and learning in a relational field. These are the moments that install a specific feeling of intensity, often registered through having 'goose bumps' (*the registration of an augmentation of affect*, or, *of the bodies' capacities to act*).

Assemblages of desire vary and extend themselves at many different levels. It is possible to use the concept in relation to a large group of preschools as done above, but it is also possible to use it in relation to smaller groups and processes. Below, assemblage of desire with all its components – machined assemblage, collective assemblage of enunciation, re- and deterritorialization, and affect – is presented and thereafter it is used as a tool to analyse what took place in the second year of the project on the OHP machine.

Assemblages of desire – components

Machined assemblage

> Desire has nothing to do with a natural or spontaneous determination; there is no desire but assembling, assembled, desire.
>
> (Deleuze and Guattari, 2004: 440)

There is never any pure or natural flow of desire. Desire is always assembled or 'machined'. This part of an assemblage of desire, called 'machined assemblage', concerns material processes of bodies and actions and serves to prevent us from thinking that desire is something biological, natural and essentially inherent in a person. In the interview mentioned above (Boutang, 2004), Deleuze presents his and Guattari's exposition of desire as something very concrete and simple. They wanted to contest the idea that you desire *something* or *someone*. You always desire in an assemblage. If you desire a dress, you desire in relation to the particular evening out you are going to. You desire in relation to friends or not friends attending the evening, etc. You never desire an object. You always desire in an assemblage of relations.

In no way should we confuse desire with the features of nature; as said, it would be a grave mistake to treat 'the child as nature' and to glorify its relation to desire as natural and spontaneous. This is not what is being talked about here. It is not spontaneous or natural desire at stake in an assemblage, but *constructivist* desire. In the interview, Deleuze on several occasions comes back to this definition of desire, desire as constructivism:

> 'If I should use the abstract term for desire I would say constructivism.'
> 'To desire is to construct an assemblage.'
> 'Desire is constructivism.'
> 'For me, anytime somebody says that they desire something it means that he is about to construct an assemblage.'
>
> (Deleuze in Boutang, 2004; my translation)

So, desire never exists outside an assemblage.[9] Desire is here presented as a factory of the unconscious production of the real; you desire within an assemblage, you construct through your desires new assemblages, you produce reality. That desire functions as machine is, then, not a metaphor. It is not a machine in the sense that we normally give to it. Since we are talking about these machines as situated in the unconscious production of real, they are not machines run by a conscious subject. There is nobody to push the button to turn on and off the machines of desire. The construction of an assemblage does not take place in a rationally planned manner. It must be treated as a little machinery that sets itself going and that nobody really controls (Deleuze and Guattari, 1984: 4–16).

Collective assemblage of enunciation

This part of an assemblage called collective assemblage of enunciation, concerns signs and speech, that is, words and ways of speaking corresponding to the material processes of bodies and actions in assemblages of desire. According to Deleuze and Guattari, all our statements depend upon a collective assemblage of enunciation that is not given in our conscious minds (Deleuze and Guattari, 2004: 93). A collective assemblage of enunciation belongs to indirect discourse; within every statement there is the presence of another statement. Or, within every word there is the presence of an order-word. The words and signs that we use function as order-words, that is, they do not inform us what to do; they create our doings. Language is not made to be informative or believed; language is made to be obeyed. In relation to this, Deleuze and Guattari say that:

> When the schoolmistress instructs her students on a rule of grammar or arithmetic, she is not informing them, any more than she is informing herself when she questions a student. She does not so much instruct as "insign", give orders or commands. A teacher's commands are not external or additional to what he or she teaches us. They do not flow from primary significations or result from information: an order always and already concerns prior orders, which is why ordering is redundancy.
>
> (Deleuze and Guattari, 2004: 83–84)

According to this quotation the schoolmistress's words are order-words. There is nothing more in language than order-words, that is, statements that are not representing or signifying anything but are direct actions. They are immediately, directly, and simultaneously attributed to the bodies of a society. The transformation that the statement is expressing is producing the effect of the transformation at once. There is a direct relation between statements and actions, and these 'speech-acts' are not run by any already existing significations or information, and they do not depend on any intersubjective communication (Deleuze and Guattari, 2004: 83–90). According to Deleuze and Guattari, order-words or speech-acts are born from the collective assemblage of enunciation. *But the important thing is that this collective assemblage is in itself continuously changing.*

Ordering is therefore always redundancy; there is always too much in ordering. In this respect there is no pre-existing structure of language. There can be no pre-existing structure of language since the collective assemblage is in a state of redundancy and continuous change. Information and communication as well as significance and subjectification are subordinate to redundancy. There is no individual enunciation and there is no subject of enunciation. All individual statements and all subjectified enunciations are such, only to the extent that they are needed and determined by a collective assemblage (Deleuze and Guattari, 2004: 87–88).

These ideas make Deleuze and Guattari introduce a certain kind of pragmatics into language. The pragmatics that is referred to here is not an external factor to language but an internal variable. The collective assemblage that language depends upon is in a state of pragmatics. Pragmatics is internal to enunciation, not a force coming from the outside affecting language. Pragmatics, not structure, constitutes the first condition of a language; language is already on the move. Language is leaking. The collective assemblage is in a continuous process of transformation, which implies that language and signs, words and ways of speaking are finding themselves in an ongoing process of creation and are not consciously or socially completely determined. Language is internally alive and accordingly, signs do not represent anything or anyone and should be treated, not as information or communication, but as little *a-signifying machines* that are capable of producing new material processes (Deleuze and Guattari, 2004: 91–94).[10]

Re- and deterritorialization

In the interview with Claire Parnet referred to above, Deleuze states that to inhabit a territory is not just about living at a particular geographical place. It is about inhabiting one's habits and manners in ways of speaking and acting. It is the creation of an environment that could be called 'chez soi' (at my place) (Boutang, 2004). Every territory finds itself re-established by lines of reterritorialization and swept away or left through movements of deterritorialization. All three concepts, territory, deterritorialization, and reterritorialization, establish a rhythmic act. The territory is always affected by movements of re- and deterritorialization and the movements of re- and deterritorialization are intertwined and simultaneous. To deterritorialize implies to leave the territory that one presently inhabits. To reterritorialize implies to form and inhabit a new territory. We live and act in one territory but from time to time we deterritorialize our current territory and start producing another one (Deleuze and Guattari, 2004: 559–562, chapter 11).

In line with this one can imagine that we are stuck in patterns of behaviour and defined and specified as individuals. We live, sustain and continue to produce ourselves, as well as being produced as child, adult, woman, man, white, black, working class, upper class etc. But now and then we produce a movement of deterritorialization out of our territory. Deterritorialization changes the specific set-up of an assemblage of desire. It changes the set-up of material bodies and speech and signs, but it always acts in tight relation to movements of reterritorialization. Still, the return to a territory can never be a return to the same, something has always changed. The rhythm of re- and deterritorialization leaves no territory unchanged (Deleuze and Guattari, 2004: 193–194).

Affect

What happens in an assemblage of desire is that bodies affect or are being affected. Affect is a concept offered us by the philosopher Spinoza, and it brings a new model to replace conscious thought: the body. By indicating that 'We do not know what a body can do', Spinoza shows us that 'the body surpasses the knowledge we have of it, *and that thought likewise surpasses the consciousness we have of it*' (Deleuze, 1988a: 18; original emphasis). Consciousness is incapable of registering affect, it only registers the *effects* of affect, that is, our feelings. Consciousness has no means to register the fact that bodies that meet can either enter into composition with each other, creating even more expansion for the respective bodies to act, or one body can start to decompose the other one, whose capacity to act is then being restricted (Deleuze and Guattari, 2004: 285–287).

When learning to swim for instance, it is possible either that my body joins the water in such a way that I will float, or the body of the water will take the upper hand and start decomposing and restricting my body's capacity to act. When our body is being restricted in its capacity to act, we feel passivity, sadness, dissatisfaction etc. When it is extending its capacities to act, we feel intensity, joy, satisfaction etc. With our conscious minds this is what we experience, but these feelings are only the effect of affect. Feelings are registrations of the body's expanded or restricted capacity to affect or be affected, to act. The point of using Spinoza's model of the body is that it can make us not overestimate consciousness. It can imply a highlighting of the *unconscious in thought* as well as the *unknown of the body* (Deleuze, 1988a: 19; original emphasis). It can make us focus on the specific potentialities in every situation.

In what follows the above-described components of assemblage of desire are put to work together with the process that took place during the second year in the project on the OHP machine.

The overhead project and assemblage of desire – the second year

Overhead projector machine and desiring machine

In the second year, the children were still working with the OHP machine practically every day. It had become a necessity in the classroom equipment, as had the costumes that the children introduced early in the project. Every time the children worked with the machine they put on the costumes. At the beginning of the second year, the teachers introduced a new material to the group: construction blocks with images of all the children glued onto them. Each child had been photographed in three pieces, head, torso and legs, to enable many different constructions of oneself and others to be made. This was part of a collective experimentation in the course for preschool teachers at the Stockholm Institute of Education, and reflected a wish to go into play and investigation about identity as a multiple feature together with the children. The teachers spent a long time preparing the material and also prepared carefully for its introduction.

On the day that the teachers introduced the material to the children, the children seemed very hesitant. The teacher said to them: 'I have a new material for you to work with, would you like to try it?' The children were at first silent and then they got up very quickly and said: 'If we are going to work we need the costumes', and they ran off to get the costumes (Figure 6.13). They started using the construction blocks for a little while, but they quickly discovered that in some of the photos on the blocks, they were not wearing a costume (Figure 6.14). When discovering this they put all the blocks with photos of children without

Figure 6.13 Getting the costumes

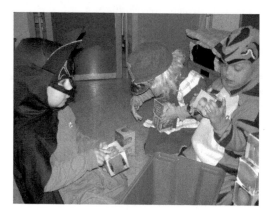

Figure 6.14 Discovering the lack of costumes on the photos

costumes away and constructed only with the blocks that had photos of children with costumes (Figure 6.15). After a short while they took all the construction blocks over to the OHP machine in the next room, where they continued their inventions with light and shadow, now with the blocks as well (Figure 6.16).

Figure 6.15 Sorting out blocks with photos with costumes

Figure 6.16 Bringing the blocks back to the machine

Analysis

What was seen in the first year of the project is even more accentuated in this sequence; the children have something going on that they won't let go of. There is something happening in between the children and in between the children and the machine that is not easily domesticated or tamed. Desiring forces are set in motion in between children and between children and machine, where children do not act as specified identities departing from their individual needs. They do not act in a way where we can easily recognize the individual and needing child. Instead, when the children choose blocks they depart from the costumes. They choose only construction blocks where costumes are figuring. The most important thing is the costumes and not whether they as specified individuals are figuring on the photos or not. They do not care about photos of themselves, they have something else going on. They have lived through one year of investigations together where the costumes have played an important part.

One interesting thing with the task of working with the new material, the construction blocks, is the costumes, because it relates to the particular desire that the children are collectively caught up in. The construction blocks in themselves do not interest the children. It is only what their possible usefulness could be in relation to the OHP machine that interests them and they therefore quickly bring the blocks over to the overhead machine. The children are working on the construction and production of sense and problems in relation to the machine and the features of light and shadow. So anything they bring in to that process must relate to the specific problem and sense under construction. That is why the blocks are quickly brought back to the machine. If they are going to serve they have to do so in relation to the machine.

The way the children relate to the OHP machine makes it something more than a machine. They make it function as organic material. It is not treated by the children as solely non-organic matter; it is treated as if it had a proper life. Everything that they bring into the machine is capable of totally overturning the machine's form and function. The way the children are caught up in this collective process of investigating make them more than desiring human individuals; they are also machines, desiring machines that in the same way as the overhead machine can be totally overturned in their form and function. Their organic bodies also function at the same time as non-organic machines. These are desiring machines that do not need an on and off button; the process takes place in between children and children and machine. The teachers, in the same way, are desiring machines, caught up in a process that nobody seems to possess. Despite the care, time and effort that the preparations of the new material demanded of them, they let go of the new project they wanted to introduce to the children.

The event takes place within an institution where teachers have accomplished an important move in relation to the logic of desiring repression; what is looked for and anticipated is what the children are after. In letting the children formulate their own problems and investigations, in supporting these through the documentation and the giving back of documentation, the logic of desire as lack has been turned around. Children are now asked: Where are your desires? What assemblages are you for the moment experimenting with? This gives space for new material processes. Children are part of producing the everyday reality of the preschool in new ways.

The costumes, pedagogical documentation and assembled desire

When the teacher comes back to the course with the documentation of the children choosing to use only the construction blocks with photos of the costumes on and bringing them over to the OHP machine, the discussion in the class turns around the importance of taking a closer look at the particular function of the costumes (Figure 6.17). The teacher decides to go back and, together with her colleagues at the preschool, look at the documentations once again with the children. They want to try to find out what it is with the costumes that has proved so important for the children. Is it a ritual that they have created for working? Is it because they are inspired by the fact that in different professions you sometimes wear specific work clothes? The teachers go back with a series of photos of the children working in costumes (Figure 6.18).

It is during one of these moments of giving back the documentation to the children that the teachers get a new idea of what the children are after with the costumes. The children look at Figure 6.19 and they say to their friend:

'We cannot see you because you are not wearing a costume. You need a costume.'

'Come on! Let's try again!'

The children run off to the machine (Figures 6.20 to 6.24).

'Look there's Batman!'

'But, where am I?'

'You are not there because you do not have any clothes.'

'But I do have clothes!'

'But not Batman, here take mine!'

'Now there's two Batman, now I am there!'

At one moment one child stands in front of the screen without a costume and says:

'Look I am seen without a costume!'

'Look, look, I am seen!'

But nobody picks up this discovery and they continue their investigations.

Figure 6.17 Discussion about the costumes

Figure 6.18 Pointing at the costumes in the photo

Figure 6.19 'We cannot see you because you are not wearing a costume'

Figure 6.20 'Look, there's Batman'

Figure 6.21 'But, where am I?'

Figure 6.22 'Now there's two Batman, now I am there!'

Analysis

Why do the children stick with the idea that it depends on the costume if you are seen or not on the screen? They have many proofs of the fact that they can be seen without a costume. One child even tries to present the idea, but it is not being picked up by the others. Maybe the children choose this ambivalence so that they can go on with their investigations. If they were to accept that you are seen with a costume the excitement of the investigation and the mystery of the problem would be gone. They want to keep their problem and the sense connected to it, still under construction and in a process of production.

Figure 6.23 'Look I am seen without a costume!'

Figure 6.24 'Look, look, I am seen!'

The particular sense and problem under construction in this process now seems a little bit clearer. It seems that the children are working on the construction and production of the sense and the problem whether and when one is seen or not. In this case the costumes do not primarily function as part of a ritual of putting them on to go to work, or to imitate adults' way of working in specific work clothes. The costumes function so as to push the problem of whether and when one is seen and not. They function as a very important tool in investigating the disappearing and reappearing effects. The children construct their problem and produce sense about light and shadow, visibility and invisibility through the costumes. They do not desire the costumes as an object; the costumes function as part of an assemblage of desire.

You always desire in an assemblage. The costumes do not represent working clothes or the particular persons. They are part of the collective construction of an assemblage around the OHP machine. Children and teachers seem to be caught up in assembled desire. Nobody seems to own the process, it takes place in between everybody involved. When used within this context of assembled desire, the documentation takes on a specific feature.

The teachers go back to the documentation; they construct new ways of understanding what the children are after, what they desire. Teachers do not use the documentation within the logic of conscious predicting, planning, supervising and evaluating. They use it together with the children and in between themselves as a living material capable of triggering new material processes. The children also make use of the documentation. We could see this already in the first year of the project; the documentation is not mainly treated by the children as a self-reflexive act. It is treated as a tool for triggering new material processes; they do things with it.

In an assemblage, desire never stands on its own. The particular desire at stake in the OHP project is functioning in a machine-like way, as assembled between teachers, teachers and children, teachers and machine, children, children and machine. The pedagogical documentation is a place where all these actors in the assemblage can momentarily gather together so as to visualize and push the problem and sense under construction further. It functions as a connective point in the relational field that assembles children, teachers and OHP machine. In this space, at this connective point, lies the possibility of children and teachers to fasten onto each other's desire.

The return of the Ghost and collective assemblage of enunciation

When the children started using the construction blocks with the OHP machine, one of the girls dragged one of the blocks over the surface of the machine. The other children were sitting behind the screen and they saw this giant shadow from the other side of the screen. This is a moment where the Ghost from the first year's investigations comes back. During the first year of the project the children used the ritual around the Ghost every time they were just about to discover or had just discovered something new. When the children now discovered that the shadows of the block could be seen from the other side of the screen, the Ghost comes back. This led them to use the Ghost, and with the help of the construction blocks, to create stories and moving images.

One child took one of the construction blocks and moved it along the overhead projector machine (Figures 6.25 to 6.27).

'Look!'

The children then began to jump around, laughing and screaming: 'The Ghost, the Ghost!'

They started to invent new stories, they pretended that the construction block was a letter sent from the Ghost and they tried to capture it (Figures 6.28 and 6.29).

'Look, a letter!'

'A letter for me, he is taking it, the Ghost!'

'It is me, it is me doing that!'

Analysis

The collective assemblage of enunciation constructs language as internally alive and pragmatic. This seems to have something to do with how the children treat language and words. The Ghost comes back throughout the entire project and it does not function as one could easily imagine; as something which scares children a little bit, but still makes them very interested. The Ghost seems to be used as a ritual sign without meaning, an 'a-signifying machine' whose only function is to come out when things get really intense. Whenever there is that particular intensity indicating that something new is about to, or has just, come about, the Ghost functions as the a-signifying trigger that pushes the children to go on with their investigations.

The word 'Ghost' does not have the particular meaning or signification we are used to. The children are using the potentiality and pragmatics

Figure 6.25 Construction block shadow

Figure 6.26 'Look!'

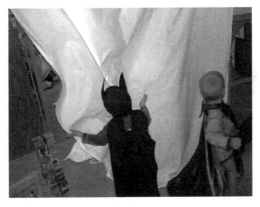

Figure 6.27 The return of the Ghost

Figure 6.28 A letter from the Ghost

Figure 6.29 'It is me, it is me doing that!'

inherent in language; they open up another order-word within the order-word and appropriate it to their own uses. This is an immediate speech-act, the a-signifying trigger 'the Ghost' functions simultaneously with the involved bodies. It triggers the ritual of bodies, jumping, dancing, screaming and pushing forward new investigations. The Ghost is a typical nonsense work uttered by the children. But here it becomes totally clear that sense and nonsense revolve around each other. It is through nonsense that sense is created.

The teachers are careful not to condemn the Ghost as nonsense that has nothing to do with sense, and they are capable of activating the pragmatic features of language. Therefore they can access the children's sense-production and problem-construction. Children are very often considered to be lacking in relation to language. A common conception amongst adults is that children do not yet possess proper language and that most of the time they get it all wrong. But in this example we see children and their learning processes being re-evaluated in relation to language; they use language pragmatically and creatively to produce sense and construct problems.

Returning to the perspective of behind and re- and deterritorialization

The Ghost is not the only thing coming back. Right in the middle of this intense period of investigating, the children go back to investigations that they did in the very beginning of the project, and they do the same kind of investigation over and over again. The perspective from behind, whose discovery was described above in the sequence with the shadow of the construction block, was really not a new discovery. The perspective from behind and the possibility to see shadows from the other side of the screen were discoveries that the teachers had identified that the children had already made in the first year of the project. But, it seems that the children rediscover this phenomenon over and over again. They seem to repeat their investigations in an identical way. They try to create shadows on the side of the screen where the light source is not directed. In the example below the light source never moves, so what the children are investigating, by moving in front of or behind the screen, is when and under what conditions you are seen or not.

First they investigate whether they are seen when they place themselves behind the screen where the light source is not directed. One child takes a place behind the screen and asks the teacher and friends (Figure 6.30):

'Can you see me now?'

'No'

'Yes you can!'

'No we can't see you!'

He then moves closer and closer to the screen and when he is slightly touching the screen, his friend shouts: 'Yes, there he is, there he is!' (Figure 6.31). He sees the contour of the screen bending under the pressure of his friend's body and, therefore, concludes that he can see him.

Figure 6.30 'Can you see me now?'

Figure 6.31 'Yes, there he is, there he is!'

Figure 6.32 'I am lying here, like Quasimodo'

A few moments later they arrange a situation where they investigate whether they are seen when they place themselves in front of the screen, where the light source is directed. The same boy who went behind the screen now lies down in front of the screen on a pile of blocks. He tells his friends to go behind the screen to see if they can see him (Figure 6.32).

'I am laying here, like Quasimodo. Take a photo! You go behind and you'll see my shadow.'

He then instructs his friend to lay down in the same way (Figures 6.33 and 6.34).

'Lay down here, and then I'll have a look at your shadow.'

'There, there you are!'

And then finally they try with a third friend who lays down in the same way (Figure 6.35).

Then they repeat the first investigation, but this time with a construction block. They try to find out whether the construction block can be seen when it is placed behind the screen. One of the girls goes behind the screen with a construction block and she tries to see its shadow (Figure 6.36). But she thinks that her friends are in the way so she tells them to move (Figure 6.37).

'No! Move away! I can't see my block!'

Analysis

This going in circles, backwards, sideways, forwards, in a mess, draws up the contours of a different kind of learning and a different kind of knowledge. In this process knowledge is not pre-existing and built in a linear logical way. It is a messy learning process and it is going in all sorts of directions. Totally different things are being drawn in to the process: 'I am laying here. Like Quasimodo. Take a photo!' The children have many things going on at the same time: the construction and production of sense and the problem of whether and when one is seen or not; the behind perspective; the figuring and trying out of Quasimodo; the importance of the teacher documenting the process.

The children are going back to things they have already done and should know by now, and supposedly be finished with or tired of. But in the learning taking place here, they repeatedly go back to the perspective from behind. They seemingly repeat the same investigation over and over again. But one has to be careful when looking at this, because every time they repeat the investigation something has changed. When one child tries first with his body and it does not work he goes on with his friends, maybe their shadows can be seen, maybe they are different? They then

Figure 6.33 Lies down in the same way

Figure 6.34 'There, there you are!'

Figure 6.35 Third friend lays down

Figure 6.36 Goes behind the screen

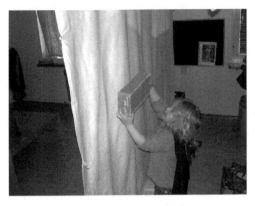

Figure 6.37 'No! Move away! I can't see my block!'

try with the construction block; maybe that will have a shadow? Just as with the rhythm of de- and reterritorialization, the children move the investigation around in a billowing movement, but it is never a question of simple imitation, they always slightly change the conditions of the investigation. The territory of the knowledge of the problem under construction through the perspective of behind is therefore always slightly changed and displaced; it is never a return to the same.

This is a non-linear kind of learning process that billows back and forth, that does not follow any progressive rational thinking. It changes as it goes on and it also continuously changes the territory of knowledge concerning the behind perspective. The problem under construction now seems quite clear; through the entire process the problem under construction seems to be about whether, and under what conditions, one is seen or not. The children are turning around this problem all the time. Throughout their preceding investigations this is the problem under construction; when they bring construction blocks to the machine, will the photos be seen or not? When insisting on the costumes, is one seen or not with or without a costume? The Ghost serves a celebrating ritual any time this particular problem takes on a new turn. And now in investigating the perspective of behind, this is the problem under construction, when is one seen or not?

The Batman costume and affect

The problem of whether one is seen or not continued to be connected to the costumes throughout the entire process. The importance of the costumes had become very clear, and it was reinforced by the situation where one child was very disappointed one morning when it turned out that he was without the particular Batman costume that he had intended to use. Everybody became deeply involved in the situation and tried to help him out (Figures 6.38 and 6.39).

'Do you want this?'

'Look, this one can also make you alive, this can also make alive.'

He turns to the others and says, 'Oh, he doesn't want it!' A friend on the other side of the table offers his costume (Figure 6.40): 'You can have mine, do you want mine?' But the boy just shakes his head: 'No.'

The other children run away to get another costume that they offer him (Figures 6.41 and 6.42). They all try to figure out how to resolve the situation:

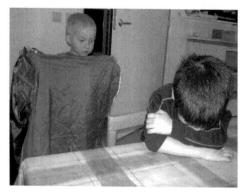

Figure 6.38 'Do you want this?'

Figure 6.39 'This can also make you alive'

Figure 6.40 Offers his costume

Figure 6.41 Running away to get another costume

Figure 6.42 'What kind of costume do you want?'

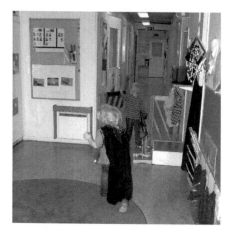

Figure 6.43 To the other classroom

Figure 6.44 Finding a tiger costume

'What kind of costume do you want?'

'Do you want the one that I am wearing?'

'Well, yes … no, I don't want it.'

'Do you want a Batman costume?' (turns to the teacher and asks:) 'Where can we find a Batman costume?' (and then immediately says:) 'I know let's go and ask the other class.'

So they all run off to the other classroom to ask them for a Batman costume (Figure 6.43). They find a tiger costume, and everybody seems very happy (Figure 6.44). One child says: 'You know if you are not seen with this costume, you can have mine.'

Analysis

In an assemblage of desire what happens is that bodies increase or decrease their capacity to act. When a body's affective capacity decreases we feel sadness, when it increases we feel joy. From this perspective the costumes serve to rise the body's potential; 'it makes you alive', as one child says. It makes you visible and thereby alive. The costumes serve so as to raise bodily potential in relation to the problem under construction; when is one seen or not? We must understand the disappointment of being without a costume through the lens of one's affective potential being decreased when without a costume; one won't be able to fully construct the problem without a costume.

And in the very same way we must understand that the reason for the children engaging so much and with such solidarity, compassion and joy, is that throughout the entire project the affective potential of their individual and collective bodies has increased. As an effect from increased affect and bodily potentiality, the children's way of feeling compassion and acting together with solidarity and with joy is born. If looking at the situation primarily from the point of view of feeling, we could say that they are nice children, and look what good results of solidarity we can have by putting children in a group around an overhead projector machine. But then we will miss out on the affective potential in this particular situation. And if we then go and try the same thing with another group, it is not at all certain that they are going to cooperate in the same way. Their desires are probably somewhere else and their assemblages are not constructed in the same way.

The bodies involved here are not only the children's physical bodies – which are of course also extended in their capacity to act, no longer sitting on one spot at circle time listening to the teacher, but instead up and around everywhere, into the other classroom, to continue the investigations. But also involved is the physical body of knowledge and learning regarding an OHP machine, and also the bodies of light and shadow are being extended. The children treat light and shadow not from the point of view of fixed entities encountering each other, but rather as plastic and elastic bodies that resonate together. They treat the bodies of light and shadow as well as their own bodies as finding themselves in a relational field.

There is no longer a predefined body of knowledge to attain by means of an equally preset and also predicted, planned, supervised and evaluated learning process. The body of knowledge in this project is acting according to Spinoza's logic; we do not yet know what a body can do. Teachers, children and machine are involved in this logic; we do not yet know what a child can do and we do not yet know what an overhead machine can do.

An interesting proposition, double shadows and subjectivity and learning as a relational field

One day when the children were investigating if you are seen or not, somebody came up with an interesting proposition: 'I know, let's take another lamp, then we'll see me.'

This is a very important moment for it opened up to a new dimension in the project; the possibility of having two light sources and thereby a double shadow. The teachers, therefore, supported the proposition and proposed the children to use another projector (Figures 6.45 to 6.48).

'Look, look there's two Batman!'

'Yes, it's my mother, Batman's mother!'

They turn off one of the projectors.

'Oh no! My mother is gone!'

Oh ! That's my little brother, hello little brother!' (hugs the small shadow of himself).

'Look, look two hands!'

'Wow! It looks like octopuses, look, look octopuses!'

The children discuss (Figure 6.49):

'Look at your mother she is huge, she is much bigger than us!'

'You are Batman.'

'No, it must be you.'

'That's me, that's shadows.'

'That's our teacher over there.'

'No it's not her!'

'It is, it is! That's me, that's you ... no, that's me. No, that's Batman ...'

'Wow, we have both machines, we have both machines!' (They sing and dance.)

Concluding analysis

The outspoken and consciously formulated pedagogical ambition with introducing the construction blocks was to get into playing with the features of multiple identities together with the children. Preparations demanding much time and effort were made by the teachers only to find that the children 'rejected' the proposition. But did they really? Is not their way of working together – sticking to their collective project on the OHP

Figure 6.45 Two light sources

Figure 6.46 'Hello little brother!'

Figure 6.47 'Look, look two hands!'

Figure 6.48 'Look octopuses!'

machine; choosing only the blocks with the costumes on; their intense and continuously varying investigations where the focus constantly is on the production and construction of sense and the problem of when and whether one is seen or not; their delicate discussions and negotiations; the creation and disappearance of different strategies and roles, Batman's

Figure 6.49 Discussion

mother, my mother, my brother, octopuses – isn't all of this an indication of the children actually being in the middle of living multiple identities?

Moreover, it seems to be a multiple identity much richer than the conceptual one we throw around and try feverishly and theoretically motivate. What the children seem to be doing is to *live* multiple identities and this take place in between everybody in this learning process. These multiple identities and the learning process involved have the features of subjectivity and learning as a relational field. The children live subjectivity and learning very much by a bodily logic of affect, where bodies and forces join or decompose each other, and where both organic and non-organic bodies are treated through a principle of plasticity and elasticity.

The proposition from the course at the Stockholm Institute of Education to go into collective experimentation by using construction blocks to play with the features of multiple identities is in this perspective quite a pale version of how the children seem to be constructing this problem. The adults' proposition is still stuck in the idea of positioning: as if you put different parts together to get yourself an identity. You do arrange and rearrange your assemblages, there is a certain constructivism connected to assembled desire. But you do not construct your assemblages by putting different already existing parts together and you certainly do not *consciously* plan and make yourself a multiple identity with constructions blocks of any kind. You act and live in assemblages, and starting out from *unconscious* desires that you cannot control, you construct assemblages through and with other people.

Throughout the project the children stick to the production of sense in relation to the problem of when and whether one is seen or not. They bring the blocks to the overhead projector machine, but constructing with them is not interesting; the problem is about whether and when one is seen or not. The costumes that the children so insistently continue using serve so as to enter the problematic field of subjectivity and learning. They use the Ghost as a 'trigger' for when interesting phenomena occur around the problem of when or whether seen or not. They wander back and forth, sideways and in circles around this problem all the time. Everything is possible; it might work with you if it did not work with me or it might work with the construction blocks if it doesn't work with us.

To be seen or not to be seen, this is a fantastic creative response to the problem of subjectivity and learning that is normally treated as a problem of being. The children resonate and vibrate together with the phenomena of light and shadow in a creative response to the problem of being. The problem is no longer 'to be or not to be', the sense and the problem is under reconstruction by the children and now concerns vision more than anything else; 'to see or not to see' or 'to be seen or not to be seen'. Everything in the children's investigations around subjectivity and learning turns around vision. But this is not vision through the gaze of recognition and representation, this gaze is an affective gaze. The children act subjectivity and learning more through the logic of immanence and affect where their bodies as well as the bodies of light and shadow pop up, not as each others' opposites, or as fixed entities encountering each other, but rather as inseparably joined and continuously moving in a relational field.

Chapter 7

Conclusions

Throughout this book attempts have been made to construct the problem of how to work with movement and experimentation in subjectivity and learning in early childhood education practice and research. Some conclusions can now be offered.

It is possible to work with movement in subjectivity and learning, starting from the idea that it is already there and always and continuously ongoing. This can be done by practice and research engaging in collective, intense and unpredictable experimentation together, where everything and everybody is seen as a relational field. Through concepts such as micro-politics and segmentarity, transcendental empiricism, event, and assemblages of desire one can work with movement and experimentation in subjectivity and learning in early childhood education research and practice in the following ways.

Through segmentarity and micro-politics it is possible to treat movement in subjectivity and learning as already there. All change of subjectivity and learning departs from flows of belief and desire that are already there. A first condition of a society is that it is leaking. The logic of conscious taming of subjectivity and learning, by predicting, preparing, controlling and supervising according to predetermined standards, never really functions well. It is all a question of 'hit and miss' and something always escapes. Therefore the formalized school and research system could benefit from adding to the conscious taming logic of subjectivity and learning, a certain kind of listening to and experimentation with these flows. Teachers, then, can be on the look out for what desires children already are caught up in and try to latch on to these together with the children and give space for lines of flight to be created. Researchers can in the same way go into practice looking for that which escapes already determined definitions and positions and engage in collective experimentations with children and teachers in making more space for lines of flight.

This is what we saw took place in the preschool practices in Stockholm and its suburbs, where it became clear how collective experimentation with lines of flight can bring to practices and to research new and interesting features of subjectivity and learning processes. Instead of using preset models and positions, people became mutually involved in processes of becoming, where each person's position and learning was caught up in a relational field and thereby continuously negotiated and in movement. This seems to be a productive way of taking into account the way power today operates through desire and affect. As long as academic or pedagogical institutions do not acknowledge their own desiring production they will inevitably be one step behind. Academic and pedagogical institutions can meet modulation of affect and desire with their own modulation of affect and desire.

Collective experimentation with lines of flight and the modulation of affect and desire take place in an environment marked by an ethico-aesthetic paradigm where you do not do it on your own. It is an environment where experimentation takes place through an ethics and politics of listening, experimentation, potentiality and a care for belonging. This seems of the highest importance today where the focus is so much on the individual. The fact that very young children are supposed, at a very early age, to develop a consciousness about themselves and their learning is a worrying thing. As can be seen, there is a danger with the lines of flight themselves that when an individual cannot connect her or his lines of flight to other lines, the lines of flight run the risk of turning into sources of demolition. Tools for individual self-reflection, measurement and evaluation are thought to function as important tools to avoid forgetting about each individual; but they are very dangerous tools if they are not complemented by environments that make it possible for each individual child to connect their lines of flights with other lines.

One cannot be too careful. There are many dangers at stake when working within an ethico-aesthetic paradigm; it is an unsafe place to be where you do not know beforehand where you will end up. As could be seen from the practices in Stockholm and its suburbs, this is a messy place to be in. Therefore the experimentation must be undertaken with vigilance. One must live with the dangers of all the lines and segments: fear, clarity, power and the great disgust.

Collective intense and unpredictable experimentation with desire and belief gives the teacher as well as the researcher the role of being, first and foremost, a 'listener' and a 'collective experimenter'. Only a listening subject can detect desires that are involved and engage properly in collective experimentation with lines of flight. The listening and experimenting teacher and researcher must no longer be placed above or outside, according to any transcendent principle.

This gives an alternative scientific methodological approach and a relation between theory and practice where theoretical concepts must not be applied; rather they have to be chosen simply on the basis that they function in relation to the practices or examples encountered. Something must happen with both concepts and practice when they are put in to use. It is a relationship where each has its distinct means, but where encounters can create new features for both practice and theory. The practices work with subjectivity and learning as a relational field. Through the examples in this study it could be proposed that this field is an immanent field. It is a field where consciousness does not function, it is a pre-conscious field. More than anything the idea of the plane of immanence and transcendental empiricism focuses on movement as already and always ongoing.

For teachers and researchers this implies starting out from the idea that things are already going on and that one's task is to go in and try to latch on to these things and experiment together with people. This implies being prepared for not knowing and for unexpected surprises, which is quite contrary to any attempt to tame subjectivity and learning through predicting, controlling, supervising or evaluating according to any predefined standards. Transcendental empiricism harbours the immanent idea of life being stronger than thought and that gives research and practice new aims and means.

Through treating pedagogical documentation as events, an alternative scientific and pedagogical methodological approach can be established, capable of harbouring movement in subjectivity and learning. Events, due to the introduction and addition of sense into language, are capable of treating subjectivity and learning as movements that are already there and continuously ongoing. Sense turns out to be a continuous production and it has an intimate relation to nonsense, problems/solutions, learning/knowledge and culture/method. This presents an alternative to doing research through commenting, interpreting and reflecting, as all these ways of approaching the event close it down, encircling it within claims of truth. But when sense is introduced as the unconditioned production of truth on the border of language and things, the event is kept complex and open ended. From the perspective of the event it is possible to treat subjectivity and learning in the empirical material as the ongoing creation and production of sense and problems and thereby in movement and open for experimentation.

In relation to pedagogical practices, children's use of nonsense to reach sense can, through the perspective put forward by the event, be acknowledged as totally appropriate. This completely changes the situation for the very young child who normally is treated through the idea of nonsense and sense as opposites and then consequently is further treated as being the one who always has everything wrong. The focus with the event is on how problems are constructed, not resolved; solutions are seen only as proportional in relation to the sense under construction. Children's doings then become important from the point of view of their production of sense and the related construction of problems. This makes it possible to re-evaluate young children's sayings and doings, to take them seriously and to see them as contributions to the world, to see them as added constructions of the world. This is seen in the OHP machine project where it turns out that the children are producing sense and constructing a problem of being in terms of vision and through plastic and elastic principles; whether and when is one seen or not?

Since they are interested in constructing problems, children will probably not back away from being confronted with what are considered to be accepted scientific problems. Why would they not be interested in these as well? It is just a question of how this encounter takes place. If teachers and researchers can live the logic of inventing and adding things to the world, through the continuous production of sense and problems, children's, and science's, problems and questions are equal and all worth working with. Teachers would not need to, and should not, back away from bringing into the process what are already known as scientific problems; the only thing to be careful with is how and when this procedure takes place.

In such learning, knowledge is variations of produced sense and constructed problems and the most interesting thing is to know how this comes about. The focus is on the process of learning and less effort is put into the outcome or the goal formulated as some predefined content of knowledge. This is not neglecting the content of knowledge, but it does imply an added definition of the content of knowledge. The content of knowledge is seen as the ongoing production and construction of sense and problems.

One could probably even talk about this approach to learning and knowledge as concerning *the art of constructing a problem*. This is a very rigorous and complex way of approaching the content of knowledge in educational systems. Moreover, it takes into account what most people have known for a long time: knowledge is not something static and unchangeable. On the contrary, and especially in today's fast-developing knowledge society, it seems troublesome to talk about learning and knowledge in such simplified ways as if it were possible to prepare, supervise, control and evaluate or measure according to predefined standards.

Still, and as seen throughout the book, this is where efforts are normally being made, with instruments for predicting, controlling, supervising and evaluating individuals, even very young children, as well as entire practices. When so much effort is put into producing and constructing such controlling and evaluative tools, one can only suspect that the question of *what* all these tools are actually supposed to measure inevitably becomes a totally forgotten and taken for granted question. In this respect it is possible to claim that the pedagogical approach with which the preschools featured in this book work, which is often dismissed as an 'anything goes pedagogy' that does not take the content of knowledge seriously, actually consists of a much more complex, rigorous and up-to-date approach to learning and knowledge. Since the children in these preschools are permitted to work within the construction of sense and problems, they participate in contemporary society's fast-developing knowledge production through their inventing and adding of versions to the world about the illustrations of sounds, about the exchanging of strategies, about light and shadow and about subjectivity and learning. They thereby learn to navigate in and handle the kind of knowledge society we live in to day.

Moreover, they learn to enjoy learning, since they do so much more than answer and resolve predefined questions and problems with equally predefined answers and solutions. This is not the same thing as a simplified idea of 'fun learning'. What the children are engaged in is the creation of a sense of being part of the world and each other; the world and other people are part of me. I am not alone. There is the possibility to think, talk, feel, play, work, dream, in short, *live* in a much larger and fulfilling sense than being reduced to an isolated island where from time to time one is judged from above in relation to things that do not even concern me.

This also has implications for the question of method. Method can no longer be seen as a pedagogical principle. Method must instead adapt itself to the sense and problem under production and construction. One can no longer apply the same single method to several cases; instead the method has to adapt itself to the entire culture surrounding the problem. And moreover, as stated above, the method has to be designed as the process of constructing a problem proceeds: 'meta'= along, 'rodos' = the road, *along the road*. One cannot plan the goal or the method beforehand since the problem is in the process of being constructed; the method must adapt and take shape in this process and the entire culture surrounding the problem must be brought in.

Preparation, though, becomes more important than ever. But this preparation concerns ensuring the space and the receptivity to be able to harbour and collectively construct different senses and problems. This can imply that when teachers or researchers prepare a project with children they need to read a lot about the content of knowledge, not so that they can give erudite lectures, but to give them as many perspectives as possible on the subject matter and to be prepared and receptive to what the children will add to these.

Teachers and researchers also need to make decisions and choices. What is important and why should they work with this content of knowledge with the children? These choices must be made in relation not only to ontological but also to political and ethical features. What kind of learning and knowledge do we want to produce together with the children in this project? How does this project relate to ongoing political and ethical features in society? How do we as adults want to contribute to the children's encounters with these features, which have either already taken place or will inevitably do so sooner or later? In the OHP machine project example for instance, one could imagine that studies of different theoretical and scientific perspectives on the features of light would be appropriate. Had not Spinoza's idea of bodies and forces encountering each other been studied in relation to this project, it might not have been possible to construct a story of how children treat the features of light and shadow through a plastic and elastic principle of vision.

The question is also, which theories? This is an ontological, political and ethical question because it depends on what kind of practice one struggles for. This choice must take place through the collective experimenting between research and practice mentioned above. This can probably only be done in local contexts and based on the very specific conditions in each case. Method in this perspective gives way to a long preparation where the entire culture surrounding the problem is being brought in, a preparation that only serves to raise receptivity and to make possible the making of choices. But then once one actually meets with the children, one must be capable of letting go.

Through the concept assemblages of desire it is possible for research and practice to highlight that children and practices have things going on all the time and that these things could be seen as the unconscious production of new realities. The question of change in relation to subjectivity and learning is no longer posed within a cause–effect relationship based on the dualism individual/society. Through turning desire on its head one no longer asks what children or practices are lacking and what they need. Rather one engages and is already engaged in, whether one is a teacher or researcher, collective assemblages of desire. The most important question is now what new realities children and teachers are already and continuously producing through desire. The practices described in this study do this by asking children 'Now, where are your desires?' and 'What assemblages are you for the moment experimenting with?' Since desire is an unconscious process of production it concerns a kind of learning that it is not possible to tame, predict, supervise, control or evaluate according to already determined standards.

This does not mean that the teacher has to give up and leave everything to the children. It is not a question of following children's desires to the extreme and letting them do whatever they choose. As said, teachers and researchers are also part of assemblages. Through assemblage of desire, production of new realities takes place within a relational field; children never stop desiring and constructing problems, but they also want to play with us, and they are very sensitive to our calling them to join us. This is very clear in the OHP machine project; the children answer the teachers' call to work with multiple identities, though in a different way than the teachers had intended. Children very quickly pick up what is the focus and interest for the teachers and they are prepared to go into a construction of problems and questions with teachers. It is a misunderstanding to believe that teachers must give up and follow the children. Since children are so sensitive to our calling them to join us, this must be met by teachers. It is only a question, again, of how and when to do this.

In this book examples have been put forward that show how teachers enter these assemblages with children in a very tentative and pragmatic way. The formalized school system does not give much place for such a teacher. Still, school already functions more or less well; children go there, most of them do manage to navigate today within the formalized school system. But we know little of what actually takes place when they learn. And we know even less about the potentialities inherent in children's ways of approaching established facts about the world. We do not seem to see what is going on, we seem to be voluntarily blind to the multiple ways that children actually do learn, and we do not explore and use these ways and means to enrich the formalized school system. Maybe it is hard for us to see children's learning, because when it takes place it does so in a much more subtle and varying way than the formalized school system is used to.

This is not again to make nature of the child, it is rather to make machine of the child. Children are exemplary in the analysis of desire as machine since they have not yet adapted or personalized all the repressive and organized schemas of desire. Under the surface of, and even within, everyday life in school, children find places to go on with their collective desires. The school system is simply not prepared for the abundant richness that goes on under the surface of organized life in school. The somewhat untameable learning processes taking place in a relational field are not comprehensible to the system because it has no way to theoretically or practically conceptualize ongoing movement and experimentation.

To see children, teachers and researchers as collectively caught up in assemblages of desire could make an important contribution to the formalized school system. It could make space for a different view on subjectivities and learning where one is permitted to learn from all sorts of different kinds of angles and means, from all sorts of different kinds of desires. In this book, subjectivity and learning have been drawn up as a relational field, where the relation is not between preset entities that function through cause–effect logic, but instead an ongoing process where the relation itself is continuously moving. Through the specific use of desire as unconscious production of real and as always assembled, it is possible to highlight forces that children are collectively caught up in and make them the starting point for a pedagogical practice.

Through language as internally alive and depending upon a collective assemblage of enunciation that is constantly varying, children's semiotic signs are possible to treat as that which they use to do things, sometimes quite apart from the signification we give specific words. Within the perspective on language as a predefined and fixed system with signifying words, children are often considered as lacking and as most of the time having it all wrong. Within the perspective of language as pragmatic and internally alive there is the possibility of a much better understanding of what kind of problems and sense children for the moment are constructing.

Through the idea of movements of re- and deterritorialization, it is possible to conceive of learning processes as anything but progressing on a straightforward line of predetermined development. Rather learning processes from this perspective billow back and forth, take short cuts and long cuts; go in circles and all sorts of other directions. But every time the territory slightly changes, it is not a question of simple imitation; the movements of re- and deterritorialization are creative acts continuously reshaping the territory.

Through affect it is possible to treat learning processes from a different logic than that of consciousness; learning has here got something to do with the capacity of involved bodies, organic as well as inorganic, to act. It is all about each event's particular potentiality and one can never formulate a pedagogical model in such an affective learning. The only thing one can do is to create more space for desiring bodies to expand their capacities; we do not know what a child or an OHP machine can do. Affect seems to be a very important concept for preschool practices. These practices are sometimes quite saturated by emotion and moral values. In fact, at its worst these practices stop almost all affective potential by taming children's desire. Children are taught how to be a good friend – 'Say I'm sorry now!' – but they rarely have the opportunity to discover real joyful passions springing from an increased affective potential.

In the practices described, children were brought into work with their questions and problems in smaller groups with different projects. These situations very often increased the affective potential of the situation and in turn created joyful passions: intense feelings of joy and solidarity. It became clear how these examples could never serve as a pedagogical principle that it was possible to imitate and impose on the next situation. Instead affect can put the focus on each specific situation's potential.

All these different ways and means to work with movements of subjectivity and learning in early childhood education research and practice must be seen as an addition to the formalized school and research system. They do not exclude any other attempts; it is just a question of constructing the problem of subjectivity and learning differently, focusing on movement and experimentation. In a formalized school and research system one must handle the ambiguity of wanting to focus on movement and experimentation and still answer to what is expected. Preschool is a political institution with goals and aims and these can also be seen to guarantee children's rights to education. But considering to what extent the focus already is on the goal and the outcome, a little bit of movement, experimenting, inventing and adding to the world might be somewhat beneficial, not least in relation to those children who seem to manage to decode and adapt to the system less well. From the point of view of this book, these children have probably been cut off in their desires; they have for one or another reason not been able to connect their lines of flight to other lines. Or maybe they live a construction of sense and problems that seems very far from established facts about the world. Working with the production of desire, sense and problems could be very beneficial for these children.

Through the examples in this book it seems that when very young children's thoughts, speech and actions are joined with the chosen theories they create together quite a forceful encounter. It becomes clear that children very often already live the features of subjectivity and learning from an immanent principle: as already and continuously moving. Through all the examples we can see that they are mostly interested in leakages. Everything already known is of less interest. They experiment and they do so collectively, immersed in the material and the problems they are constructing. We can see how they treat sense as an ongoing production intimately related to nonsense and how they prefer to stay in the process of constructing problems. In these ways, they focus more on the process of learning than on the goal, the knowledge to attain. In that process they will not subordinate the culture to method, but will rather use everything available surrounding the problem.

Children are involved in assembled desires all the time; they get caught up and use their bodies as well as language as a-signifying triggers of new events. They billow back and forth and in circles in their learning processes and continuously reshape the territory of learning and knowledge. They look for each situation's potentiality, starting out from the idea that we do not know either what one's own body or what an OHP machine can do. Light and shadow as well as subjectivity and learning are treated as bodies and forces encountering each other in a continuously moving relationship.

This is where it becomes clear that 'children are Spinozists' (Deleuze and Guattari, 2004: 282). In the project on the OHP machine one gets overwhelmed by how the children by and large outflank the adults' way of conceiving of subjectivity and learning processes. This is not making nature of the child again, or putting Deleuze and Guattari on to children. It is just focusing on a different image of thought that both these theories and the children in the examples seem to work with. If there were to be such a thing as a concluding conclusion to this study it would be that, when it comes to the problem of how to work with movement and experimentation in subjectivity and learning, it seems that the field of early childhood education research and practice actually has something to learn from children.

> If little children managed to make their protests heard in nursery school, or even simply their questions, it would be enough to derail the whole educational system.
>
> (Deleuze, 2004a: 208)

Epilogue
Out of order

A virtual child in crystal time

A problem is a set-up of points of singularities. Learning is about joining
the singular points of a problem in order to enter a problematic field.
The child learning to walk and the surfer learning to surf join their
bodies with the points of singularities in the sea and the ground. Writing
a dissertation, such as the one this book is based on, is also about entering
into composition with a problem: to join one's distinctive points with the
singular points of the problem confronted.

You do not choose a problem. Rather it is the other way around: it
chooses you. *Something in the world forces you to think.* The entire research
process is about constructing the problem only to find by the end that
the problem must be posed in relation to other means and in a different
way, maybe with the help of new and different examples or concepts.
The specific study reported in this book has focused on putting to work
a number of concepts – micro-politics and segmentarity, transcendental
empiricism, event and assemblages of desire – and it has now led to
the need to approach the problem of how to work with movement and
experimentation in subjectivity and learning in early childhood education
practice and research in a different way. What seems to be needed for
continuous work with this problem is a reformulation and reactivation
of time and space.

To further account for movement and experimentation in subjectivity
and learning, a possible opening is to be found in some additional concepts:
a-lives, virtuality, crystal time and becoming. Thorough work with these
concepts must wait for another project and only initial ideas can be drawn
up at this point. It is not by accident that this study ends with an invitation
to a new project. This is how we work, on the border of our knowledge,
in between knowing and not knowing. That's where everything happens.

A-lives

Stella Nona when learning to walk is *a* child. The surfer when learning to surf is *a* surfer. Underneath their bodies of child and surfer they are a-lives without selves. They are no longer individuals, they are processes of individuation. Children keep telling us this in sticking to the indefinite article; they ask questions of *a* person, *a* rhythm, *a* light, *a* shadow. Children, surfers, light, shadow and rhythm are all perfectly singular at the same time as they are common, they are impersonal and still singular. Even ground and waves are a-lives; they are common but perfectly singular. The sea moves all the time, waves move infinitely, but still they each have their perfectly singular movement.

Stella Nona when learning to walk resembled many other children learning to walk, and still her singular way of joining the ground cuts her out of the child image where she is defined according to predetermined attributes and installs her in the repetitive act of a child learning to walk. But this is a repetitive act and a child learning grounded in continuous movement. In that respect no child learns how to walk similarly to other children. Each child learns how to walk as a singularity without self. Selves cannot account for movements; they are stuck in definition and position. Selves can only be accounted for on a plane of transcendence. That's when they are already set, already defined, already positioned.

On the plane of immanence, on the contrary, there are only forces and bodies with different speeds and slowness entering into composition with each other or decomposing each other. Bodies, forces of different speeds and slowness are a-lives. On the plane of immanence there are only pre-individual singularities and impersonal commons. A-lives are always indefinite. That is why we should listen carefully to children's questions about *a* person, *a* rhythm, *a* light, *a* shadow. They are not asking out of ignorance; they are asking out of order, in movement (Deleuze, 2001; Deleuze and Guattari, 2004: chapter 10).

Virtuality

A life contains only virtuals. It is made up of virtualities, events, singularities. What we call virtual is not something that lacks reality but something that is engaged in a process of actualization following the plane that gives it its particular reality.

(Deleuze, 2001: 31)

In a-lives and on the plane of immanence there are only virtuals, which actualize themselves into the definitions and positions that we come to know. When we see the child learning to walk and the surfer learning to surf as predetermined entities with a given and progressing line for each development, we recognize only one dimension of reality – the actual dimension of reality. And of course the actual child is the perfectly real and concrete child we encounter every day. The point is not to deny the existence of real children in preschools, but from the perspective drawn up here reality contains more than one actualized dimension; it also carries with it a virtual dimension.

The virtual dimension is not opposed to the real; it is only opposed to the actual. The virtual dimension has its proper reality; it is no less real than the actual dimension. A virtual child is as real as an actualized child, only not yet defined, and not perceptible on a plane of transcendence. A virtual child can only be perceived, and cannot be but perceived, on a plane of immanence. A virtual child is the image of a child doubled, but completely without resemblance: not a copy. The actual, even though it is the virtual actualized, has no resemblance whatsoever to the virtual. The virtual does not precede the actual; virtual and actual are two dimensions of reality, intimately intertwined but still distinct. That the child could be considered also from the point of virtuality could come with the advantage of a certain potentiality for children to be otherwise. The taking into account of more than one dimension to reality destabilizes what we already know. A virtual child would be a child of movement and its subjectivity and learning processes would be considered from the point of view of a virtual, abundant richness, always moving and ready to transform.

The virtual, though, even as it contains a certain potentiality, is not the same thing as the possible; the possible is still opposed to the real. The possible is just yet another version of what we already know and it is only capable of 'realizing itself'. Within the possible we could make the mistake of mixing Stella Nona up with the surfer, as if the image told us that she was possible also as surfer. But that is not good enough, that is still to keep a too-tight relation to a real that is already given. The virtual never realizes itself, it only actualizes, and the actualization never resembles the virtual. For the same reason the virtual is not fantasy, it is not the opposite of real.

Maybe it would be beneficial to treat children's play from the point of view of the duo virtual/actual rather than fantasy/real? Children, when playing, are probably plunging into the most intense actualization of virtuality. As long as we do not consider this, play is something that is not worth taking seriously; it is like a metaphor, a game with words that does not take itself seriously. The point is to play joyfully and seriously.

Children's play is poorly understood, invaded by psychology or dismissed as meaningless and of no value. In both cases play is treated as fantasy and has too close a relation with the real as given. Children's play as plunging into an intense actualization of virtuality could open up to new dimensions of reality. A virtual child is a perfectly real child, but one that we do not yet know, one that is never given, one that is in the process of actualization. In this way it can never be confounded with a child from cyberspace or a digitalized child. Virtuality has nothing to do with cyberspace and the digital, as long as the aims, means and procedures of cyberspace and the digital stay within the distinction of opposing virtual to real and confounding it with possibility. You do not find a virtual child in cyberspace; it is right before your eyes, only on another plane in another dimension and in another time (Deleuze 1994a, 2001; Deleuze and Guattari, 2004: chapter 10; Massumi, 2003: 137–138; Zourabichvili, 2003: 22).

Crystal time

A virtual child functions only in another dimension of time than the one the child image obeys. In the child image where the child develops into an adult and even into a surfer, according to predetermined stages, we see only the actualized child because time is considered as chronologically linear. In crystal time, time is no longer conceived of as chronological linear time; time is at each instant doubled and divided into two dissymmetrical jets, one heading for the past, the other towards the future. The past is the virtual dimension of reality and the present is the actual dimension of reality. And even though the actual present and the virtual past are distinctively different there is no chronological succession; the actual does not come after the virtual past, they are completely simultaneous. The present passes on and even though new presents arrive it is not enough to say that they replace the past that is no longer, because it is the past of each specific present that causes the present to pass on.

> Thus the image has to be present and past, still present and already past, at once and at the same time. If it was not already past at the same time as present, the present would never pass on. The past does not follow the present that it is no longer, it coexists with the present

it was. The present is the actual image, and *its* contemporaneous past is the virtual image, the image in mirror.

(Deleuze, 1989: 79; original emphasis)

The past is not something that has been and that no longer exists. Rather, all past is the past of this specific present. Every moment carries the whole of the past, and it is this past, contemporaneous with and specific to this very present, that makes the present pass on. If the past is seen as old past, as no longer present, the present is immobilized, it becomes a static entity that can never move; movement is lost again. To be able to account for movement in the present, the past cannot be an anecdote; it must coexist with the present. It is in the crystal we see this split of time, into one actual dimension of reality (the present) and one virtual dimension of reality (the past). It is time seen through the crystal that can give subjectivity and learning the features of movement before intermediate stops on the way towards the goal. This would also be subjectivity and learning taking on the features of becoming (Deleuze, 1989: chapter 4, 2002: chapters 4 and 5; Zourabichvili, 2003: 19–26).

Becoming – imperceptible and movement out of order

Stella Nona in the picture with the surfer is not becoming surfer; neither is the surfer becoming child, if by that we mean the molar definition of the surfer and the child. Rather there is something in the walking and the surfing that touches each other, that has something to do with each other. The surfer joins the movements and forces of the sea and the child joins the movements and the forces of the ground. There are particles of walking that are close to particles of surfing and vice versa. Children playing dogs are not imitating dogs or identifying with them. Rather they pick something out from the 'dogginess' of a dog that they join with their bodies.

> In a way, we must start at the end; all becomings are already molecular. That is because becoming is not to imitate or identify with something or someone. Nor is it to proportion formal relations. Neither of these two figures of analogy is applicable to becoming: neither the imitation of a subject nor the proportionality of a form. Starting from the forms one has, the subject one is, the organs one has, or the functions one fulfils, becoming is to extract particles between which one establishes the relations of movements and rest,

speed and slowness that are *closest* to what one is becoming, and through which one becomes.

(Deleuze and Guattari, 2004: 300; original emphasis)

You become only molecularly, children do not become the dog; they pick out something from 'dogginess' bringing forward a molecular dog. Children, though, are capable of many more becomings than adults, not because they are naturally apt for becomings, but simply because they have not yet decoded and adapted to the molar positions of adults and dogs. Therefore it is more correct to say that it is rather becoming itself that is a child. Children do not become adults; it is rather the child that is the becoming of every age. This does not mean 'to stay young' or 'to be childlike'; it concerns the extraction of a becoming specific to every age.

From this point of view, neither children learning to walk, nor surfers learning to surf, develop or evolve, rather they *involve*. In the image of them together, respectively joining sea and ground, a bloc of becoming is created, that has nothing to do with children growing up to be adults or potentially surfers or surfers regressing to a child-like state. Becoming takes place in between, it has no beginning and no final end; it is entered from the middle.

There exists a final kind of becoming though, maybe a kind of ultimate becoming. This is the becoming-imperceptible. Becoming-imperceptible is total immersion, it is 'the immanent end of becoming, its cosmic formula' (Deleuze and Guattari, 2004: 308). This is when one is connected to everything, dissolved in a continuously changing relationship with everything. To be nobody and at the same time everything instead of being somebody and at the same time nothing. This is where movement is to be found, in the imperceptible.

> One is then like grass; one has made the world, everybody/everything, into a becoming, because one has made a necessarily communicating world, because one has suppressed in oneself everything that prevents us from slipping between things and growing in the midst of things [...] Movement has an essential relation to the imperceptible; it is by nature imperceptible. Perception can grasp movement only as the displacement of a moving body or the development of a form. Movements, becomings, in other words, pure relations of speed and slowness, pure affects, are below and above the threshold of perception.
>
> (Deleuze and Guattari, 2004: 309)

By saying that we look at a child's developing into an adult, we pretend to look only at movements but we never do, we look only at the intermediate stops on the road towards the goal; we look for movement in the wrong place. The wrong place is always the transcendent plane, the plane of organization and development. This plane conditions our perception so that we cannot perceive movement. It renders some things perceptible and others not, but it always hides its principle of doing this. We cannot perceive movement because it takes place when the child falls and not when it walks. It takes place before the position we have given the child as a 'walking child'. That is why it is only on the other plane, on the plane of immanence, that we can perceive movement; actually on the plane of immanence *we cannot but perceive movement.* Because on this plane the principle of composition is perceived at the same time as that which it composes. Perception on the plane of immanence can no longer see the ground and the child, the surfer and the sea as separated, rather they are perceived from the point of view of movement in that relation.

> Perception will no longer reside in the relation between a subject and an object, but rather in the movement serving as the limit of that relation, in the period associated with the subject and the object. Perception will confront its own limit; it will be in the midst of things, throughout its own proximity, as the presence of one haecceity in one another, the prehension of one by the other or the passage from one to the other: Look only at the movements.
>
> (Deleuze and Guattari, 2004: 311)

'Look only at the movements'. Easy to say, much harder to do. And it is true that there is a great jump from the idea of immanence presented as a plane where concepts are connected and related, and an everyday practice in preschools. But really, if immanence as an idea can bring the features of a continuous collective, intense and unpredictable experimentation to everyday practices, why not use it? And anyway what other choice do we have, once we have entered something from the middle, than to continue experimenting? Maybe what is needed more than anything, is a certain amount of vigilance and humbleness in front of subjectivity and learning as something we cannot fully grasp, paired with a trust in the moment and a willingness to experiment with the potentialities already inherent in this moment.

We also sometimes need to leave the walking child and the surfer in peace. We have persisted with our attempts to tame and make them function long enough. We struggle to tame life, to make it function and it never does, which is the same thing as saying that it functions. Life persists and insists in its own proper way. We sense it sometimes when everything has fallen apart and broken down around us and in us; that's when life is at its most intense and even beautiful; it really functions. Machines function only when they break down, the order is order only as a moment temporarily stagnated from out of order. It is when out of order movement moves.

Appendix I

Dear Parents

My name is Liselott Olsson and I am currently a doctoral student at the Stockholm Institute of Education, where I am preparing a doctoral thesis on young children's learning. During later years I have been giving in-service training courses for teachers in early childhood education. During these courses we work with pedagogical documentations coming from the participants' own preschool classes in order to make visible and become curious about children's learning processes and their capacities to construct knowledge.

In the courses, as well as in my research, what is focused on is what happens when teachers make an effort to really listen to children's own interests and strategies of learning through documenting their learning processes with photos and observations. The purpose of my research is to create knowledge about children's and teachers' desire to learn through collective experimentation.

The teachers in your child's class are currently attending one of the courses described above. The material that the teachers in your child's class have produced is interesting and of good quality and I would like to use this material in my forthcoming doctoral thesis, as well as in different research contexts, such as in teaching at the Stockholm Institute of Education, in articles published in scientific journals, in papers presented at conferences both in Sweden and internationally.

The purpose of this letter is to ask for your permission to use photos, as well as observations of the documented project on 'The overhead projector'/'The rhythm of the heart', that takes place in your child's class. Please fill in the coupon below where you can choose whether or not to consent to the use of the material described above.

I am adopting the principles for research in the humanities and social sciences put forward by the Swedish Research Council. If you have any questions or want to discuss something, please contact me.

I consent to the material from the project on 'The overhead projector'/ 'The rhythm of the heart', in which my child is participating, being used in the way described above.

I do not consent to the material from the project on 'The overhead projector'/'The rhythm of the heart', in which my child is participating, being used in the way described above.

_____

Signature

Appendix 2

Dear Teachers

I am currently a doctoral student at the Stockholm Institute of Education where I am preparing a doctoral thesis on young children's learning. In my research, the focus is what happens when teachers make an effort to really listen to children's own interests and strategies of learning through documenting their learning processes with photos and observations. The purpose of my research is to create knowledge about children's and teachers' desire to learn through collective experimentation.

The material that have been produced in your project is interesting and of good quality and I would like to use this material in my forthcoming doctoral thesis, as well as in different research contexts, such as in teaching at the Stockholm Institute of Education, in articles published in scientific journals, in papers presented at conferences both in Sweden and internationally.

The purpose of this letter is to ask for your permission to use photos, observations as well as individual and collective analyses of the documented project on 'The overhead projector'/'The rhythm of the heart', which takes place in your class. Please fill in the coupon below where you can choose whether to consent or not to the use of the material according to the description above.

I am adopting the principles for research in the humanities and social sciences put forward by the Swedish Research Council. If you have any questions or want to discuss something, please contact me.

> I consent to the material from the project on 'The overhead projector'/'The rhythm of the heart', being used in the way described above.

I do not consent to the material from the project on 'The overhead projector'/'The rhythm of the heart', being used in the way described above.

_____

Signature

Notes

Prologue

1 This prologue is written as a way of entering the problem that the present book tries to construct: how to work with movement and experimentation in Early Childhood Education practice and research. It starts out from the practical and theoretical resources presented and worked through later on, some preschools in Stockholm and its suburbs in Sweden, and the French philosophers Gilles Deleuze and Félix Guattari. In the prologue a certain academic liberty has been taken, there are no references or quotations made. The prologue was written at the end of the research process and hopefully serves so as to create the ambiance and state the focus of the book that follows: movement and experimentation in subjectivity and learning.

2 Thanks to Elisabeth Grosz for pointing out the risk of this prologue being read as a metaphorical or analogous description of child and surfer.

3 Artist and PhD student at the Royal College of Technology in Stockholm, Sweden, Monica Sand, has been exploring walking in precisely this way, as a question of rhythm rather than as a movement forward. She uses a text from poet and songwriter Laurie Anderson to show how walking rather could be understood as a rhythm of falling and catching yourself.

> You're walking. And you don't always realize it,
> but you're always falling.
> With each step, you fall forward slightly.
> And then catch yourself from falling.
> Over and over, you're falling.
> And then catching yourself from falling.
> And this is how you can be walking and falling
> *At the same time*'
> (Anderson, 1982)

In her dissertation Sand (2008) is working in various ways with the relation between bodies, space, time and knowledge production through the activation of the in between, seen as a rhythm rather than as a fixed space. In her work she is challenging not only the function of walking, but also the meaning of progress. She takes as a starting point the movement of walking, to trouble the entire idea of development and knowledge production in a movement forwards and upwards.

She also shows, by referring to the story of Penelope and Odysseus, how we believe that it is the physical movement that indicates progress and production. Odysseus is the hero, travelling the seven seas performing heroic deeds; Penelope is just sitting around waiting for him. As the time goes by the more convinced everybody is that he will not be back. The suitors start to flock around Penelope and try to force her to make a choice among them for her new husband. Penelope then starts to weave; she promises her suitors that the day the weaving is completed she will make her choice. But since Penelope does not really fancy marrying any of the suitors she starts to undo the weaving during the night-time. She weaves during daytime and undoes the weaving at night. At first sight, these actions appear to accomplish nothing: she does not get ahead, she produces nothing, and she is still just waiting. But the way Sand reads it, Penelope is creating a rhythm that produces space and time for herself. She does not do heroic deeds, she is not advancing, but she is producing.

Sand uses these ideas of challenging progress and development in one of her installations. In a bridge in the town of Gothenburg on the west coast of Sweden she sets up a 40 metre high swing and lets a dancer swing there all hours of the day and night. When you swing, at the very moment the swing is at its highest point, turning to swing back again you are, for a short moment, weightless. Sand reads the movements of swinging as a rhythm very much like the rhythm of walking and weaving. Swinging is an activity that does not lead anywhere, you do not get ahead and you do not produce anything, and yet, from where does this extraordinary feeling come, that everyone that once has been on a swing remembers? Sand reads this feeling as a moment of liberation, a moment away from gravity that constantly pulls us back to earth. Gravity, according to her, can in this sense be translated to culture and the dominating ideas we have, for example, about identity. In this sense life contains moments of being captured in gravity, culture or a specific definition of one's identity, but it also contains moments away from gravity, culture and already defined identities. These moments away from gravity or culture, though, are not connected to any progress or development as we normally think of it. Rather they are forgotten spaces, but still perfectly open for being activated again (Sand, 2008).

4 I have worked as a preschool teacher and preschool head teacher in one of the communes, Trångsund, during the period 1992-2001. During the years 2002-7, I have been a PhD student at the Stockholm Institute of Education and I have also been working as a teacher educator at the Stockholm Institute of Education where, through in-service training courses, I have been working closely with many of the communes involved in the processes mentioned in this book.

5 Already at this point it was recognized that developmental psychology is a much more complex field than one could imagine when seeing the results of a deconstructive work. It is important to see that developmental psychology is in itself a complex and varying field that cannot easily be reduced to homogenous discourses. However, it is possible to say something about how preschools have picked up, made use of and also transformed these theories.

I Practical resources

1 The Stockholm Institute of Education, from the 1st of January 2008, joined Stockholm University.
2 For instance, Foucault's writings on the history of subjectification have been connected to the every day life of preschools. Researchers and teachers have in this way been able to identify some discursive regimes involved in their practice. This has also made it possible to reinvent these practices in other ways.
3 This notion is also inspired by the preschools in Reggio Emilia and their idea of 'learning as a relational place' (Giudici, Rinaldi, Krechevsky, 2001).

2 Theoretical resources

1 It might be important already at this stage to state that the 'new' should be treated with some caution. The 'new' runs the risk of seducing us with its apparent freshness, but through many of Deleuze and Guattari's work there runs a thread that speaks of a certain kind of suspiciousness against what we consider to be 'new'; technical innovations, the development of new forms of communication in the information society, new drugs, medicine etc. All these 'new' innovations are not necessarily new. Very often they turn out to be 'more of the same'. Maybe the 'new' is better understood as that which is 'coming about', that is, it is when experimenting and doing so without controlling parameters or the outcome that unrecognizable and unrepresentative things can happen.
2 This is something that is very easily forgotten when Deleuze and Guattari are exported or imported elsewhere; they become somewhat abstract and mystical thinkers. But repeatedly Deleuze and Guattari make references to real and concrete events when they draw up their philosophy. It is through confronting thought with examples that their philosophy is constructed. Through working with Liane Mozère, who was active in Paris in one of the many political projects in which Deleuze and Guattari were involved, this impression has been reinforced and it has led to a conception of this philosophy as a truly empiricist project. However, it is of the greatest importance to really go into serious studies of the texts and concepts, especially since the corpus of work inspired by Deleuze and Guattari is steadily increasing and widely debated. For this reason this book relies mainly on the original texts of Deleuze and Guattari.
3 This is of course not the only way of using Deleuze and Guattari's philosophy. According to Fredrika Spindler (Deleuze seminar at the Stockholm Institute of Education 17th October 2007), there are at least two general ways of dealing with Deleuze and Guattari; either in the pragmatic way described here, using parts of their work to connect with other fields and practices; or in a more philosophical way, where one accounts for their work in relation to the history of philosophy.
4 It does not seem particularly intelligent to use only the odd concept of a philosopher or theory; it probably implies a rather hasty attitude where overlooking and misuse seem quite probable. But going into the work of any

of these philosophers (which would of course be the most proper way of doing it) would demand at least the time and effort of a second book.

5   In the epilogue openings are made towards a new and next project going into the concepts of time and space in relation to movement and experimentation. In the epilogue it also becomes clear that when constructing a problem you often find yourself, by the end of the process, without many clear and perfected solutions. But rather, you discover the need to go into a new reformulation of the problem through other means. This is of course what has happened here as well; the particular study on which this book is based started off by constructing the problem of movement and experimentation through the chosen concepts, only to discover by the end that one now needs to look closer into the concepts of time and space.

6   Some of Deleuze and Guattari's texts have been read in French and English, especially Logique du sens (1969)/The Logic of Sense (2004b), a difficult but very important book for this study. It was necessary to use both the French and English version of this book to be able to use the concept 'event' in the present study. Because of the use of both French and English versions and due to the extensive use of Deleuze and Guattari in this study, it seemed fair to acknowledge also the original versions of their work in the bibliography. But in order to not confuse the reader, all references and quotations refer to the English translations throughout the study, apart from a few exceptions: on page 36 when describing Deleuze's earliest published work there are five references to original work. These concern Deleuze's thesis Différence et Répétition (1968a), his work on Hume (1953), Nietzsche (1962), Bergson (1966) and Spinoza (1968b). In the bibliography are presented both the original French versions and the translated works. There is also two cases where there is no translation available. This concerns Deleuze's article in Le Magazine Littéraire (1994b) and Guattari's book Ecrits pour L'Anti-Œdipe (2004).

7   Both Zourabichvili (2003) and Sauvagnargues (2005) write with a focus on Deleuze's thinking, but they both also make a point of insisting upon the close relationship in between Deleuze and Guattari.

8   For anyone interested in how Deleuze and Guattari's philosophy can be and has been used in the field of education there are a few interesting examples. For instance, Kaustuv Roy (2003, 2005) has produced some valuable field work in curriculum theory, where Deleuze's philosophy has been used in experimentation with the practice in an innovative urban school. Curriculum as representation and recognition is here challenged by the creation of 'nomadic spaces', where teachers, teacher educators and students can enter new expressions and new ways of thinking, talking and doing. Inna Semetsky (2003, 2004a, 2004b) has produced various work where Deleuze's concepts are worked through in relation to classroom practices. She has also made interesting connections between Deleuze and John Dewey.

9   CERFI: Centre d'étude, de recherche et de formation institutionnelles, was born out of another organisation FGERI : Fédération des groupes d'études et de recherches institutionelles, that joined over 300 psychiatrists, psychologists, teachers, town planners, architects, economists, film-makers, academics and other people. CERFI published the journal Recherches founded by Guattari in 1966.

10   Detailed references for the concepts will be given as they are worked through in respective chapters.

3 Micropolitics and segmentarity in early childhood education

1   In relation to this there could also be some interesting openings for feminist scholars. For instance, Elisabeth Grosz (1995) proposes that it could be a challenge for contemporary feminist research perspectives to take into consideration the Deleuzian and Guattarian philosophy. According to Grosz, the feminist critique and resistance practices need new ways of addressing the subject capable of not getting stuck in and reinforcing the already set dualism man-woman. She is arguing that there might be a challenge for feminist critique and resistance practices in turning to the different ideas of time and space presented in Deleuze and Guattari's philosophy. In a seminar in Bergen, Norway (May 2007) Grosz spoke about how Deleuze and Guattari's ideas, building on Nietzsche, Bergson and Spinoza can give a different view of how sexual difference is constructed; as internal difference rather than difference through opposition, contradiction, negation or analogy. Accordingly the question of the status of the female sex, so important for feminists, could be answered in the following way; 'I'll be the sex that my next encounter makes possible' (quote from Grosz in lecture, Bergen, Norway May 2007).

2   See also Hardt's and Negri's Empire (2002) where they claim that post-modern and postcolonial theories in their critique of modernity focus on only one strand of modernity; the taming logic of transcendence. They do not account for the other strand in modernity; the truly revolutionary immanent logic at stake at the very same time. According to Hardt and Negri, when it comes to contemporary governing through an immanent logic, these theories, do not function effectively since they address their movement of resistance towards what can only be considered to be the shadows of one mode of modernity; with its transcendent logic and disciplining order. If society today no longer works and governs through this transcendent order but has woken up and appropriated the very revolutionary mode of modernity, that is, its immanent logic of creation and modulation of desire, they ask how effective this critique then can be. According to Hardt and Negri, there might even be a risk that these theories actually sustain and reinforce the transcendent forces of governing:

> We suspect that postmodernist and postcolonialist theories may end up in a dead end because they fail to recognize adequately the contemporary object of critique, that is, they mistake today's real enemy. What if the modern form of power these critics (and we ourselves) have taken such pains to describe and contest no longer holds sway in our society? What if these theorists are so intent on combating the remnants of a past form of domination that they fail to recognize the new form that is looming over them in the present? What if the dominating powers that are the intended object of critique have mutated in such a way as to depotentialize any such postmodernist challenge? In short, what if a

new paradigm of power, a postmodern sovereignty, has come to replace the modern paradigm and rule through differential hierarchies of the hybrid and fragmentary subjectivities that these theorists celebrate? In this case, modern forms of sovereignty would no longer be at issue, and the postmodernist and post colonialist strategies that appear to be libratory would not challenge but in fact coincide with and unwittingly reinforce the new strategies of rule!

(Hardt and Negri, 2002: 137-138)

It seems that in relation to the features of contemporary economics and politics, as well as in relation to the issues evoked in post-modern and postcolonial times, there is great potential for going into their work in more depth than is being done in this book, through connecting these features to the field of early childhood education. For anyone tempted by such a project there would probably be many interesting resources in Hardt's and Negri's Empire (2002), as well as in Negri's Time for Revolution (2003).

3 See further Chapter Five on the event and how it connects the continuous production of sense to problems, learning, and the entire culture surrounding a problem, and how it sees these as more important than pre-established and given solutions, knowledge and methods. The event could in this case present a quite different approach to the whole idea of 'good practice', as well as the idea of the possibility to consciously and rationally work progressively with 'good practice'.

4 This could be a possible way of approaching something that lies outside the present study, namely the developing movement of 'sustainable development'. Guattari's way of thinking about the necessity to work with issues of the psyche, the social and the environment at the same time and through adapting an aesthetic approach to life seems to be an interesting perspective to bring in to the efforts conducted within this movement. For anyone interested in such a project there would probably be some interesting resources to be found in Chaosmosis an ethico-aesthetic paradigm (1995).

4 Pedagogical work and transcendental empiricism

1 This brief review of the birth and development of the new research discipline pedagogical work builds on the account by Monica Vinterek, in the *Journal of Research in Teacher Education*, 3-4, 2004.

2 Deleuze and Guattari also speak of 'radical empiricism' (Deleuze and Guattari, 1994: 47).

3 To speak in this way, about transcendence and transcendent thinkers on the one hand, and immanence and immanent thinkers on the other hand, is not a very fruitful way of approaching the question of immanence and transcendence. One tends to get easily stuck within this created dualism. Rather, what Deleuze and Guattari seem to want to acknowledge throughout all their works is that immanence and transcendence cannot exist without each other. Just as with micro and macro-politics, they are interrelated and proportional. But maybe one can, just as Smith (2003) does in note 29, talk about 'elective affinities'. When it comes to the present book, the treatment of transcendence and immanence serves only the pragmatic purpose of

making clear that, to be able to theoretically account for collective, intense and unpredictable experimentation, one must acknowledge a certain devaluation of transcendence.

4 Compare with the definition of desire as unconscious production of real and the concept of affect, as concerning the question of what a body can do, thereby proposing a new model for thought capable of focusing on the *unconscious in thought and the unknown of the body* (see further Chapter Six).

5 The plane of immanence is a very complex notion and it is not possible to think of it as a scientific method or even a concept. It is more of a horizon against which all thinking takes place. The plane of immanence is also where there is infinite movement (Deleuze and Guattari, 1994: 36-37). Due to this complexity, in the present study openings towards this plane of immanence where movement is infinite is made only in the epilogue. In this chapter, the plane of immanence is not completely worked through; what is being talked about is how transcendental empiricism, with the focus on the specific features of consciousness and empiricism, might be able to account for the collective, intense and unpredictable experimentation that takes place in between teachers and researchers in the preschools.

6 At this point it might be appropriate to draw up the contours of the difference between Deleuze and Guattari's philosophy and phenomenology. However, in doing this, there is no ambition of making a thorough exposition of this highly complex relation. The purpose of this book is not to position Deleuze and Guattari in relation to the entire history of philosophy. Its concerns are much more modest: to try out this philosophy in relation to the field of early childhood education. So at this point it is not possible to expose this relationship in its entirety; only a few indications of the different preoccupations of phenomenology and Deleuze and Guattari's philosophy can be given here.

Following Deleuze and Guattari (1994: 44-47), phenomenology never really succeeds in erasing the dualism between subject and object. Rather, phenomenology installs the transcendent principle *within* the subject's lived experience. In this way the claim is still that there is a subject with an inner essence as well as an objective world possible to enter. Now, Deleuze and Guattari push the problem further by insisting on the immanence of the world and the subject, that is: the subject is already immanent with the world. Neither the subject nor the world exists in any essential or fixed state. As we could see thought is created through encounters and relations, where the relation itself is in a continuously changing state. What is being drawn up is an idea of the world and the subject as ongoing production, where the dualism between subject and object no longer functions. Zourabichvili (2003: 33-36) also argues that it is because of the fact that there is no longer any essential Ego or Subject within Deleuze's philosophy that he is capable of pushing the problem of experience further than phenomenology.

In *What is philosophy?* (1994: 44-47), Deleuze and Guattari expose three strategies to reintroduce transcendence (and thereby sustain the subject/object dualism) throughout the history of philosophy. First, Platonism that separates the Idea as the transcendent principle from the field of immanence viewed as a field of simple appearances. Secondly, Descartes who through the formulation of the conscious cogito and the 'I think', inscribe the transcendent principle exactly in this conscious I or Ego. Finally, phenomenology's way of attempting to think the lived experience within the subject, as an immanent principle and no longer making immanence immanent to the Idea or to the Subject. But what happens is that, since phenomenology does not give up the idea of the essential and conscious subject, transcendence is claimed right in the heart of lived experience, that is; phenomenology is seeking transcendence right in the heart of immanence. As it is going to be argued in this chapter, the particularity with an immanent and transcendental empiricism, as a relation between theory and practice, is that it never permits one to explain, contain or be the cause of the other in any transcendent way. It is rather the question of an encounter, a speaking with, that forces both theory and practices to *experiment* and *do* new things.

7 This might be the point were it is possible to draw up some initial ideas of the relation between Deleuze/Guattari and another French philosopher, Jacques Derrida. There is no attempt to position these two ways of thinking as contradictory or opposite. Firstly because Deleuze/Guattari and Derrida were all part of a generation of thinkers in France, and their relationship is of a highly complex nature that would need a much more thorough exposition than it is possible to give here. Secondly, the focus of this study is on putting Deleuze and Guattari to work in relation to the field of early childhood education and not on their relationship with the entire history of philosophy. Still, there are a few initial ideas about the relationship between Deleuze and Derrida that could be presented as points of departure for further investigation.

In Patton and Protevi (2003), Smith, drawing on Giorgio Agamben's essay *Potentialities: Collected Essays in Philosophy* (1999), writes about two different trajectories in contemporary French philosophy: a trajectory of transcendence, which includes Derrida, and goes back through Husserl to Kant; and a trajectory of immanence that includes Deleuze and goes back through Nietzsche to Spinoza. Smith chooses to compare the two thinkers, Deleuze and Derrida, by looking for their 'elective affinities', concerning the terms transcendence/immanence in relation to some philosophical themes. Derrida and Deleuze relate differently to the subjectivist tradition (that is following Descartes in installing the transcendent principle in the consciousness of the subject). Through his declaration of the death of the metaphysics and metaphysic's structural closure, Derrida seems to appeal to a transcendent trajectory. Metaphysics is for Derrida a closed system and there is no outside to it; the only way to overcome metaphysics is to deconstruct it from within, hence the Derridean method of deconstruction. Deconstruction is seen as impossible, but at the same time it is this very impossibility that conditions the deconstruction from within. One can, working on the border of exhausted concepts and the formal transcendent structure (always present within metaphysics) create a certain sliding that will bring forward that which could not be presented in the history of philosophy.

Deleuze on the other hand has never been interested in the death of metaphysics. He proposes that the philosophical task, if one is not content with the existing metaphysics, is to create a different one. Deleuze's method is one of creation and experimentation out of the possibilities already existing even within metaphysics. There is no attempt to overcome metaphysics, but rather Deleuze sees his work as being immanent to metaphysics; one can always pick up old themes and reactivate them, and creation and transformation are always possible within metaphysics. Metaphysics itself is seen as an open-ended and continuously changing system. 'Put crudely, then, if Derrida sets out to undo metaphysics, Deleuze sets out simply to *do* metaphysics' Smith, (2003:50). Furthermore, Derrida uses the concept 'difference' as that which transcends ontology, whilst for Deleuze difference is already an immanent principle within ontology.

In short, for Derrida the subject and the world are stuck in structures and the subject can only quasi-liberate itself through working within the transcendent always present. For Deleuze the subject and the world are finding themselves in structures but these are already somewhat leaking, that is, they are already run by an immanent principle. Hence Derrida's method of deconstruction takes place through a transcendent logic and Deleuze's way of working with creation and experimentation takes place through an immanent logic. Zourabichvili (2003:42-43) also points out the difference between Deleuze and Derrida at the level of different approaches to the history of philosophy; Derrida by insisting on the *deconstruction* of the logos and Deleuze by a certain perversion, that is; to *create* a different logos. Bonta and Protevi (2004: 12-16) describe how these two different approaches are departing from two different approaches to Being. In Derrida and his critique and attempts to overcome the metaphysics of presence, Being is functioning as a higher organizing principle, that is, a transcendent principle. Whilst Deleuze develops an ontology that continuously avoids all presence through the replacement of essences in favour of virtual multiplicities (see further this book's epilogue 'A virtual child in crystal time').

8 See further Chapter Six.

9 I started up these courses with my colleague Ann Åberg, preschool teacher and co-writer of the book *Lyssnandets Pedagogik* ('The Pedagogy of Listening') (Åberg, and Lenz-Taguchi, 2005).

10 This might be the place to say something about the relationship between Deleuze and Foucault. Again, the attempt is not to present any complete exposition of the relation between them. Neither is there any attempt to make their relationship a contradictory one. There seems to be no point, since it has become obvious, both in the discussion referred to above, but also through the book *Foucault* (1988b) that Deleuze wrote on Foucault, that the relationship between Deleuze and Foucault was one of a real friendship. In a special issue of *Le Magazine Litteraire* (Deleuze, 1994b) their relationship and continuing discussion is demonstrated. It becomes visible that, during periods of their lives, Deleuze and Foucault had a close and intense communication. But even though they shared their endeavours, they sometimes had different ways of going about it. The most striking difference between them becomes obvious in the published letter that Deleuze wrote to Foucault in 1977 after Foucault's writing of *La Volonté de savoir* (1976), the introduction to the three volumes of *Histoire de la sexualité* (1976; 1984a; 1984b) a book that was poorly understood and that would lead to some sort of a crisis in Foucault's work. Deleuze writes a very friendly and supportive

letter to Foucault that is far away from being a critique or even a positioning. It is his way of drawing up the difference between himself and Foucault and a way of inviting a continuing dialogue. This difference concerns the concept of power used by Foucault and the concept of desire used by Deleuze.

For Deleuze, power is indeed part of our lives and the system we live in. We are regulated and repressed in many ways and, just as Foucault says, not least by the way power is associated with knowledge, shaping regimes of truth. But, for Deleuze, desire, and especially and always desire without lack in assembled desire, contains power, but only as one of its components. Power is only an effect of desire, or better, within desire:

> Of course, an assemblage contains the dispositions of power (for instance feudal power), but these would need to be situated as part of the different components of an assemblage. Following a first axis, there exists within an assemblage of desire the distinguishing of the state of things and enunciations (this would be the same thing as the two formations or multiplicities that Michel talks about). Following another axis, one can distinguish territories or reterritorializations as well as movements of deterritorializations that follow an assemblage [...] The dispositions of power would come forward anytime there are reterritorializations at stake, even if they are abstract. The dispositions of power would then, be one of the components of an assemblage. But assemblages also contain points of deterritorialization. In short, it is not the dispositions of power that assembles or constitutes, but power formations swarm amongst assemblages of desire following one of their dimensions.
>
> (Deleuze, 1994b: 60-61; my translation)

We see in this quotation the definition of an assemblage of desire as that which contains both movements of de- and reterritorialization, where power is at work in the reterritorializing movements. But, Deleuze's focus is on the fact that each assemblage always and also contains de-territorializing movements. It is a question of focusing, in the systems we live in, that which leaks and flees from the system. The first definition of a society for Deleuze is not power or stable structures, but the fact that these structures are always leaking and escaping:

> I would say for my own part: a society, a social field does not contradict itself, but what is primary is that it is leaking, it is first and foremost leaking everywhere, the lines of flight are primary [...] There is no problem for me in the status of resistance: since lines of flights are the primary determinations, since desire makes the social field function, it is rather that power, at the same time, is produced by these assemblages and crush or plug them. I share Michel's horror of those who call themselves marginal: the romanticism of madness, of delinquency, of perversion, of drugs, is less and less tolerable for me. But lines of flight, which is to say assemblages of desire, are not created by marginal elements for me. It is on the contrary on the objective lines which traverse a society that marginal elements install themselves here and there, to complete a circle, a tournament, a recoding. I thus have no need of a status of

resistance: if the first given of a society is that everything is leaking and deterritorializing.

(Deleuze, 1994b: 61-62; my translation)

We could then speak of two different starting points or affinities in understanding the structures of a society. This might also be a reason why research being carried out from a Foucauldian perspective will quite often (and one might suspect, with a great deal of miscomprehension of Foucault's own intents, since the last parts of his work and especially *The Care of the Self Volume 3 of The History of Sexuality* (1986) is dedicated to the way the subject itself is part of 'wanting power') focus on structures as stable and quite easily identifiable. Working from the perspective of the primacy of desire and through assemblages of desire will, as seen in Chapter 3 and which is going to be seen in Chapter Six, give power a secondary role and the focus will be on that that flees and leaks from structure.

5 Pedagogical documentation treated as events, a culture, a use, a style

1 The event is also called a 'haecceity' (Deleuze and Guattari, 2004: 287).
2 The event is a concept that is connected to Deleuze's ideas of time. But, as already said, the time aspect is in the present study only opened up for in the epilogue. In this chapter the event is treated solely through its relation to language and linguistic propositions. The concept is here treated pragmatically with the purpose of being able to account for movement in subjectivity and learning through an additional affirmative scientific method.
3 Deleuze here points out that in the famous story where Descartes analyses a piece of wax, it is not the wax itself he is examining, he is not even interested in the wax in itself; what he is examining is how the manifesting I within the Cogito is grounding the designing judgement that identifies the wax (Deleuze, 2004b: 17).
4 It is important to point out here how Deleuze continuously avoids 'being' or 'existing', and replaces it with 'insisting' or 'becoming'. This makes it possible to focus on the genesis and production of sense and truth at every moment (see further on this in the epilogue 'A virtual child in crystal time').
5 This way of working can be found in Deleuze's writings on Nietzsche. Deleuze considers Nietzsche to be a philosopher of pluralism and empiricism that does not believe in the 'great events', but rather 'in the silent plurality of senses of each event' (Deleuze, 1983a: 4).
6 From Monica Sand's dissertation (2008) where she uses this definition of method, inspired by a seminar with the philosopher Marcia Sa Cavalcante Schuback.
7 According to Sauvagnargues (2005), Deleuze's way of working consists of a continuous mutation of concepts. When engaging in such a mutation one needs to contextualize it in the above-mentioned way:

> The attentive examination of the mutation of concepts forces a taking into account of the context of their elaboration, the contemporary debates, the chronology of lecture, the references, that is, to take into

account the ethologic of the problem: the environment within which it is constituted.

(Sauvagnargues, 2005: 258; my translation)

8 'Something happens' or 'quelque chose se passe' is a phrase that Deleuze often uses in his texts and interviews to describe an encounter, for instance between philosophy and another field such as film, art or even origami. In the interview earlier mentioned with Claire Parnet (Boutang, 2004), Deleuze talks about an encounter he experienced when writing *The Fold, Leibniz and the Baroque* (1993). During the writing of the book Deleuze receives letters from people occupying themselves with folding paper, insisting that he is writing about what they are doing. But it is not only these people who insist that The Fold talks about what they are doing. Deleuze also receives letters from surfers stating that he is writing about what they are doing when surfing; folding in and out of waves. Deleuze talks in the interview about these events as encounters where 'something happened'.

9 Regarding ethics, also take into consideration what is said in Chapter 4 about the relation of theory and practice, where theory is considered as a practice working *with* another practice by experimentation and creation. Also take into consideration what is said under the heading 'The role of the researcher', as working with participants in the practice in the manner of a co-production.

10 A more profound analysis inspired by Beck (1992) and Massumi (2005) in relation to the field of early childhood education could be another future and very important project for anyone interested. One can imagine that childhood probably is a field that functions as a strong indicator of the development of the risk society and where many of the strategies of the risk society are played out, due to the strong and general connection between children and 'our future'.

6   Assemblages of desire in early childhood education

1 The five children were the ones involved in the project, but since the overhead projector, as well as the documentation, were placed in the centre of the room, obviously other children participated in their own ways.

2 Guattari writes in his book *Chaosmosis an ethico-aesthetic paradigm* (1995) that he prefers to call the discovery of the psyche, made by Freud, an invention, and not in any judging or devaluing sense. To look at the psyche as an invention rather than as a discovery completely changes the picture, since, if it is a discovery it is impossible to question it. If the psyche has been discovered it seems to be something pre-existing, something innate that has always been around just waiting to be discovered. But, if the psyche is seen as an invention it has got no pre-existing features, it cannot be innate within the subject but must rather be seen as Freud's own construction. That Guattari does not try to devalue Freud's invention of the psyche does not mean that he accepts it as an eternal or innate truth. He says that over the course of the years it has lost its inventive character and has run into a dogmatic structuralized version of itself compared to the early years of freshness and creation (Guattari, 1995: 10).

3 It might be important to think about the fact that Deleuze and Guattari
   address psychoanalysis in their particular time and space. Since then
   obviously things have happened and contemporary psychoanalysis is
   probably not a coherent field saturated by the Oedipus complex, but
   supposedly a much more vast and varied field. In the present study Deleuze
   and Guattari's writings and relations to psychoanalysis are used only so as to
   be able to account for how the preschools presented in this study accomplish
   a shift in relation to how desire is conceived of and worked with.

4 Having been a psychoanalyst at the clinic La Borde, and trying out
   alternative ways of working, Guattari gives an example in his book *Chaosmosis
   an ethico-aestethic paradigm* (1995) of how one can break this vicious circle of
   interpretation. He presents 'a new ethico-aesthetic paradigm'. Within this
   paradigm one can see the relationship of the psychoanalyst and her or his
   patient as an act of creation instead of relying on any form of predetermined
   schema of interpretation delivered by the inventions of psychology. The
   psychoanalyst has an ethical choice to make, that depends upon her or
   his ontological perspective. Either she or he will make of the patient and
   hers or his problems a scientific object, explained and interpreted by what
   we already know of these problems; the psychoanalyst will then propose
   already established means to cure the patient: to make the patient normal.
   Or the analyst will bring her or himself, the patient as well as the problems
   to a level of construction and creation where any means whatsoever is worth
   trying out, such as for instance the phrase uttered 'en passant', 'I think I
   would like to take a driving licence'. This seemingly unimportant phrase
   can be picked up and used and turns out to be a tool for the patient to break
   out of a vicious circle of reproduction and create completely new frames
   of references for living her or his life; getting to see different persons and
   landscapes, accessing new sense and motor skills etc. In relation to this it is,
   according to Guattari, important to make a choice about whether to see the
   patient as an object or to engage in creative production with the patient:

   > Of course, I am not equating either psychosis to the work of art or the
   > psychoanalyst to the artist! I am only emphasising that the existential
   > registers concerned here involve a dimension of autonomy of an
   > aesthetic order. We are faced with an important ethical choice: either
   > we objectify, reify, "scientifise" subjectivity, or, on the contrary, we try to
   > grasp it in the dimension of its processual creativity.
   >
   > (Guattari, 1995: 13)

5 Or rather, from the way that the field of early childhood education has
   picked up and used developmental psychology. Again, we have to be careful
   when judging starting out from our local and contemporary experiences
   of developmental psychology. Obviously these theories when used in the
   preschool context have been transformed and turned around in many senses
   and directions.

6 Compare with the notion of 'the child as reproducer of culture, identity and
   knowledge'.

7 Compare with the notion of 'the natural child'.

8 This might be the point to draw up some initial ideas of how Deleuze
   and Guattari relate to other theories of the individual/society relation in

political practises. According to Bonta and Protevi (2004), one important contribution that Deleuze and Guattari's work brings to the research field of social sciences is to be found in the way that they have used what is popularly known as 'complexity theory'. Complexity theory can be described as investigations on how systems of different kinds – organic, inorganic, and social – can consist, at the same time, of levels of internal complexity and systematic behaviour, but without relying on external factors or organizing agents. Systems, in this view, are self-organizing and self-producing, though not in a homeostatic way, or according to any established order. Rather they randomly produce and organize freely and openly. Bonta and Protevi argue that Deleuze and Guattari's politically informed use of complexity theory in the field of social sciences has made it possible to undo, and add something to, one of the most important dilemmas of social science research, namely the debate on structure/agency. According to Bonta and Protevi, attempts have been made, not least by Giddens (1984), to overcome this dualism, but they consider that the question remains unresolved and that the fighting over the respective possibilities and impact of structure or agency on the fields and aims of research in social sciences continue to persist. They show how the work of Deleuze and Guattari relates to the structure/agency debate and how they add a different way of thinking where neither side is being dismissed but instead enriched by their way of pulling out of both sides important features that they rework and combine in a new and different way. They mention on the structuralist side four examples, by referring to a functionalist/naturalist variant of General Systems Theory (Parsons) or its successor 'autopoetic theory' (Luhman), and the structuralism of the Lévi Strauss school or any of its 'postmodernist variants'. On the agency side they refer to anti-positivist Hermeneutics and different recently developed 'resistance practices'.

According to Bonta and Protevi, Deleuze and Guattari could be named functionalists in the way that they describe systems as working with a certain machinism and order, but they contest that this order and machinic behaviour is pre-given and determining. They talk about open-ended systems randomly producing and organizing freely and openly. According to Bonta and Protevi, Deleuze and Guattari can also be described as naturalists in the way that they use the same concepts to describe inorganic as well as organic systems, but they refuse any biological nailing down of the human subject as natural and organic.

Concerning the structural position of Lévi-Strauss and the subsequent postmodernist variants, Bonta and Protevi propose that Deleuze and Guattari bring up the question of the sign and its impact on the field of social science research in a new and different way. Due to their politically informed use of complexity theory and their rethinking of sense and reference in relation to the sign, they avoid being trapped in what Bonta and Protevi call 'the postmodernist trap', where meaning can only be understood through the sign's position in a signifying chain and reference only through the relation of signifiers to each other. By insisting on the findings of complexity theory concerning the possibility for certain physical and biological systems at critical thresholds to sense differences in their environment that trigger self-organizing processes, signs are no longer reduced to linguistic entities and sense or meaning is no longer hijacked within the never ending logic of the reference of signifiers to each other (signifying chains). Instead the meaning and function of the sign is its capacity of triggering new material processes.

On the agency side Bonta and Protevi refer to anti-positivist variants of Hermeneutics and lately the development of different 'resistance practices'. According to Bonta and Protevi, Deleuze and Guattari confirm the possibility of human subjects to participate in the creation of themselves and the world. But they do not see this creation as something essentially human, any life, animals, even non-organic life participate in the creation of the world through the very same kind of non-deterministic movements that takes place in a complex system. Bonta and Protevi further argue that at the same time as Deleuze and Guattari confirm the possibility of human subjects creating themselves and the world, they do not deny the possibility of emergence above the level of subjectivity; systems are not seen merely as a result of individual actions.

> Thus, in its politically-informed complexity theory, where signs are triggers of material processes and emergence extends to subjectivity from "desiring machines" below and from subjectivity to social machines above, *ATP* provides an escape route from the conceptual gridlock of "structure" as either a merely homeostatic self-regulation or a postmodernist "signifier imperialism" and "agency" as a mysterious exception somehow granted to individual human subjects in defiance of natural laws and blithely free of social structure.
>
> (Bonta and Protevi, 2004: 6)

9 This is probably also why the concept 'agencement' is accentuated in *A Thousands Plateaus* (2004), since it takes into account this constructivist part of desire and by that avoids the misunderstandings that followed on *Anti-Oedipus* (1984) where desire was understood as spontanéism. For a comment on the misunderstandings, that followed *Anti-Oedipus* see further the interview with Claire Parnet (Boutang, 2004).

10 A-signifying machine is a concept Deleuze is using in a written answer to a harsh critic. He uses it to talk about two different ways of reading a book: either you treat the book as a signifying box, that contains information and you try to interpret it, comment upon it, write a book about the book etc; or you treat the book as a little a-signifying machine and the only thing you ask from it is, is it functioning? And is it functioning for me? If not, says Deleuze; put it away and take another book. Either something happens when you read a book, or not, and it has nothing to do with any signifying information or communication that is contained in the book. In this sense reading a book is more of an encounter that takes place in between reader and book (Deleuze, 1995a).

References

Åberg, A. and Lenz Taguchi, H. (2005) *Lyssnandets pedagogik* ('A Pedagogy of Listening'), Stockholm, Liber förlag.

Agamben, G. (1999) *Potentialities: Collected Essays in Philosophy*, Stanford CA: Stanford University Press.

Ahlström, K.-G. and Kallós, D. (1996) 'Svensk forskning om lärarutbildning. Problem och frågeställningar i ett komparativt perspektiv' ('Swedish research on teacher education. Problems and questions in a comparative perspective'), *Pedagogisk Forskning i Sverige (Pedagogical Research in Sweden), 1(2)*, 65–88.

Anderson, L. (1982) 'Big Science, Songs from United States I–IV', LP.

Barsotti, A., Dahlberg, G., Göthson, H. and Åsén, G. (1993) 'Pedagogik i en föränderlig omvärld – ett samarbetsprojekt med Reggio Emilia' ('Education in a Changing World – a project in cooperation with Reggio Emilia'). Forskningsprogram. HLS, Institutionen för barn- och ungdomsvetenskap, Avdelningen för barnpedagogisk forskning i Solna.

Barsotti *et al.* (forthcoming) *Transculturalism and Communication*, Stockholm: Stockholm University.

Beck, U. (1992) *Risk Society: Towards a New Modernity*, London: Sage.

Blackman, L. and Walkerdine, V. (2001) *Mass Hysteria Critical Psychology and Media Studies*, New York: Palgrave.

Bloch, M., Holmlund, K., Moqvist, I. and Popkewitz, T. (2003) (eds) *Governing Children, Families and Education: Restructuring the Welfare State*, New York: Palgrave McMillan.

Bonta, M. and Protevi, J. (2004) *Deleuze and Geophilosophy: A Guide and Glossary*, Edinburgh: Edinburgh University Press.

Boutang, P.-A. (2004) 'L'abécédaire de Gilles Deleuze' with C. Parnet, DVD Paris: Editions Montparnasse.

Cannella, G. (1997) *Deconstructing Early Childhood Education: Social Justice and Revolution*, New York: Peter Lang Publishing.

Carlgren, I. (1996a) 'Lärarutbildningen som yrkesutbildning' ('Teacher education as vocational training'), in Utbildningsdepartementet (Swedish Department for Education) *Lärarutbildning i förändring (Teacher Education in Transformation)*, Ds 1996: 16, Stockholm: Fritzes.

Carlgren, I. (1996b) 'Skolans utveckling och forskning' ('School's development and research'), in Utbildningsdepartementet (Swedish Department for Education) *Lärarutbildning i förändring (Teacher Education in Transformation)*, Ds 1996: 16, Stockholm: Fritzes.

Dahlberg, G. (2003) 'Pedagogy as a loci of an ethics of an encounter', in M. Bloch, K. Holmlund, I. Moqvist and T. Popkewitz (eds) *Governing Children, Families and Education: Restructuring the Welfare State*, New York: Palgrave McMillan.

Dahlberg, G. and Bloch, M. (2006) 'Is the power to see and visualize always the power to control?', in T. Popkewitz, K. Pettersson, U. Olsson and J. Kowalczyk (eds) *"The Future is not what it appears to be"*. *Pedagogy, Genealogy and Political Epistemology. In honour and in memory of Kenneth Hultqvist*, Stockholm: HLS Förlag.

Dahlberg, G. and Hultqvist, K. (2001) (eds) *Governing the Child in the New Millennium*, London: Routledge Falmer.

Dahlberg, G. and Lenz Taguchi, H. (1994) *Förskola och skola- om två skilda traditioner och visionen om en mötesplats* ('Preschool and school – two different traditions and a vision of an encounter'), Stockholm: HLS Förlag.

Dahlberg, G. and Moss, P. (2005) *Ethics and Politics in Early Childhood Education*, Oxfordshire: RoutledgeFalmer.

Dahlberg, G. and Olsson, L. M. (forthcoming) *The Magic of Language – Young Children's Relations to Language, Reading and Writing*, Stockholm University.

Dahlberg, G. and Theorell, E. (forthcoming) *Children's Dialogue with Nature – The Challenges of the Knowledge Society and the Possibilities for Learning*, Stockholm University.

Dahlberg, G., Moss, P. and Pence, A. (2007) *Beyond Quality in Early Childhood Education and Care: Postmodern Perspectives*, 2nd edn. London: Falmer Press.

Damkjaer, C. (2005) *The Aesthetics of Movement: Variations on Gilles Deleuze and Merce Cunningham*. Doctoral thesis. Stockholm: Stockholm University.

De Landa, M. (2002) *Intensive Science and Virtual Philosophy*, London: Continuum.

Deleuze, G. (1953) *Empirisme et subjectivité. Essai sur la nature humaine selon Hume*, collection 'Épiméthée', Paris: Presses Universitaires de France

Deleuze, G. (1962) *Nietzsche et la philosophie*, collection 'Bibliothèque de philosophie contemporaine', Paris: Presses Universitaires de France'

Deleuze, G. (1965) *Nietzsche*, Paris: Presses Universitaires de France.

Deleuze, G. (1966) *Le bergsonism*, collection 'SUP-Le Philosophe', Paris: Presses Universitaires de France.

Deleuze, G. (1968a) *Différence et Répétition*, collection 'Épiméthée', Paris: Presses Universitaires de France.

Deleuze, G. (1968b) *Spinoza et le problème de l'expression*, collection 'Critique', Paris: Les Éditions de Minuit.

Deleuze, G. (1969) *Logique du sens*, Paris: Les Éditions de Minuit.

Deleuze, G. (1970) *Spinoza. Philosophie pratique*, Paris: Les Éditions de Minuit, revised and extended 2nd edn (1981).

Deleuze, G. (1972) 'Hume', in *La Philosophie: De Galilée à Jean Jacques Rousseau*, Paris: Les Éditions de Minuit.

Deleuze, G. (1983a) *Nietzsche and Philosophy*, trans. Hugh Tomlinson, London: Athlone Press.

Deleuze, G. (1983b) *Cinéma 1, L'Image-Mouvement*, Paris: Les Éditions de Minuit.

Deleuze, G. (1985) *Cinema 2, L'Image-Temps*, Paris: Les Éditions de Minuit.

Deleuze, G. (1986) *Foucault*, collection 'Critique', Paris: Les Éditions de Minuit.

Deleuze, G. (1988a) *Spinoza: Practical Philosophy*, trans. Robert Hurley, San Fransisco: City Light Books.

Deleuze, G. (1988b) *Foucault*, trans. Séan Hand, Minneapolis, MN: University of Minnesota Press.

Deleuze, G. (1988c) *Le Pli, Leibniz et le baroque*, collection 'Critique', Paris: Les Éditions de Minuit.

Deleuze, G. (1989) *Cinema 2 The Time-Image*, trans. Hugh Tomlinson and Robert Galeta, London: Athlone Press.

Deleuze, G. (1990) *Pourparlers*, Paris: Les Éditions de Minuit.

Deleuze, G. (1991) *Empiricism and Subjectivity*, trans. Constantin Boundas, New York: Columbia University Press.

Deleuze, G. (1992a) *Cinema 1 The Movement-Image*, trans. Hugh Tomlinson and Barbara Habberjam, London: Athlone Press.

Deleuze, G. (1992b) *Expressionism in Philosophy: Spinoza*, trans. Martin Joughin, New York: Zone Books.

Deleuze, G. (1993) *The Fold, Leibniz and the Baroque*, trans. Tom Conley, London: Athlone Press.

Deleuze, G. (1994a) *Difference and Repetition*, trans. Paul Patton, London: Athlone Press.

Deleuze, G. (1994b) 'Désir et plaisir'('Desire and Pleasure'), *Le Magazine Litteraire*, *325*, 58–65.

Deleuze, G. (1995a) *Negotiations*, trans. Martin Joughin, New York: Columbia University Press.

Deleuze, G. (1995b) 'L'Immanence: Une vie', *Philosophie, 47*, Les Éditions de Minuit.

Deleuze, G. (2001) *Pure Immanence: Essays on a Life*, trans. A. Boyman, New York: Urzone.

Deleuze, G. (2002) *L'île déserte et autres textes. Textes et entretiens 1953–1974*, Paris: Les Éditions de Minuit.

Deleuze, G. (2004a) *Desert Islands and Other Texts 1953–1974* (ed. D. Lapoujade), trans. Michael Taormina, Los Angeles: Semiotext(e).

Deleuze, G. (2004b) *The Logic of Sense*, trans. Mark Lester, London: Continuum.

Deleuze, G. (2006) *Bergsonism*, trans. Hugh Tomlinson and Barbara Habberjam, Brooklyn, NY: Zone Books.

Deleuze, G. and Guattari, F. (1972) *L'Anti-Oedipe. Capitalisme et schizophrénie*, collection 'Critique', Paris: Les Éditions de Minuit.

Deleuze, G. and Guattari, F. (1980) *Mille plateaux. Capitalisme et schizophrénie 2*, collection 'Critique', Paris: Les Éditions de Minuit.

Deleuze, G. and Guattari, F. (1984) *Anti-Oedipus: Capitalism and Schizophrenia*, trans. Robert Hurley, Mark Seem and Helen R. Lane, London: The Athlone Press.

Deleuze, G. and Guattari, F. (1991) *Qu'est-ce que la philosophie?*, Paris: Les Éditions de Minuit.

Deleuze, G. and Guattari, F. (1994) *What is philosophy?* trans. Hugh Tomlinson and Graham Burchill, London: Verso.

Deleuze, G. and Guattari, F. (1999) *A Thousand Plateaus: Capitalism & Schizophrenia*, London: The Athlone Press.

Deleuze, G. and Guattari, F. (2004) *A Thousand Plateaus: Capitalism and Schizophrenia*, trans. Brian Massumi, 2nd edn. London: Continuum.

Deleuze, G. and Parnet, C. (1977) *Dialogues*, Paris: Flammarion.

Deleuze, G. and Parnet, C. (1987) *Dialogues*, trans. Hugh Tomlinson and Barbara Habberjam, London: Athlone Press.

Elfström, I. (forthcoming) *Pedagogisk Dokumentation och/eller Individuella Utvecklingsplaner-om att synliggöra och bedöma förskolebarns kooperativa och enskilda lärande* ('Pedagogical Documentation and/or Individual Development plans – making visible and assessing preschool children's cooperative and individual learning'), manuscript for doctoral thesis, Stockholm University.

Erixon Arreman, I. (2002) 'Pedagogiskt arbete – En social konstruktion för att fylla en social funktion' ('Pedagogical work – A social construction for a social function'), *Tidskrift för lärarutbildning och forskning (Journal of Research in Teacher Education)*, *1*, 39–58.

Fendler, L. (2001) 'Educating flexible souls', in K. Hultqvist and G. Dahlberg (eds) *Governing the Child in the New Millennium*, London: Routledge Falmer.

Foucault, M. (1963) *Naissance de la clinique*, Paris: Presses Universitaires de France.

Foucault, M. (1973) *The Birth of the Clinic: An Archaeology of Medical Perception*, trans. A. M. Sheridan Smith, London: Tavistock Publications.

Foucault, M. (1975) *Surveiller et punir: Naissance de la prison*, Paris: Éditions Gallimard.

Foucault, M. (1976) *La Volonté de savoir*, Paris: Éditions Gallimard.

Foucault, M. (1977) *Discipline and Punish: The Birth of the Prison*, trans. Alan Sheridan, London: Allen Lane.

Foucault, M. (1979) *The History of Sexuality: Volume 1. An Introduction*. trans. Robert Hurley, London: Allen Lane.

Foucault, M. (1984a) *L'Usage des plaisirs*, Paris: Éditions Gallimard.

Foucault, M. (1984b) *Le souci de soi*, Paris: Éditions Gallimard.

Foucault, M. (1984c) 'Preface', in G. Deleuze and F. Guattari, *Anti-Oedipus: Capitalism and Schizophrenia*, London: Continuum.

Foucault, M. (1985) *The Use of Pleasure: Volume 2 of The History of Sexuality*, trans. Robert Hurley, New York: Vintage Books.

Foucault, M. (1986) *The Care of the Self: Volume 3 of The History of Sexuality*, trans. Robert Hurley, New York: Pantheon Books.

Foucault, M. (2002) 'Les intellectuels et le pouvoir' in G. Deleuze, *L'île déserte et autres textes. Textes et entretiens 1953–1974*, Paris: Les Éditions de Minuit.

Foucault, M. (2004) *Desert Islands and Other Texts 1953–1974* (ed. D. Lapoujade), trans. Michael Taormina, Los Angeles: Semiotext(e).

Giddens, A. (1984) *The Constitution of Society: Outline of the Theory of Structuration*, Berkeley: University of California Press.

Giudici, C., Rinaldi, C. and Krechevsky, M. (2001) (eds) *Making Learning Visible: Children as Individual and Group Learners*, Cambridge, MA: Project Zero and Reggio Emilia: Reggio Children.

Grosz, E. (1995). *Space, Time and Perversion: Essays on the politics of bodies*, New York: Routledge.

Guattari, F. (1992) *Chaosmose*, Paris: Éditions Galilée; trans. Paul Bains and Julian Pefanis (1995) *Chaosmosis an ethico-aesthetic paradigm*, Bloomington and Indianapolis: Indiana University Press.

Guattari, F. (1995) *Chaosmosis an ethico-aesthetic paradigm*, trans. Paul Bains and Julian Pefanis, Bloomington, IN: Indiana University Press.

Guattari, F. (2004) *Ecrits pour L'Anti-Œdipe* ('Writings for Anti-Oedipus'), Paris: Éditions Lignes & Manifestes.

Gustafsson, B., Hermerén, G. and Petersson, B. (2006) 'Good Research Practice – What is it? Views, guidelines and examples', Vetenskapsrådets rapportserie, Swedish Research Council. Online. Available HTTP: <http://www.vr.se/mainmenu/researchethics.html> (accessed 10 January 2007).

Hardt, M. and Negri, A. (2002) *Empire*, Cambridge, MA: Harvard University Press.

Hultqvist, K. (1990) *Förskolebarnet en konstruktion för gemenskapen och den individuella frigörelsen* ('The preschool child a construction for the spirit of community and the emancipation of the individual'), Stockholm: Symposion.

Lenz Taguchi, H. (2000) *Emancipation och motstånd: Dokumentation och kooperativa läroprocesser i förskolan* ('Emancipation and resistance: Documentation and co-operative learning processes in the preschool'). Doctoral thesis. Stockholm: LHS Förlag.

Lind, U. (2005) 'Identity and Power, "Meaning", Gender and Age: Children's creative work as a signifying practice', *Contemporary Issues in Early Childhood* *6(3)*, 256–268.

Lind, U. (forthcoming) *Blickens ordning. Bildspråk och estetiska lärprocesser som kunskapsform och kulturform* ('The order of seeing: Pictorial language and aesthetic learning processes as forms of knowledge and culture'), manuscript for doctoral thesis, Stockholm University.

MacNaughton, G. (2005) *Doing Foucault in Early Childhood Studies: Applying Post-structural Ideas*, New York: Routledge.

Massumi, B. (2002) *Parables for the Virtual: Movement, Affect, Sensation*, Durham NC: Duke University Press.

Massumi, B. (2003) 'Navigating Movements: An Interview with Brian Massumi', *21cMagazine*, 2, 1–25. Online. Available HTTP: <http://www.21magazine.com/issue2/massumi.html> (accessed 29 March 2006).

Massumi, B. (2005) 'Peur, dit le spectre'('Fear says the spectrum'), *Multitudes*, *23*, 135–152. Montigny le Bretonneux: *Multitudes*. Online. Available HTTP: <http://multitudes.samizdat.net/spip.php?article2241> (accessed 22 February 2007).

Moulier Boutang, Y. (2005) 'Les vieux habits neufs de la République. En défense d'émeutiers prétendument "insignifiants"' ('The new old clothes of the

Republic. Defending the supposedly "insignificant" rioters'), *Multitudes*, *23*, 5–11. Montigny le Bretonneux: *Multitudes*. Online. Available HTTP: <http://multitudes.samizdat.net/spip.php?article2220> (accessed 22 February 2007).

Mozère, L. (1992) *Le Printemps des Crèches: histoire et analyse d'un mouvement* ('Springtime in the crèche. The history and analysis of a movement'), Paris: L'Harmattan.

Mozère, L. (2002) 'Devenir-enfant Narrative'('Becoming-child Narrative'), paper presented at Reconceptualizing Early Childhood Education Conference, Tempe, AZ, January.

Mozère, L. (2006) 'What's the Trouble with Identity? Practices and Theories from France', *Contemporary Issues in Early Childhood*, *7(2)*, 109–118.

Mozère, L. (2007a) 'In Early Childhood: What's language about?', *Educational Philosophy and Theory*, *39(3)*, 291–299.

Mozère, L. (2007b) '"Du côté" des jeunes enfants ou comment appréhender le désir en sociologie?'('On children's side or how to understand desire in sociology'), in G. Brougère and M. Vandenbroeck (eds) *Repenser l'éducation des jeunes enfants* ('Rethinking early childhood education'), Bruxelles: Peter Lang.

Mozère, L. (2007c) 'Devenir-enfant'('Becoming-child'), in L. Mozère (ed.) *Gilles Deleuze et Félix Guattari: Territoire et Devenir* ('Territory and Becoming'), Strasbourg: Éditions du Portique.

Negri, A. (2003) *Time for Revolution*, London: Continuum.

Nordin-Hultman, E. (2004) *Pedagogiska miljöer och barns subjektsskapande* ('Pedagogical environments and children's construction of subjectivity'). Doctoral thesis. Stockholm: Liber Förlag.

Patton, P. and Protevi, J. (2003) *Between Deleuze and Derrida*, London: Continuum.

Popkewitz, T. and Bloch, M. (2001) 'Administering freedom: a history of the present – rescuing the parent to rescue the child for society', in K. Hultqvist and G. Dahlberg (eds) *Governing the Child in the New Millennium*, London: Routledge Falmer.

Querrien, A. (2005) 'Défendre la société contre tous les racismes'('Defending society against all kinds of racisms'), *Multitudes*, *23*, 13–19. Montigny le Bretonneux: *Multitudes*. Online. Available HTTP: <http://multitudes.samizdat.net/spip.php?article2221> (accessed 22 February 2007).

Rajchman, J. (2001) *The Deleuze Connections*, Massachusetts: MIT.

Reggio Children (1997) *Shoe and Meter*, Reggio Emilia: Reggio Children.

Rinaldi, C. (2005) *In Dialogue with Reggio Emilia: Listening, Researching and Learning*, London: Routledge.

Rose, N. (1999) *Powers of Freedom: Reframing Political Thought*, Cambridge: Cambridge University Press.

Roy, K. (2003) *Teachers in Nomadic Spaces: Deleuze and Curriculum*, New York: Peter Lang.

Roy, K. (2005) 'On Sense and Nonsense: Looking Beyond the Literacy Wars', *Journal of Philosophy of Education*, *39(1)*, 99–111.

Sand, M. (2008) *Konsten att gunga: experiment som aktiverar mellanrum* ('Space in motion: the art of activating space in between'), doctoral thesis.

Sauvagnargues, A. (2005) *Deleuze et l'art* ('Deleuze and art'), collection 'Lignes d'art', Paris: Presses Universitaires de France.

Semetsky, I. (2003) 'The problematics of human subjectivity: Gilles Deleuze and the Deweyan legacy', *Studies in Philosophy and Education*, *22*, 211–225.

Semetsky, I. (2004a) 'Becoming-Language/Becoming-Other: Whence ethics?', *Educational Philosophy and Theory*, *36(3)*, 313–325.

Semetsky, I. (2004b) 'The Role of Intuition in Thinking and Learning: Deleuze and the pragmatic legacy', *Educational Philosophy and Theory*, *36(4)*, 433–454.

Smith, D. W. (2003) 'Deleuze and Derrida, Immanence and Transcendence: Two Directions in Recent French Thought', in P. Patton and J. Protevi (eds) *Between Deleuze and Derrida*, London: Continuum.

Smith, K. (2005) 'Rhizoanalysis: a tactic for creating new co-ordinates for observation as a political practice for social justice', in G. MacNaughton, *Doing Foucault in Early Childhood Studies: applying post-structural ideas*, New York: Routledge.

Spindler, F. (2006) 'Att förlora fotfästet : om tänkandets territorier' ('To lose one's foothold: about the territories of thinking'), in S. Gromark and F. Nilsson (eds) *Utforskande arkitektur*, Stockholm: Axl Books.

Umeå Universitet (2005) 'Studieplan för forskarutbildning i Pedagogiskt arbete vid Umeå Universitet' ('Curriculum for postgraduate studies in Pedagogical work at Umeå University'), (Fastställd 2000-05-08) Umeå.

Vinterek, M. (2004) 'Pedagogiskt arbete. Ett forskningsområde börjar anta en tydlig profil' ('Pedagogical work. A research field begins to take on a clear profile') *Tidskrift för lärarutbildning och forskning* (*Journal of Research in Teacher Education*), *3–4*, 73–90.

Walkerdine, V. (1997) *Daddy's Girl Young Girls and Popular Culture*, London: Macmillan Press.

Wenzer, J. (2004) 'The Deterritorialization of the Being Child', in H. Brembeck, B. Johansson and J. Kampman (eds) *Beyond the Competent Child: Exploring Contemporary Childhoods in the Nordic Welfare Societies*, Frederiksberg: Roskilde University Press.

Wenzer, J. (2007) *Resonanser: en neomaterialistisk analys av independentscenen i Göteborg* ('Resonances: a neo-materialist analysis of the indie scene in Gothenburg'). Doctoral thesis. Gothenburg: Gothenburg University.

Zourabichvili, F. (2003) *Le vocabulaire de Deleuze* ('Deleuze's vocabulary'), collection 'Vocabulaire de…', Paris: Editions Ellipses.

Index